THE
BLACK
BOOK

Middleton Harris

with the assistance of

Morris Levitt
Roger Furman
Ernest Smith

Random House New York

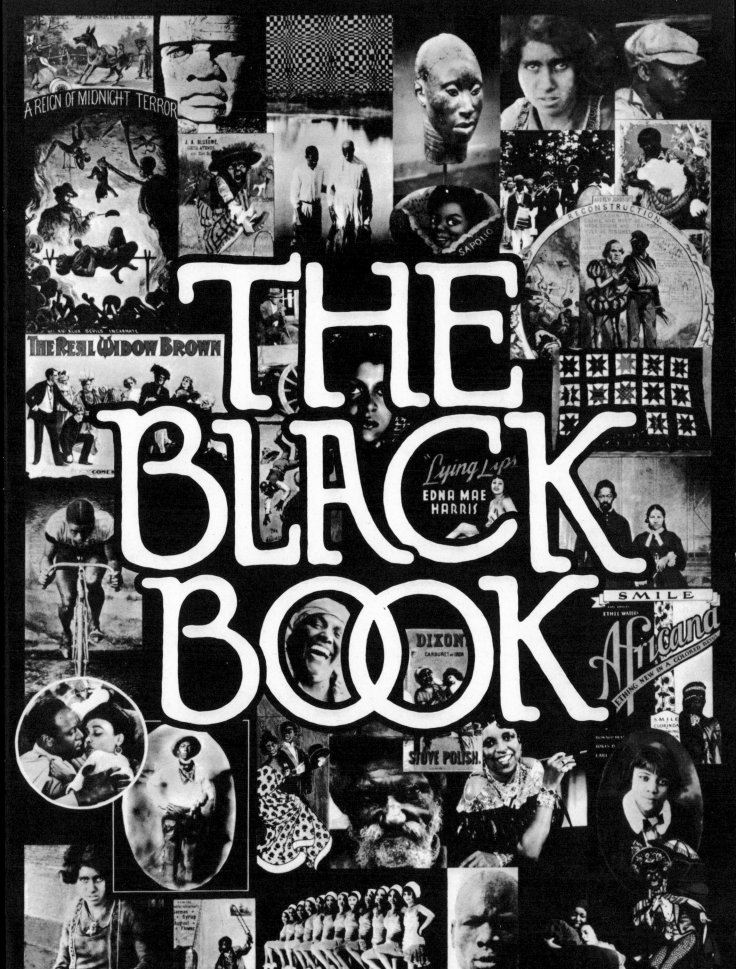

Library of Congress Cataloging in Publication Data
Main entry under title:
The Black book.
    1. Negroes—History—Miscellanea. I. Harris,
M. A., 1908–
E185.B56 1973 973′.04′96073 73-5026
ISBN 0-394-48388-X (hardbound)
ISBN 0-394-70622-6 (paperbound)

Manufactured in the United States of America

98765432

Design: Jack Ribik
Design Concept: Charles Schmalz
Production Manager: Dean Ragland

**Grateful acknowledgment is made to the
following for permission to reprint previously
published material:**

Bantam Books, Inc.: For four recipes from *The Tuesday Soul
Food Cookbook*. Copyright © 1969 by Tuesday Publications,
Inc.

Farrar, Straus & Giroux, Inc., and Maxfield Parrish: For
text excerpts and one musical score from *Slave Songs of the
Georgia Sea Islands*, by Lydia Parrish. Copyright 1942 by
Lydia Parrish, Copyright renewed 1969 by Maxfield Parrish, Jr.

Grove Press, Inc., and Faber & Faber, Ltd.: For an excerpt
from pages 17–21 of *My Life in the Bush of Ghosts*, by Amos
Tutuola. All rights reserved.

Macmillan Publishing Company, Inc.: For an excerpt from
page 173 of *Black Song, The Forge and the Flame*, by John
Lovell.

Raymond J. Martinez: "Charles the Grinder" from *Myste-
rious Marie Laveau and Folk Tales Along the Mississippi* by
Raymond J. Martinez. Copyright © 1956 by Raymond J.
Martinez. Published by Hope Publications.

G. P. Putnam's Sons and the author's agents, Lenniger
Literary Agency, Inc.: For text excerpts from *The Complete Book of Voodoo*, by Robert W. Pelton. Copyright ©
1972 by Robert W. Pelton. Reprinted by permission of the
publishers, the author and his agents.

The University of Chicago Press and Benjamin A. Botkin:
For excerpts from pages 174–177 of *Lay My Burden Down:
A Folk History of Slavery* by B. A. Botkin. Copyright 1945.

The University of Georgia Press: For excerpts from *Drums
and Shadows* by The Georgia Writers' Project.

Introduction

Suppose a three-hundred-year-old
black man had decided, oh, say when he was about ten,
to keep a scrapbook—a record of what it was like for himself and his people
in these United States. He would keep newspaper articles that interested him,
old family photos, trading cards, advertisements, letters, handbills,
dreambooks, and posters—all sorts of stuff.

He would remember things, too,
and put those in: stories he'd heard, rumors, dates. He'd remember the
first March on Washington, how John Quincy Adams defended Joseph Cinque,
the black slaveship rebel—and won; the Jewish Hospital that opened its doors
to the wounded during the Civil War Draft Riots.

He would know about black goldminers,
and pirates and factory owners and inventors. And he would keep records
of blacks who owned slaves, lyrics of songs he'd sung, voodoo recipes he'd tried—
all of that he would put in his book.

And he would end up with
a folk journey of Black America: a book just like this one—beautiful, haunting,
curious, informative, and human.

No such man kept such a book.
But it's okay—because it's here, anyway.
I sure wish I'd had it when I was in school. Then I'd know what to say when
Mrs. Broadbird said my speech was slang.

I sure wish I'd had it in my house back in Philadelphia—then whenever I
played the "dozens" I'd know where they came from.

More important—I wish I'd had it
when I went to the barbershop. Then it wouldn't have been necessary for that
dude to leave his chair with half a haircut to run home and get his birth certificate
to prove he was around when Josh Gibson
was playing baseball.

But here it is—at last—THE BLACK BOOK.
Everybody has one, you know. The difference in this one is that here nobody
changed the names to protect the guilty.

Browse in it. The pickins'ain't always easy, but they're always good.

September, 1973 Bill Cosby

Acknowledgments

Many people contributed
to this text — with stories, pictures, recollections and general aid.
They are: Mary Singleton, Donna Woods, Ramah Wofford, George Carl
Wofford, Verta Mae Grosvenor, June Rephan,
Eleanor Charles.

Special mention must go to
Judith Wragg Chase, who made available photographs of the items in
her Old Slave Mart Museum, and to Shareen Brysac
for her photo research.

Above all, our thanks to those millions of black people
who lived this life and held on.

PHOTO CREDITS

Brown Brothers: 22, 54, 149, 154, 166, 181, 187, 189

Culver Pictures: 38, 55, 58, 170, 171

Denver Public Library Western Collection: 49, 52, 53

Granger Collection: 69, 153, 159, 164, 173

Magnum Photos: 1, 4, 6, 7

Negro History Associates: 2–3, 12, 13, 15, 21, 24, 25, 27, 29, 30, 33, 36, 37, 38, 39, 40, 41, 43, 47, 48, 52, 53, 54, 68–69, 83, 122, 123, 124, 125, 126, 127, 128, 130, 131, 133, 151, 152, 156, 157, 158, 160, 162, 165, 166

New York Historical Society, New York: 132

New York Public Library Picture Collection: 13, 15, 16–17, 30, 61, 64, 65, 71, 78, 139, 141, 142, 156, 162–163

Collection Old Slave Mart Museum, Judith Wragg Chase, Director: 105–109

Clarence Robinson: 174, 175, 176, 177, 179

Ernest R. Smith: 167, 168, 169, 170, 171, 172, 173, 174, 175, 176, 177

State Department Archives of History: 156

United Press International: 182

Verta Mae Grosvenor Collection: 92, 94, 96

THE
BLACK
BOOK

I was there when the Angel drove out the Ancestor I was there when the waters consumed the mountains

—Bernard Dadie

It is now established beyond effective contradiction that for easily a century before Columbus, and perhaps for a still longer period, French merchants of Dieppe and Rouen regularly sent their ships to the Guinea Coast of Africa and probably to the bays of South America, for gold, ivory, spices, skins, precious stones, and other exotic desirables. It is known that this commerce was organized on almost the scale of a modern American corporation. Yet, for a reason, all this business went on without pomp of advertising and as much as possible under the seal of secrecy.

The reason was a very simple one, we are told:

War was a settled industry of that time likewise. Or it was a favorite diversion of petty kings, who sought relief from the tedium of life on the field of honor. But honor, and war in defense of it, cost money; and for the revenue necessary to wage it in the style to which they were accustomed, these kings by habit levied first and heaviest on the merchant class. Few others had money in amounts to justify the cost and bother of collection. Hence the merchants acquired the habit of keeping as far as possible from public notice the origin and extent of their fortunes. Their ships slipt out of Dieppe or Rouen; they slipt in in again some time afterward; and few or none outside the circles of trade knew where those ships had been between departure and return.

It is now known that these shipping magnates maintained a well-ordered clearing-house or admiralty office at Dieppe, as a place of business record and for the exchange of marine intelligence. This center was in systematic running order for a period of time yet to be ascertained, but the span of its existence certainly covered several centuries, and as certainly its founding antedates by a wide margin the birth of Christopher Columbus. In this admiralty office each returning captain filed a full and detailed account of his voyage, for the knowledge of his employers and for the guidance of

Huge stone sculptures like this one were found in Mexico. They are over 2,500 years old.

his fellow captains. These masters of ships were men of high intelligence, the crack navigators of their time, keen on the job, each striving to outdo his rivals in the extension of trade into new quarters. All captains were licensed in regular order. It was, in every respect, a settled business.

On [Columbus'] return from the third voyage to the new land he had reached he reports *the presence of Negroes there.* Interesting as this is, even more telling is the account he gives, after the first voyage itself, of having received from the "Indians," as it pleased him to call the natives, a present of certain "guanines."

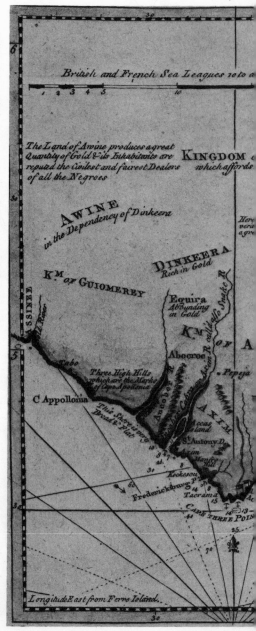

The Gold Coaſt is extended about Sixty ſix Marine Leagues, beginning with the Gold River 9 Miles West of Aſſinee, & Ending with the Village of Ponni about 30 Miles from Accra It takes its Name from the vaſt quantity of Gold that is imported from the inland Countries, and Sold to the Europeans by the Negroes; The Shore itſelf producing but very little of that Mineral. The Dutch have the Principal Settlements on that Coaſt and their Town of Elmina may be lookt upon as the Capital among the European Factories; Next to this is the Engliſh Fort and Factory of Cape Coaſt. The Soil of the Gold Coaſt is very fertile and abounds with all sorts of Fruit; The European Inhabitants never the leſs Complain very much of ye unwholeſomeneſs of the air, and give the worſt character to the Natives. When their Trade is flouriſhing and the Inland Nations are in Peace, it is Computed that they Export for about 230 000 ℓ. of Gold, the two Thirds of which quantity are for ye Engliſh and the Dutch. The Gold is generally found in two sorts of Places Ftˢᵗ in and about some Rivers and Waterfalls whoſe Violence waſhes down great quantities of Earth which Carries the Gold with it. 2ᵈ in particular Hills where the Negroes Dig Pits and ſeparate it from the Earth. This Gold is of two sorts; one is call'd Gold Duſt which is almoſt as fine as flower, and is the Beſt; The other ſort call'd Mountain or Rock Gold is in pieces of Different Sizes. The Negroes are very Subtle artiſts in the Sophiſticating of Gold, and if we may believe the European Traders They can ſo Neatly falſifie and Counterfeit Gold Duſt and Rock gold that several unexperienced Factors are frequently Cheated.

"...and he (Columbus) wanted to find out what the Indians of Hispaniola had told him, that there had come to it from the south and southeast Negro people, who brought those spear points made of a metal which they call guanin, of which he had sent to the king and queen for assaying, and which was found to have in thirty-two parts, eighteen of gold, six of silver, and eight of copper."

—Raccolta, parte I, vol. I, p. 96 (as quoted by Leo Weiner in his text Africa and the Discovery of America.)

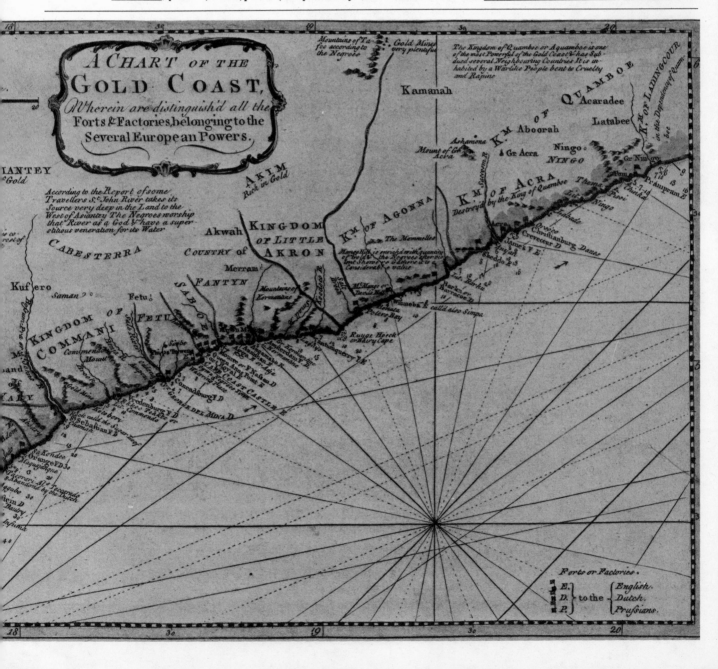

"Guanin" was the native African name of the time for pebbles or slobs of gold, the form in which it was imported to Europe from the Guinea Coast. Quite naturally, Columbus, on being handed these same things in America, pricked up his ears. For be it remembered that Columbus, like all the rovers before him, had as his primary object, not the discovery of land merely, but the discovery of gold, ivory, spices, any article salable at a profit at home. New lands were only a happy incident to the business. They pleased one's king, lured new investors, and made good advertising. But gold was the thing, and Columbus lost no time in asking his Indians where they kept it.

Very troublesome to Columbus their reply must have been, for according to his own report, they told him, "From black merchants that came to us from the Southeast."

From The Literary Digest, May 16, 1925

Peter Martyr, historian of Balboa's expeditions, wrote, "Balboa in 1513 found Negroes in Panama. These were the first Negroes seen in the Indies. Balboa found them at war with the Indians and thought that they had sailed from Ethiopia."

Emperor Septimius Severus was a native of Africa who married a Syrian and was succeeded by his son Caracalla, half African, half Syrian; Macrinus was a Moor; Pertinax was the son of an emancipated slave.

White nations named certain sections of the African Coast after their leading export: The Grain Coast (from Sierra Leone to Cape Palmas); The Ivory Coast (from Cape Palmas to modern Ghana); The Gold Coast; the Slave Coast (from the Volta River to the Niger Delta).

A cargo of slaves of the Ebo tribe had been landed at a suspiciously secluded spot on the west side of the island. They preferred death to a life of captivity, and as they walked into the water the leader said: "The water brought us here. The water will take us away."

In those days of unknown year, because I was too young to keep the number of the year in my mind till this time, so there were many kinds of African wars and some of them are as follows: general wars, tribal wars, burglary wars and the slave wars which were very common in every town and village and particularly in famous markets and on main roads of big towns at any time in the day or night. These slave-wars were causing dead luck to both old and young of those days, because if one is captured, he or she would be sold into slavery for foreigners who would carry him or her to unknown destinations to be killed for the buyer's god or to be working for him.

But as my mother was a petty trader who was going here and there, so one morning she went to a market which was about three miles away from our town, she left two slices of cooked yam for us (my brother and myself) as she was usually doing. When it was twelve o'clock p.m. cocks began to crow continuously, then my brother and myself entered into our mother's room in which she kept the two sliced or cut yams safely for us, so that it might not be poisoned by the two wives who hated us, then my brother took one of the yams and I took the other one and began to eat it at the same time. But as we were eating the yam inside our mother's room, these two wives who hated us heard information before us that war was nearly breaking into the town, so both of them and their daughters ran away from the town without informing us or taking us along with themselves and all of them knew already that our mother was out of the town.

Even as we were very young to know the meaning of "bad" and "good" both of us were dancing to the noises of the enemies' guns which were reverberating into the room in which we were eating the yam as the big trees and many hills with deep holes on them entirely surrounded the town and they changed the fearful noises of the enemies' guns to a lofty one for us, and we were dancing for these lofty noises of the enemies' guns.

But as these enemies were more approaching the town the lofty noises of their guns became fearful for us because every place was shaking at that moment. So when we could not bear it then we left our mother's room for the veranda, but we met nobody there, and then we ran from there to the portico of the house, but the town was also empty except the domestic animals as sheep, pigs, goats and fowls and also some of the bush animals as monkeys, wolves, deer and lions who were driven from the bush that surrounded the town to the town by the fearful noises of the enemies' guns. All these animals were running and crying bitterly up and down in the town in searching for their keepers. Immediately we saw that there was nobody in the town again we stepped down from the door to the outside as all the while we stood at the door looking at every part of the town with fearful and doubtful mind.

So first of all we travelled to the north of the town as there was a road which led to the town of our grandmother which was not far away from ours.

But as these animals were giving us much trouble, fear, and disturbing us so at last we left to run to the north and then to the south where there was a large river which crossed the road on which we should travel to some protective place to hide ourselves.

And as the enemies were approaching nearer, we left the river at once and when we went further on this road we reached a kind of African fruit tree which stood by the road, then we stopped under it to find a shelter, but as we were hastily turning round this tree perhaps we would see a shelter there, two ripe fruits fell down on it, then my brother took both and put them into his pocket and started to carry or lift me along on this road as I was too young to run as fast as he could. But

as he himself was too young to lift or carry such weight like me, so by that he was unable to lift me to a distance of about ten feet before he would fall down four times or more.

When he tried all his power for several times and failed and again at that moment the smell of the gunpowder of the enemies' guns which were shooting repeatedly was rushing to our noses by the breeze and this made us fear more, so my brother lifted me again a very short distance, but when I saw that he was falling several times, then I told him to leave me on the road and run away for his life perhaps he might be safe so that he would be taking care of our mother as she had no other sons more than both of us and I told him that if God saves my life too then we should meet again, but if God does not save my life we should meet in heaven.

But as I was telling him these sorrowful words both his eyes were shedding tears repeatedly, of course I did not shed tears at all on my eyes as I put hope that no doubt I would be easily captured or killed. And it was that day I believed that if fear is overmuch, a person would not fear for anything again. But as the smoke of the enemies' guns was rushing to our view, then my brother left me on that road with sorrow, and then he stopped and put his hand into his pocket and brought out the fruits which fell down from the tree under which we were about to hide ourselves before; he gave me both fruits instead of one. After that he started to run as fast as he could along this road towards the enemies unnoticed and he was still looking at me as he was running away.

So after I saw him no more on the road I put both fruits into my pocket and then got back to that fruit tree under which we picked them and I stood there only to shelter myself from the sun. But when the enemies were at a distance of about an eighth of a mile to that place where I stood I was unable to hear again because of the noises of the enemies' guns and as I was too young to hear such fearful noises and wait, so I entered into the bush under this fruit tree. This fruit tree was a "SIGN" for me and it was on that day I called it—THE "FUTURE SIGN."

Now it remained me alone in the bush, because no brother, mother, father or other defender could save me or direct me if and whenever any danger is imminent. But as these enemies had approached us closely before my brother left because of me he was captured within fifteen minutes that he left me, but he was only captured as a slave and not killed, because I heard his voice when he shouted louder for help.

African Word	Afro American Word	Meaning
Yaw Kay	OK	All right
Hipi	Hip	Aware
Cat	Cat	Person
Goy	Guy	A young man of no standing
Dega	Dig	Understand
Kuta	Cooter	Tortoise
Podzo	Poor Joe	Blue Heron
Taki	Tackies	Small wild horses
Tota	Tote	Carry
Dzogal (to rise)	Joggle board	Seesaw
Saut (to run around the Kaaba)	Shout	Religious ecstasy
Banzar	Banjo	Musical instrument with neck of wood fitted with four strings

And they sold us like beasts, and they counted our teeth . . . and they felt our testicles and they tested the lustre or dullness of our skin . . .

—Cesaire

Public Sale of Negroes,

By RICHARD CLAGETT.

On Tuesday, March 5th, 1833 at 1:00 P. M. the following Slaves will be sold at Potters Mart, in Charleston, S. C.

Miscellaneous Lots of Negroes, mostly house servants, some for field work.

Conditions: ½ cash, balance by bond, bearing interest from date of sale. Payable in one to two years to be secured by a mortgage of the *Negroes,* and appraised personal security. *Auctioneer will pay for the papers.*

A valuable Negro woman, accustomed to all kinds of house work. Is a good plain cook, and excellent dairy maid, washes and irons. She has four children, one a girl about 13 years of age, another 7, a boy about 5, and an infant 11 months old. 2 of the children will be sold with mother, the others separately, if it best suits the purchaser.

A very valuable Blacksmith, wife and daughters; the Smith is in the prime of life, and a perfect master at his trade. His wife about 27 years old, and his daughters 12 and 10 years old have been brought up as house servants, and as such are very valuable. Also for sale 2 likely young negro wenches, one of whom is 16 the other 13, both of whom have been taught and accustomed to the duties of house servants. The 16 year old wench has one eye.

A likely yellow girl about 17 or 18 years old, has been accustomed to all kinds of house and garden work. She is sold for no fault. Sound as a dollar.

House servants: The owner of a family described herein, would sell them for a good price only, they are offered for no fault whatever, but because they can be done without, and money is needed. He has been offered $1250. They consist of a man 30 to 33 years old, who has been raised in a genteel Virginia family as house servant, Carriage driver etc., in all which he excels. His wife a likely wench of 25 to 30 raised in like manner, as chamber maid, seamstress, nurse etc., their two children, girls of 12 and 4 or 5. They are bright mulattoes, of mild tractable dispositions, unassuming manners, and of genteel appearance and well worthy the notice of a gentleman of fortune needing such.

Also 14 Negro Wenches ranging from 16 to 25 years of age, all sound and capable of doing a good days work in the house or field.

A TYPICAL NEGRO.

We publish herewith three portraits, from photographs by M'Pherson and Oliver, of the negro Gordon, who escaped from his master in Mississippi, and came into our lines at Baton Rouge in March last. One of these portraits represents the man as he entered our lines, with clothes torn and covered with mud and dirt from his long race through the swamps and bayous, chased as he had been for days and nights by his master with several neighbors and a pack of blood-hounds; another shows him as he underwent the surgical examination previous to being mustered into the service —his back furrowed and scarred with the traces of a whipping administered on Christmas-day last; and the third represents him in United States uniform, bearing the musket and prepared for duty.

This negro displayed unusual intelligence and energy. In order to foil the scent of the blood-hounds who were chasing him he took from his plantation onions, which he carried in his pockets. After crossing each creek or swamp he rubbed his body freely with these onions, and thus, no doubt, frequently threw the dogs off the scent.

At one time in Louisiana he served our troops as guide, and on one expedition was unfortunately taken prisoner by the rebels, who, infuriated beyond measure, tied him up and beat him, leaving him for dead. He came to life, however, and once more made his escape to our lines.

By way of illustrating the degree of brutality which slavery has developed among the whites in the section of country from which this negro came, we append the following extract from a letter in the New York *Times*, recounting what was told by the refugees from Mrs. Gillespie's estate on the Black River:

The treatment of the slaves, they say, has been growing worse and worse for the last six or seven years.

Flogging with a leather strap on the naked body is common; also, paddling the body with a hand-saw until the skin is a mass of blisters, and then breaking the blisters with the teeth of the saw. They have "very often" seen slaves stretched out upon the ground with hands and feet held down by fellow-slaves, or lashed to stakes driven into the ground for "*burning*." Handfuls of dry corn-husks are then lighted, and the burning embers are whipped off with a stick so as to fall in showers of live sparks upon the naked back. This is continued until the victim is covered with blisters. If in his writhings of torture the slave gets his hands free to brush off the fire, the burning brand is applied to them.

Another method of punishment, which is inflicted for the higher order of crimes, such as running away, or other refractory conduct, is to dig a hole in the ground large enough for the slave to squat or lie down in. The victim is then stripped naked and placed in the hole, and a covering or grating of green sticks is laid over the opening. Upon this a quick fire is built, and the live embers sifted through upon the naked flesh of the slave, until his body is blistered and swollen almost to bursting. With just enough of life to enable him to crawl, the slave is then allowed to recover from his wounds if he can, or to end his sufferings by death.

GORDON AS HE ENTERED OUR LINES.

GORDON UNDER MEDICAL INSPECTION.

GORDON IN HIS UNIFORM AS A U. S. SOLDIER.

Good Prices for Negroes.—We learn from the Sumter (Ala.) Democrat, that on the 24th instant, Hon. A. A. Coleman, executor of the late Benjamin Ivy, with Wm. K. Ustick as Auctioneer, sold fifty-two negroes of indiscriminate ages, sizes and conditions, for the large sum of $50,000, lacking only thirty dollars, being an average of over $960. Eighteen of these negroes were under ten years of age; eight were forty years old and upwards, and they were sold in families without separation, frequently as many as five or six selling together. Negro men brought from $1400 to $1675; boys from twelve to fourteen years old from $1250 to 1400; girls from nine to fourteen years of age, from $1050 to $1400.

One of the most extraordinary sales of slaves—not so much on account of their number as the prices obtained for them, although even the number was very large—was made at public auction at the village of Autaugaville during four days of last week. One hundred and seventy slaves belonging to the estate of Richard Morton, were sold, on twelve months' time, with interest added, for the enormous sum of *one hundred and sixty thousand dollars*, being an average of $941 and a fraction over. In the large number composing the lot were old and young, halt and lame, and one was deaf and dumb. A girl aged 14, black and a field hand, brought $1935. A young fellow was bid off for $2160. Evidently, the 'Flush times of Alabama' have come again.—*Montgomery Confederation.*

NEGROES.

On last Monday, a great many negroes were sold in this place—only four of them, however, at sheriff sale, and those under a disputed title. Somewhere between 50 and 75 must have been put upon the block. They were sold in all manner of ways—for cash, on one and two years' credit, and sometimes with interest, and sometimes without. They brought high prices, especially those that were sold on a credit. It is unnecessary to specify prices, but they were large. These high prices, doubtless bring many of the negroes into market, although some of them were estate negroes. And it is likely that the same prices will range for several years at least. Cotton is bringing very high figures. In fact, a cotton plantation is now about the best thing in which capitalists can invest. We have frequently expressed the opinion that the culture will never again overtake the consumption, so as materially to reduce the prices. We reiterate the same opinion now. And so long as that is the case, the price of negroes must range high. Besides, there is great demand for negro labor on railroad work. That demand, also, must continue for some years, and perhaps increase. Hence, in our judgment, the price of negroes will not decline for years to come. Even the introduction of a million of Africans would not materially affect prices. Some will, undoubtedly, be smuggled in, but there is no possibility of re-opening the slave trade, lawfully, until a dissolution of the Union.

Negro property is getting to be a monopoly—the high price of it makes it so. And we are sorry to see that a great many of our largest holders are opposed to the re-opening the African slave trade, either lawfully or otherwise. They are acting upon a mistaken principle. They fear that it will reduce the value of their negroes. We have already expressed the opinion, that the introduction of a million would have no material effect. But suppose it did, negro property would be so much the safer. For there would be a larger mass of our own citizens interested in its perpetuity, and it would command still more respect abroad. All our people are still true to the South, because they are influenced by principle; but can we hope that will always be the case, when the great majority of the slaves shall become a perfect monopoly, as it is now fast doing, in the hands of a few rich men, comprising not one twentieth of our population; and when there will no longer be any hope of a laboring man ever possessing a slave?

We have no time or space now to discuss this subject; but it is one of fearful importance, and there is no use in shutting our eyes to its magnitude. It will have to be met before the end of the century. In our opinion, the very existence of the South depends upon the re-opening of the African Slave Trade.—*Tuskegee, (Ala.) Republican.*

Runaway Negro Camp.—On Friday last, a runaway negro camp was discovered on an 'island,' in Big Swamp, situated between Bladen and Robeson counties. On Saturday morning, a company of twelve or fifteen started out to hunt them, and after starting them from their camp, one of the negroes fired at Mr. David C. Lewis, wounding him, from the effects of which he died on Sunday morning. On Friday, a man named Taylor was shot at twice from the same place, but missed. The negroes had cleared a place for a garden, had cows, &c., in the swamp. None arrested. The swamp is about four miles wide, and almost impenetrable.—*Wilmington (N. C.) Journal, 14th.*

☞ A negro has been tarred and feathered, by his colored brethren, at Washington, Pa., in consequence of it being clearly proved that he was in the employ of slaveholders, in hunting up fugitives.

From the American Baptist.

A VISIT TO THE SLAVE MOTHER WHO KILLED HER CHILD.

Last Sabbath, after preaching in the city prison, Cincinnati, through the kindness of the Deputy Sheriff, I was permitted to visit the apartment of that unfortunate woman, concerning whom there has been so much excitement during the last two weeks.

I found her with an infant in her arms only a few months old, and observed that it had a large bunch on its forehead. I inquired the cause of the injury. She then proceeded to give a detailed account of her attempt to kill her children.

She said, that when the officers and slave-hunters came to the house in which they were concealed, she caught a shovel and struck two of her children on the head, and then took a knife and cut the throat of the third, and tried to kill the other,—that if they had given her time, she would have killed them all—that with regard to herself, she cared but little ; but she was unwilling to have her children suffer as she had done.

I inquired if she was not excited almost to madness when she committed the act. No, she replied, I was as cool as I now am ; and would much rather kill them at once, and thus end their sufferings, than have them taken back to slavery, and be murdered by piece-meal.

She then told the story of her wrongs. She spoke of her days of suffering, of her nights of unmitigated toil, while the bitter tears coursed their way down her cheeks, and fell in the face of the innocent child as it looked smiling up, little conscious of the danger and probable suffering that awaited it.

As I listened to the facts, and witnessed the agony depicted in her countenance, I could not but exclaim, Oh, how terrible is irresponsible power, when exercised over intelligent beings ! She alludes to the child that she killed as being free from all trouble and sorrow, with a degree of satisfaction that almost chills the blood in one's veins ; yet she evidently possesses all the passionate tenderness of a mother's love. She is about twenty-five years of age, and apparently possesses an average amount of kindness, with a vigorous intellect, and much energy of character.

The two men and the two other children were in another apartment, but her mother-in-law was in the same room. She says she is the mother of eight children, most of whom have been separated from her ; that her husband was once separated from her twenty-five years, during which time she did not see him ; that could she have prevented it, she would never have permitted him to return, as she did not wish him to witness her sufferings, or be exposed to the brutal treatment that he would receive.

She states that she has been a faithful servant, and in her old age she would not have attempted to obtain her liberty ; but as she became feeble, and less capable of performing labor, her master became more and more exacting and brutal in his treatment, until she could stand it no longer ; that the effort could result only in death, at most—she therefore made the attempt.

She witnessed the killing of the child, but said she neither encouraged nor discouraged her daughter-in-law,—for under similar circumstances she should probably have done the same. The old woman is from sixty to seventy years of age, has been a professor of religion about twenty years, and speaks with much feeling of the time when she shall be delivered from the power of the oppressor, and dwell with the Savior, ' where the wicked cease from troubling, and the weary are at rest.'

These slaves (as far as I am informed) have resided all their lives within sixteen miles of Cincinnati. We are frequently told that Kentucky slavery is very innocent. If these are its fruits, where it exists in a mild form, will some one tell us what we may expect from its more objectionable features ? But comments are unnecessary.   P. S. BASSETT.

Fairmount Theological Seminary,
    Cincinnati, (Ohio,) Feb. 12, 1856.

John Newton, captain of a slave trading vessel, read the Bible daily. On board the ship with hundreds of human souls in the hold, he pursued his studies for the ministry and held prayer service on deck twice daily. He wrote a hymn: "How Sweet the name of Jesus Sounds."

Anti-slavery Quakers had Negro pews. (See Frederick Douglass memoirs.)

Southern slave-holding interests owed New York merchants $200,-000,000 in the middle of the nineteenth century.

Sir John Hawkins, a slaver licensed by Queen Elizabeth, transported his human cargo in ships named *Jesus*, *Angel*, and *Grace of God*.

Brown University at Providence, Rhode Island, was established in 1764 from the fortune made by the Brown brothers whose wealth was based on the profits made from their ships in the African slave trade.

A judge sentenced a slave to be severely lashed for purchasing stolen goods. Before the sentence was carried out, the slave addressed the court, saying that the thief from whom he had purchased the goods was a white man. Then he asked the court if the thief would be punished if caught.

"Of course he will be punished," the judge replied.

"Then," said the slave, "you must punish my master also. The goods I bought had no parents, but my master purchased me knowing I was stolen from my mother and father."

Punishment was set aside.

From Pennsylvania Packet and Daily Advertiser, May 20, 1788.

In 1800, when condemned to die for plotting a slave revolt in Virginia, Gabriel Prosser looked the judge in the eye and said, "You only do to me what the British would have done to George Washington had they caught him."

The value of a slave condemned and executed, or dying before execution, shall be paid by the public to the owner.

If a Negro shall be convicted of an offense within the benefit of clergy, judgment of death shall not be given, but he shall be burnt in the hand in open court, and suffer such other corporal punishment as the court shall think fit.

If a Negro give false testimony, he shall without further trial have one ear nailed to the pillory for one hour and then the ear cut off and the other nailed and cut off in like manner, and moreover receive on his bare back thirty-nine lashes, well laid on, at the public whipping post, or such other punishment as the court shall think proper, not extending to life or limb.

"If he knows enough to be hanged, he knows enough to vote."

Frederick Douglass on the question of Negro Suffrage.

Nat Turner, the black revolutionist of 1831, rebuked another slave for bowing and scraping before a white man.

"But we are slaves," said the fellow.

Turner replied, "You deserve to be."

DAYTON, Ohio, Aug. 7, 1865.

To my old Master, Col. P. H. Anderson, Big Spring, Tenn.

SIR: I got your letter and was glad to find that you had not forgotten Jourdon, and that you wanted me to come back and live with you again, promising to do better for me than anybody else can. I have often felt uneasy about you. I thought the Yankees would have hung you long before this for harboring rebs, they found at your house. I suppose they never heard about your going to Col. Martin's to kill the Union soldier that was left by his company in their stable. Although you shot at me twice before I left you, I did not want to hear of your being hurt, and am glad you are still living. It would do me good to go back to the dear old home again and see Miss Mary and Miss Martha and Allen, Esther, Green and Lee. Give my love to them all, and tell them I hope we will meet in the better world, if not in this. I would have gone back to see you all when I was working in the Nashville Hospital, but one of the neighbors told me that Henry intended to shoot me if ever he got a chance.

I want to know particularly what the good chance is you propose to give me. I am doing tolerably well here; I get $25 a month, with victuals and clothing; have a comfortable home for Mandy, (the folks call her Mrs. Anderson) and the children Milly, Jane and Grundy, go to school and are learning well; the teacher says Grundy has a head for a preacher. They go to Sunday school and Mandy and me attend church regularly. We are kindly treated; sometimes we overhear others saying, "Them colored people were slaves" down in Tennessee. The children feel hurt when they hear such remarks, but I tell them it was no disgrace in Tennessee to belong to Col. Anderson. Many darkies would have been proud, as I used to was, to call you master. Now, if you will write and say what wages you will give me, I will be better able to decide whether it would be to my advantage to move back again.

As to my freedom, which you say I can have, there is nothing to be gained on that score, as I got my free-papers in 1864 from the Provost Marshal General of the Department of Nashville.—Mandy says she would be afraid to go back without some proof that you are disposed to treat us justly and kindly—and we have concluded to test your sincerity by asking you to send us our wages for the time we served you. This will make us forget and forgive old scores, and rely on your justice and friendship in the future. I served you faithfully for thirty two years, and Mandy twenty years. At $25 a month for me, and $2 a week for Mandy, our earnings would amount to $11,680. Add to this the interest for the time our wages has been kept back, and deduct what you paid for our clothing and three doctor's visits to me, and pulling a tooth for Mandy, and the balance will show what we are in justice entitled to. Please send the money by Adams Express, in care of V. Winters, Esq., Dayton, Ohio. If you fail to pay us for faithful labors in the past we can have little faith in your promises in the future.—We trust the good Maker has opened your eyes to the wrongs which you and your fathers have done to me and my fathers, in making us toil for you for generations without recompense. Here I draw my wages every Saturday night, but in Tennessee there was never any pay for the negroes any more than for the horses and cows. Surely there will be a day of reckoning for those who defraud the laborer of his hire.

In answering this letter please state if there would be any safety for my Milly and Jane, who are now grown up and both good looking girls. You know how it was with poor Matilda and Catherine. I would rather stay here and starve and die, if it come to that, than have my girls brought to shame by the violence and wickedness of the young masters. You will also please state if there has been any good schools opened for the colored children in your neighborhood; the great desire of my life now is to give my children an education, and have them form virtuous habits.

From your old servant,
JOURDON ANDERSON.

P. S.—Say howdy to George Carter, and thank him for taking the pistol from you when you were shooting at me.

SPIRIT OF SLAVERY.

Prejudice against the Colored Man.

At the recent Anniversary of the New-York State Anti-Slavery Society.

Rev. THEODORE S. WRIGHT, of New-York, spoke on the following resolution:

Resolved, That the prejudice peculiar to our country, which subjects our colored brethren to a degrading distinction in our worshipping assemblies, and schools, which withholds from them that kind and courteous treatment to which as well as other citizens, they have a right, at public houses, on board steamboats, in stages, and in places of public concourse, is the spirit of slavery, is nefarious and wicked and should be practically reprobated and discountenanced.

Mr. President, with much feeling do I rise to address the society on this resolution, and I should hardly have been induced to have done it, had I not been requested. I confess I am personally interested in this resolution. But were it not for the fact that none can feel the lash but those who have it put upon them; that none know where the chain galls but those who wear it, I would not address you.

This is serious business, sir. The prejudice which exists against the colored man, the free man, is like the atmosphere, every where felt by him. It is true that in these United States, and in this State, there are men, like myself, colored with a skin like my own, who are not subjected to the lash; who are not liable to have their wives and infants torn from them; from whose hand the Bible is not taken. It is true that we may walk abroad; we may enjoy our domestic comforts, our families; retire to the closet; visit the sanctuary, and may be permitted to urge on our children and our neighbors in well doing. But sir, still we are slaves---every where we feel the chain galling us. It is by that prejudice which the resolution condemns; the spirit of slavery; the law which has been enacted here, by a corrupt public sentiment, through the influence of slavery which treats moral agents, different from the rule of God, which treats them irrespective of their morals or intellectual cultivation. This spirit is withering all our hopes, and oft times causes the colored parent as he looks upon his child, to wish he had never been born. Often is the heart of the colored mother, as she presses her child to her bosom, filled with sorrow to think that, by reason of this prejudice, it is cut off from all hopes of usefulness in this land. Sir, this prejudice is wicked.

If the nation and church understood this matter, I would not speak a word about that killing influence that destroys the colored man's reputation. This influence cuts us off from every thing; it follows us up from childhood to manhood; it excludes us from all stations of profit, usefulness and honor; takes away from us all motive for pressing forward in enterprises, useful and important to the world and to ourselves.

In the first place, it cuts us off from the advantages of the mechanic arts almost entirely. A colored man can hardly learn a trade, and if he does, it is difficult for him to find any one who will employ him to work at that trade, in any part of the State. In most of our large cities, there are associations of mechanics, who legislate out of their society colored men. And in many cases where our young men have learned trades, they have had to come down to low employments, for want of encouragement in those trades.

It must be a matter of rejoicing to know that in this vicinity colored fathers and mothers have the privileges of education. It must be a matter of rejoicing, that in this vicinity colored parents can have their children trained up in schools.--- At present, we find the colleges barred against us.

I will say nothing about the inconvenience which I have experienced myself, and which every man of color experiences, though made in the image of God. I will say nothing about the inconvenience we find in travelling; how we are frowned upon and despised. No matter how we may demean ourselves, we find embarrassments every where.

But sir, this prejudice goes farther. It debars men from heaven. While sir, slavery cuts off the colored portion of the community from religious privileges, men are made infidels. What, they demand, is your Christianity? How do you regard your brethren? How do you treat them at the Lord's table? Where is your consistency in talking about the heathen; traversing the ocean to circulate the Bible every where, while you frown upon them at the door? These things meet us, and weigh down our spirits.

And, sir, the constitution of society, moulded by this prejudice, destroys souls. I have known extensively, that in revivals which have been blest and enjoyed, in this part of the country, the colored population were overlooked. I recollect an instance. The Lord God was pouring out His Spirit. He was entering every house, and sinners were converted. I asked, Where is the colored man? where is my brother? where is my sister? who is feeling for him and her? who is weeping for them? who is endeavoring to pull them out of the fire? No reply was made. I was asked to go around with one of the elders, and visit them. We went and they humbled themselves. The church commenced efficient efforts, and God blessed them as soon as they began to act for these people as though they had souls.

And sir, the manner in which our churches are regulated destroys souls. Whilst the church is thrown open to every body, and one says, come, come in and share the blessings of the sanctuary, this is the gate to heaven—he says to the colored man, *be careful where you take your stand.* I know an efficient church in this State, where a respectable colored man went to the house of God, and was going to take a seat in the gallery, and one of the officers contended with him, and says— "you cannot go there sir."

In one place the people had come together to the house of the Lord. The sermon was preached —the emblems were about to be administered— and all at once the persons who managed the church, thought the value of their pews would be diminished, if the colored people sat in them. They objected to their sitting there, and the colored people left and went into the gallery, and that too when they were thinking of handling the memorials of the broken body and shed blood of the Saviour! And, sir, this prejudice follows the colored man, every where and depresses his spirits.

Thanks be to God, there is a buoyant principle that elevates the poor down-trodden colored man above all this:—It is that there is society which regards man according to his worth; It is the fact, that when he looks up to Heaven, he knows that God treats him like a moral agent, irrespective of caste, or the circumstances in which he may be placed. Amid the embarrassments which he has to meet, and the scorn and contempt that is heaped upon him, he is cheered by the hope that he will soon be disenthralled, and soon, like a bird set forth from its cage, wing his flight to Jesus, where he can be happy, and may look down with pity on the man who despises the poor slave for being what God made him, and the man who despises him because he is identified with the poor slave. Blessed be God for the principles of the Gospel! Were it not for these, and for the fact that a better day is dawning, I would not wish to live. Blessed be God for the anti slavery movement. Blessed be God that there is a war waging with slavery, that the granite rock is about to be rolled from its base. But as long as the colored man is to be looked upon as an inferior caste, so long will they disregard his cries, his groans, his shrieks.

I rejoice, sir, in this Society; and I deem the day when I joined this Society, as one of the proudest days of my life. And I know I can die better, in more peace to-day, to know there are men who will plead the cause of my children.

Does a man, who walks erect, with the conscience, and heart and reason of a man, need to be told that this abominable trade, or rather piracy, endangers the peace of the nation? To say nothing about our good name, which was lost long ago, does any one suppose that this nation can carry on open war upon God and man, and continue to prosper?

SLAVE TRADE.

The internal Slave Trade.

The New-York Journal of Commerce, of Oct. 12, 1835, published a letter "from a very good and sensible man in Virginia," in which we find the following language:—"The negroes have to thank their kind friends for this (Lynch Law.) an for 20,000 moved from the state this year into perpetual slavery, and not one liberated where hitherto there have been annually numbers set free." "The kind friends," ironically referred to, are the abolitionists. It seems then, that the abolitionists last year caused Virginia to sell into "perpetual slavery," 20,000 of her own native citizens, for which she probably received, at the market price, not less than $10,000,000—a very large amount of crime this, to be committed out of spite towards a set of reporters. But large as it is, we have no doubt it is far exceeded by the iniquitous traffic of the present year. There is every reason to believe that more slaves have been this year torn from their homes in the single state of Virginia, than were ever brought into the whole United States in any one year during the continuance of the foreign traffic. The enormous price of slaves at the southwest has given such activity to the internal slave trade as was never known before. The northern slave states now receive more money by selling of their people, than by all their other productions put together. To speak within bounds, *more people have this year been sold and driven away to the cotton, rice and sugar plantations of the remote south than inhabit the city of Boston.*

OUTRAGE AT PRINCETON, N. J.—At the late commencement of Princeton College, a presbyterian clergyman of respectability, and an alumnus of the Theological Seminary at Princeton was brutally attacked and kicked out of doors, by the son of a Southern slaveholder, and supposed to have been a student in the college. When an account was first published, it caused some sensation and inquiry, as the color of the clergyman was not stated.—President Carnahan therefore published a statement "that the facts appear to have been manufactured." He then proceeded to state that "a respectable colored man" had been indeed turned out by somebody, but not by a student of the college—that "that respectable gentleman," on the spot, "saw no acts of violence," &c.

The "respectable colored man" was Rev. THEODORE S. WRIGHT, of New York, the gentleman who spoke lately at the annual meeting of the New York State A. S. Society, in Utica, and who preached the next Sabbath in the 2d Presbyterian church. Many of our readers will long remember him. It is a little remarkable that Pres. Carnahan should not have stated that the "colored man" was a clergyman of the Presbyterian church. The young man who committed the assault is said to have been previously dismissed from the college. Mr. Wright has given an account of the affair in an excellent letter addressed to Rev. Dr. Alexander.—*Friend of Man.*

In 1764, George Washington purchased Jack and a woman named Cleo; in 1758 he got Gregory. Soon afterward he acquired Hannah and child, Will, and a man with one hand named Charles. Judy and her child were later purchases, as were Adam, two men each named Frank, and Will, who were purchased from Mrs. Mary Lee in 1768. Will became famous as Billy Lee, the general's inseparable manservant from then on until the general's death in 1799. He was painted by Savage in the picture of the Washington family and he was the only slave freed outright under terms of Washington's will.

In 1766, Washington advertised for the capture of a runaway, Tom, who was only one of any number who "eloped" and were pursued with vigor. It was probably that same Tom to whom Washington referred in a letter of July 2, 1766, addressed to a ship captain, John Thompson, in which Washington shipped the slave to the West Indies in exchange for some rum and sundries. Another slave named Waggoner Jack went on the same voyage in 1791 in exchange for a cask of wine.

On November 14, 1835, according to the *Alexandria Gazette*, a reporter in Fairfax County, Virginia, observed a group of blacks working at Mount Vernon and asked their names. He was told they were Joseph Smith, Sambo Anderson and his son William, George Lear, Duck and Morris Jasper, Levi and Jo Richardson, William Moss, William Hayes and Nancy Squander.

They were tending the graves of George and Martha Washington, for they were freed after the death of Mrs. Washington. Under the terms of the general's will, all the slaves were to be freed after the death of his wife. However, his nephew, Supreme Court Justice Bushrod Washington, sold twenty-one of them, he claimed, to pay taxes on the estate.

I have heard from an eyewitness that on more than one occasion when the Sage of Monticello (Thomas Jefferson) left that retreat for the Presidential abode in Washington, on more than one occasion there

Thomas Jefferson's slave

would be, on top of the same coach, a yellow boy running away. When told that one of his slaves was running away without leave, Jefferson said, 'Well, let him go his way—his right is as good as his father's.'

It has also been credibly reported over the signatures of respectable citizens that a reputed daughter of Thomas Jefferson has been exposed for sale in New Orleans as a slave.

—William Goodell,
Slavery and Anti-Slavery, 1853.

Mr. Jefferson freed a number of his servants in his will. I think he would have freed all of them if his affairs had not been so much involved. . . . He freed one girl some years before he died and there was a great deal of talk about it. People said he freed her because she was his own daughter; she was ———— daughter. I know that I have seen him come out of her mother's room many a morning when I went up to Monticello very early. When she was nearly grown, by Mr. Jefferson's direction, I paid her stage fare to Philadelphia and gave her fifty dollars. I have never seen her since and don't know what became of her.

Statement by Edmund Bacon, for twenty years the manager of Thomas Jefferson's estate. From Jefferson at Monticello: The Private Life of Thomas Jefferson, by Reverend Hamilton W. Pierson, New York, 1862.

Free Negroes in Slave States.—A foreign correspondent of the "Atlas" furnishes that paper with the following copy of an interesting correspondence (*supposed to have taken place*) between Alexandre Dumas and a celebrated Southern Democrat :

Among his other characteristics, Dumas is a great traveller. Having visited the other quarters of the globe, he is anxious to go to America. Being, however, a mulatto, he is said to be afraid that he will be taken and sold as a slave. This has given rise to the following correspondence, of which I give you the first English translation* :

From Alexandre Dumas to the Hon. J. C. C—n.
Paris, April 1st, 1847.

Sir : I shall make no apology for addressing you the present letter. I see your name enrolled among the leading Democrats of the United States. I cannot but feel assured that the request I am about to make will be cheerfully granted. My name cannot be unknown to you. I am the author of Monte Christo and other works, which have heralded my fame throughout Europe. I rank among my personal friends many individuals of noble and even royal birth. I am the familiar associate of the leading literary and scientific characters of Paris. I am a member of the Institute, and wear the cross of the Legion of Honor. Yet my mother was a negro, and I am not ashamed to confess that my person makes open declaration of my lineage.

I have travelled in other quarters of the globe, yet resembling my renowned namesake, who sighed to conquer new worlds, I am anxious to visit your transatlantic continent. In this, I am less moved by vain curiosity than a desire to breathe the pure atmosphere of civil liberty, and to mingle my ardent sympathies with those of a free and happy people. One thing alone deters me from immediately realizing this cherished wish of my heart. I am told that my African blood will subject me to inconveniences in the United States, and that I may be even taken and sold as a slave, according to the existing laws. This, of course, I hold to be an atrocious slander, propagated by the envious monarchists of the old world. Yet I have deemed it prudent to address you on the subject, and solicit your advice. If there be any difficulty in my travelling through the United States, might it not be removed by my being invested with some diplomatic functions, which I have no doubt my friend and admirer, the Duke de Montpensier, would readily obtain for me. An early reply to this note will confer upon me a lasting obligation. Accept, sir, the assurances of my highest consideration.   A. DUMAS.

From the Emancipator and Free American.

TYLER-ISING.

About five or six years ago, a Baptist minister of the North, a man of the highest integrity and scrupulousness of conscience, spent a few days at Richmond, Virginia, where he was hospitably entertained at the house of a Baptist lady. Among the servants who waited, our friend's attention was particularly drawn to one young man of very genteel address, and pleasant appearance, whose complexion was so very light as to make it difficult to believe he bore any African blood in his veins. Our friend was so much interested in his appearance, and so well pleased with his behavior, that he sought an opportunity of conversing with him in regard to the welfare of his soul. During the interview, some conversation of the following tenor took place; which has been brought to remembrance by the events of the last six months.

Minister.—Are you free, my friend ?
Servant.—No, master, I belong to the lady who keeps the house.
M.—Then you are a slave ?
S.—Yes, master, I am a slave.
M.—Were you born in this house ?
S.—No, master, I was bought. My mistress bought me of my old master, Governor Tyler, down at Williamsburgh.
M.—Were you born on Governor Tyler's plantation ?
S.—Yes, master, I was born there.
M.—What is your name ?

S.—My name is John, sir ; my mother called me *John Tyler*, because she said Governor Tyler was my father. You know such things happen sometimes on plantations.
M.—Governor Tyler your father ? and did he sell you ?
S.—Yes, master, planters do it, you know, the same as others.
M.—Were there any other children of your mother that were thought to be your master's children ?
S.—Yes, sir, several.
M.—And what became of them ?
S.—I reckon they are all sold before now.

Now, we would not express the slightest belief that the man who is now the acting President of the United States ever had children by his slaves, or

ever sold his own children ; although, from what is known of his pecuniary circumstances, and from the general practice among the slaveholders in lower Virginia, it is altogether probable he has supported his family by selling the increase of his slave stock. But we have the fullest confidence, the certainty, that such a conversation as we have described did take place in Richmond, and that the genteel, slender-built, light-complexioned young slave, did tell Mr. ——, a Baptist minister, that he believed himself to be the son of Governor Tyler. Whether the slave told the truth or not, Governor Tyler knows; we do not, and therefore tell the story as it was told to us, for what it is worth.

In the year 1837, or the beginning of 1838, a colored man passed through Poughkeepsie, on his way

SLAVE TAX RECEIPTS for State of Virginia — 1860 and 1862

Peter S. Roller   TO Y. C. AMMON, S. R. C. Dr. To Taxes for 1862.
To Revenue on 3 Tract   251 — 207 — 6   1 Lot $ 127.19
Do   1 Whites 21 years old, 7.34, 6.70 2.05 3.10
Do   Free Negroes 21 years old, $1.20 Cents,   38.88
Do 6280 Taxable Property, 60 Cents on the $100,   33.06
To   Military Tax, 20 per cent.   6.25
To   5 County Levy 75 Cents, Parish Levy 50 Cents,
To   Railroad Tax,   28.98
Rec'd Pay, C. Miller   Deputy for Y. C. AMMON, S. R. C. $ 234.36

Peter S. Roller   TO J. R. KOOGLER, S. R. C. Dr. To Taxes for 1860.
To Revenue on 4 Tract 252 5³ 39³ 387 1 Lot $ 89.52
                    4958, 81. 456, 3513   144
Do   4 Slaves over 12 years old, $1.20 Cents,   4.80
Do   1 Whites over 21 years old, 80 Cents,   80
Do 2959 Other Taxable Property, 40 Cents on the $100,   11.83
To   3 County Levy $1.05 Cents, Parish Levy 1.25 Cents,   6.40
To   Railroad Tax,

Free blacks who were jailed and unable to pay their fines were often sold back into slavery.

to Canada, who called his name *Charles Tyler*, and who seemed to have a good deal of knowledge of things at Washington. He told the friend who gave him food and clothing for his journey, that his master had been in Congress, and that he was body servant. Some months afterwards, another man passed by the same route, who called himself Gideon, and said his master was a Mr. Leigh, of Virginia, who had been in Congress. Gideon said his wife had been sold away by his master, and, as he understood, was sent to New Orleans. He also said he knew Charles Tyler; and that he had belonged to Governor Tyler; and that Governor Tyler thought so much of him, that he would rather have lost every one of his other slaves, than that Charles should leave him. Charles Tyler remained in Canada, gaining the good will of all, until Lord Durham, then Governor General, returned to England, when he took Charles with him, as his waiter, or in some other confidential capacity; and it is supposed he is still in England, perhaps in the services of the Durham family. Perhaps Governor Tyler would do well to instruct *his* worthy ambassador extraordinary and minister plenipotentiary, EDWARD EVERETT, to make a peremptory demand for the surrender of his property, thus wrongfully withheld by the humbug of British law. It would be a capital offset to the British demand for the surrender of McLeod, while he was known to be in the custody of American law. In point of merit, the two demands would be precisely on a par.

GOOD.—A very respectful memorial, signed by sixty ministers of the Maine Conference of the Methodist Episcopal church, has been sent to Mr. Tyler, protesting against the President of a Christian republic holding slaves, &c.

One of the presiding elders remarked, that not many years ago, President Tyler inherited from his father a number of slaves, from whom he selected some fifteen or twenty for his own use, and *disposed of the remainder.* "Those fifteen or twenty have have multiplied till now the President has seventy or eighty slaves. Having nothing for them to do, he proposed to some of them, not long since, to go on a plantation and work; this they steadily declined doing—and they are literally eating up the President."

Notwithstanding all this, Mr. Tyler seems to think it not such a dreadful thing to be eaten up—for in the Virginia Convention, 1829, he went with the slavery party against a *free basis* representation.— *Philanthropist.*

FURTHER PARTICULARS CONCERNING THE SCHOONER AMISTAD.

The following letter from the New London Gazette office, gives further particulars concerning the Spanish schooner, and as every thing relating to this subject is read with interest, we lay it before our readers.

NEW LONDON GAZETTE OFFICE, August 30th, 1839.

We regret to see in some of your papers complaints that they were not duly supplied with the particulars concerning the capture of the Amistad. As one of the conductors of the press in your city, from whom we have received repeated marks of editorial courtesy, expresses some surprise that we had not furnished him with the earliest intelligence on this subject, we deem it due to ourselves to state, that when we were called on by Captain Gedney at 12 o'clock on the night of the 26th, the first thing we did, after despatching an express for the Marshal, was to write a minute account to one of your daily papers, with a request that yourself and others should be supplied immediately with a copy of the same. As we had seen no publication of this, it, probably owing to the tardiness and irregularity of the mail, was not received till after the publication of the Gazette. In addition to this, the first papers that we printed at this office on the evening of the 28th, were sent by private conveyance to Stonington to the agents of the New York boats, who delivered them promptly the next morning. This much to exenerate ourselves from any imputation of a want of professional courtesy.

It is a source of regret that several of your papers, with no other authority than mere rumor, have published accounts, which, if credited, must deprive those to whom it is due, of their just share of credit in this capture. It has been stated that Captain Gedney was not on board the Washington at the time the schooner was seized. The truth is, that he was on board, and was, at the time the schooner was discovered, engaged in running a line of soundings. The Amistad was first observed by Lieut. R. W. Meade, who at that time had charge of the deck. Capt. Gedney scrutinized her with his glass, and observing wagons and people on the shore, concluded that she was a smuggler, and accordingly despatched a boat, with six men, and arms, in charge of Lieut. Meade and Passed Midshipman D. D. Porter, for the purpose of seizing her. On approaching the schooner, the two Spanish gentlemen made their appearance on deck, and exclaimed, "Bless the Holy Virgin, you are our preservers." The boat laid aboa d the prize, and Lieut. Meade and Mr. Porter, followed by two of the men, jumped on deck, and drove the Africans below. Lieut. Meade then demanded in Spanish who was their captain, and where were their colors; when a torn Spanish ensign was produced, and by his orders it was set in the main rigging as a signal of distress to Capt. Gedney to send another boat alongside. The joy of the two passengers was unbounded. One of them, Senor Montez, the elder, who had been threatened every day during his captivity with death, threw his arms around Mr. Meade, who, under the circumstances, and from the by no means gentle nature of the embrace, being led to think that his intention was any thing but amicable, presented a pistol at his face, with a threat that unless he relaxed his hold he would shoot him. He was, however, soon convinced of the sincerity of his intentions by the tears of delight and thankfulness of the poor old man. Mr. Meade and two men remained in charge of the prize, while Mr. Porter, with four others, went ashor to arrest the leader and his accomplices, who were on the beach. On their approach, the blacks leapt into their boat, and pulled towards the schooner, when Mr. Porter discharged a pistol and they hove to. They were taken on board the brig, when Cingues, watching a convenient opportunity, leapt overboard, diving and swimming like a fish, till he was caught with a boat-hook. Meantime, Capt. Gedney came up with the Washington, and took the prize in tow for New London.

It has been stated that the schooner was taken by boys; this is also incorrect; she was taken by able-bodied men, who were prepared for the worst, and who would have been hard customers to deal with in case of a brush. On board the Washington there are several naval apprentices, and it is not out of place here to bear testimony to their neat and healthy appearance as well as their orderly deportment. We have cause to hope that from the adoption of this system, our navy, whilst it protects our commerce throughout the world, will at the same time be educating a class of mariners, in seamanship and character equal to those of any other nation, at the same time providing for a large class of indigent boys, who otherwise would become the inmates of our prisons.

The advantage of the surveying squadron to our revenue in preventing smuggling is also proved. In fact, we have long been of the opinion that it would be well for the service and for our commerce, if the revenue cutters were placed in charge of the junior officers of the navy, who would be thus qualifying themselves for more important duties. We have no doubt that they would prove equally as efficient as those who now make a sinecure of what was originally intended as a safeguard against frauds on the revenue.

You have doubtless received ere this a report of the investigation in presence of Judge Judson.— Segnor Montez is writing a history of his sufferings, which a friend has kindly offered to translate for us, and should it develop any additional facts of importance, they shall be transmitted to you at once. The negroes have been taken to New Haven, where they will await in jail their trial, which is to take place at Hartford on the 17th day of September next. The schooner is discharging at New London, where probably both vessel and cargo will be sold at auction.

If the Washington had not fallen in with the Amistad at the time and under the circumstances she did, the lives of the two passengers must inevitably have been sacrificed, and the cargo and vessel destroyed. They had supplied themselves with water, and were going to sea that night. Cingues had always declared that in case they were likely to be taken, he should kill the passengers, and that he would die sooner than be taken, and he enjoined upon his comrades to take his knife and avenge his death—that they had better die in self-defence, than be hung as they would be if taken.

The old gentleman says he never shall recover from the effects of his trouble, and that if he had been chained for ten years in a dungeon, it would not thus have broken him down. For some time previous to their deliverance, their only drink was the water of the sea. For more minute particulars, I would refer you to the Sun, of your city.

The schooner is of faultless model, and foul as her bottom is at present, she would have been able to work to windward of almost any of our cutters.

Names of the slaves as furnished by Lieutenant Meade:

Cingues, the chief.
Quash, his brother.
Faquorna, assisted in killing the captain.
Quimboo, also one of the murderers.
Maum, helped to kill the captain and cook.
Faa, concerned also in murder.
Gabao, one of the ringleaders, fat and short.
Funny, cook, apparently amiable.
Pana, alias Juan, speaks little English.
Llamani, very severe with passengers and cabin boy.
Guana, Sissi, Con, Sua, (sick) Zabray.
Paulo Dama, great friend of cabin boy—saved his life.
Conorno, cannibal, with six large tusks projecting at right angles from his mouth.
Jaoni, Pie, Naquai, Cuba, Baa, Berry, Prumuco, Faha, Huebo, Fuerre 1st, Fuerre 2d, Saa, Faguana, Chockamaw, Fasoma, Panguna, Kinna, Carri, Cuperi.
Antonio Gonzalez, cabin boy.
Cane, boy, 9 years old.
Females—Ferne, Kene, Margra, about 13 years of age.

NEW LONDON, Aug. 29, 1839.

A CARD.—The subscribers, Don Jose Ruiz and Don Pedro Montez, in gratitude for their most unhoped for and provid ntial rescue from the hands of a ruthless gang of African buccaneers, and an awful death, would take this means of expressing, in some slight degree, their thankfulness and obligation to Lieut. T. R. Gedney, and the officers and crew of the U. S. surveying brig Washington, for their decision in seizing the Amistad, and their unremitting kindness and hospitality in providing for their comfort on board their vessel, as well as the means they have taken for the protection of their property.

We also must express our indebtedness to that nation whose flag they so worthily bear, with an assurance that this act will be duly appreciated by our most gracious sovereign Her Majesty the Qneen of Spain.

DON JOSE RUIZ.
DON PEDRO MONTEZ.

Notice issued by the slavers aboard the Amistad

THE AFRICAN PRISONERS.

NEW HAVEN, Sept. 9, 1839.

To the committee on behalf of the African Prisoners:

I arrived here last Friday evening, with three men who are natives of Africa, and who were joined the next day by two others, to act as interpreters in conversing with Joseph Cinquez and his comrades. On going to the jail, the next morning, we found, to our great disappointment, that only one of the men, J.F., was able to converse with the prisoners. He is about 30 years of age, a native of Geshee or Gishe, which is about 100 or 150 miles from the mouth of the river Gallinus, in the interior, which is about a day's journey south of Sierra Leone. He was kidnapped when about 12 years of age, and was liberated in Columbia, by Bolivar. He is able to converse a little in the Mandingo dialect, but understands better that of Gallinao, which some of the prisoners can speak. Most of the prisoners can understand him, although none of them can speak his Geshee dialect. You may imagine the joy manifested by these poor Africans, when they heard one of their own color address them in a friendly manner, and in a language they could comprehend!

The prisoners are in comfortable rooms.— They are well clothed in dark striped cotton trowsers, called by some of the manufacturers "hard times," and in striped cotton shirts. The girls are in calico frocks, and have made the little shawls that were given them into turbans. The prisoners eyed the clothes some time, and laughed a good deal among themselves before they put them on. Their food is brought to them in separate tin pans, and they eat it in an orderly manner. In general, they are in good health. One of their number, however, died on Tuesday last, and two or three more are on the sick list and considered dangerous. They probably suffer for want of exercise in the open air. The four children are apparently from 10 to 12 years of age. The boy and two of the girls (who appeared to be sisters) are Mandingos, and the other girl is from Congo. They are robust, and full of hilarity, especially the Mandingos. The sheriff of the county took them to ride in a wagon on Friday. At first their eyes were filled with tears, and they seemed to be afraid, but soon they enjoyed themselves very well, and appeared to be greatly delighted. The children speak only their native dialects. Neither Cinquez nor any of his comrades have been manacled since they have been here. Their demeanor is altogether quiet, kind and orderly.

Most of the prisoners told the interpreter that they are from Mandingo. The district of Mandingo, in the Senegambia country, is bounded by the Atlantic Ocean, and is directly north of Liberia. Two or three of the men, besides one of the little girls, are natives of Congo, which is on the coast just south of the equator. The man with some of his teeth like tusks, is from Gahula in Congo. The teeth are said to be sharpened and made thus prominent by artificial means. One of the men from Mandingo, named Dama, talks Mandingo, and is a good looking and intelligent man. Cinquez is about five feet eight inches high, of fine proportions, with a noble air. Indeed, the whole company, although thin in flesh, and generally of slight forms and limbs, especially, are as good looking and intelligent a body of men as we usually meet with. All are young, and several are quite striplings. The Mandingos are described in books as being a very gentle race, cheerful in their dispositions, inquisitive, credulous, simple hearted, and much given to trading propensities. The Mandingo dialects are spoken extensively, and it is said to be the commercial language of nearly the whole coast of West Africa. We found that the following words are nearly the same in the Gallinas of the interpreter, in the Mandingo of the prisoners, in the Mandingo of Mungo Park, and in Jallowka of the German author, Adeburg, viz:—Sun, moon, woman, child, father, head, hand and foot. The numerals do not agree so well. If any person, who reads this statement, can furnish the Committee information concerning the Mandingo language, and its different dialects, particularly for vocabularies, they may render important service in the future examination of these unfortunate Africans. Professor Gibbs, of Yale College, has Adeburg's Mithridates, Park's Travels, and Mollien's Travels in Africa, and Professor Silliman has Prichard's Physical History of Mankind, which are at the service of the Committee.

Previous to this the Captain was very cruel and beat them severely. They would not take it, to use their own expression, and therefore turned to and fought for it. After this they did not know which way to go. But at length they told the Spaniards to take them to Sierra Leone. "They made fools of us," said Shinquau, "and did not go to Sierra Leone." In the day time they said they could tell very well which way to go by the sun, but at night the Spaniards deceived them, and put the vessel the other way. After this, said they, we got here, and did not know where we were.

Captain Green, of Sag Harbor, who was one of the first men the prisoners met ashore before their capture by Lieut. Gedney, of the U. S. brig Washington, and who has given me a circumstantial account, differing in many respects from what has been published, of all that took place, says that the Africans asked him by one of their number who speaks a little broken English, "What country is this?" He replied, this is America. They immediately asked, "Is it a slave country?" Captain Green answered, it is free here, and safe, and there are no Spanish law here. Shinquau then gave a sort of whistle, when they all sprang upon their feet and shouted. Captain Green and his associates sprang to their wagon for their guns, supposing the Africans were about to attack them. But Shinquau came up, delivered up his cutlass and gun, and even offered his hat, &c., and the rest did the same, indicating that they would give all up, that Capt. G. might take charge of the schooner and everything on board. They however begged of him to take them to Sierra Leone. Shinquau positively assured Capt. G. at the time, and he repeats it now, that they threw nothing overboard. The stories about his loosening his girdle, and letting three or four hundred doubloons drop into the sea, and of diving and keeping under water forty minutes, are considered fabulous. The Africans assert that there was a quantity of doubloons in the trunks that were carried on shore on Long Island, and Capt. Green says he heard the money rattle as the trunks were returned to the schooner by order of Lieut. Gedney. On examining the contents of the trunks afterwards no gold was found! Some person, or persons, are supposed to have the money, *but who, is a secret.* While on shore, at Long Island, Shinquau and his companions, although hungry, and with arms in their hands, would not kill a single animal, or take an article even to satisfy their hunger, without paying generously for it. They appeared, it is true, to know very little about the value of money, and gave a doubloon for a dog, and a small gold piece for some victuals.

The African prisoners are orderly and peaceable among themselves. Some of them sing well, and appear to be in good spirits and grateful for the kindness shewn them. Col. Stanton Pendleton, at whose house I stop, is the jailor, and is kind and attentive to the prisoners. He provides them wholesome food in sufficient quantities, and gives every reasonable indulgence to the numerous visitors, from the neighboring towns and elsewhere, who throng the prison continually to see these interesting strangers from a distant land. Col. P. has allowed me to take copies of the warrants of commitment. The little girls, and the negro boy, Antonio, are committed as witnesses, "for neglecting to become recognized to the United States with surety," and Shinquau and his comrades are bound over "for murder on the high seas."

I have read an ingenious and well written article in the Evening Post signed Veto, in which the learned writer presents a pretty full examination of the case of the schooner Amistad. He says that it seems but too probable that the slaveholders, Messrs. Ruez and Montez, conscious of the invalidity of their claim in the Civil Courts, have drawn this criminal prosecution (the charge of murder) to give time to their government to make a demand: and he rather singularly says "this raises a far more difficult question." If Veto will turn to Niles' Register for 1823, he will find an elegantly written and very able opinion of Chief Justice Tilghman, of Pa., on this subject, in which that eminent jurist, in giving his own judgment against the claim of a foreign government in the case of a fugitive charged with treason or for said District, against Simon, Lucis, Joseph, Peter, Mortine, Manuel and fifty two others (whose names are enumerated) for the murder of Ramon Ferrer on the 20th day of June, 1839, on the high seas within the admiralty and maritime jurisdiction of the United States, it was ordered and adjudged by the undersigned that they against whom said information and complaint was made, stand committed to appear before the Circuit Court of the United States for the District of Connecticut, to be holden at Hartford, in said District, on the 17th day of September, 1839, to answer to the crime of murder, as set forth in said information and complaint.

You are therefore commanded to take the said persons, named as above, and charged with said crime, and them safely keep in the jail in New Haven, in said District, and them have before the Circuit Court of the United States to be holden at Hartford, in said District, on the 17th day of September A. D. 1839. Hereof fail not, &c. Dated at New London, Aug. 29, 1839.

(Signed)   ANDREW T. JUDSON,
Judge of the United States for the District of Connecticut.

Joseph Cinque, leader of the Amistad revolt

If I'da hada my way I'da burn this building down Great God Amighty If I'da hada my way.

LOUISIANA EXPERIENCES.

[From "Camps and Prisons, Twelve Months in the Department of the Gulf," by Col. A. J. H. Duganne.]

WHAT THE NEGROES THOUGHT.

ANOTHER gray-wooled negro approaches. He holds his hat in hand, discovering a white forehead, strongly marked features, intelligent eyes. I inquire his name, and learn that he is known as "Uncle Phil," that he is a plantation preacher; that he was formerly a slave and overseer's assistant on the Johnson estate.

"You must know all about the place then, Uncle Phil?"

"Yes, sah!" (Uncle Phil speaks good English, with but little twang of negro patois.) I have lived in this Lafourche county sixty years, sah. It was a grand country for rich white people, sah!"

"You were an old servant of Col. Johnson, I suppose."

"I was one of his slaves, sah!" rejoined Uncle Phil in an impressive tone, as he looked up at me.

"You were so well acquainted with the plantation," I said, "it would gratify me to walk about with you."

Uncle Phil touched his weather-stained palmetto hat, and led the way through stacks of out-houses, from saw-mill to sugar-mill, displaying to my uninterested gaze the troughs, the coolers, vacuum-pans, and mighty iron kettles, the reservoir of syrup, piles of hogsheads damp with mould, the broken cane wagons, the shattered "carrier" that once bore its saccharine freight from field to engine house.

"You understand this business well, Uncle Phil," I remarked, while listening to the negro's brief and lucid explanations of the complicated sugar-making process.

"I was sugar-maker here for many a year, sah," answered Uncle Phil.

"You could carry on a sugar plantation yourself," I suggested.

"I think so," responded the old man, quickly; "at least, so far as sugar-making goes; I understand that, sah."

I hazarded another conjecture : that Uncle Phil might manage a hundred of his fellow laborers without using whip or stocks; and that he could, peradventure, make as much sugar with them as his quondam owner did in "flush times" of Lafourche parish.

The negro turned, and steadily met my glance. "I think, sah," he replied, "that a hundred *men* might do as much as a hundred *slaves!*"

"You suppose, then, that emancipated slaves could carry on the labors of these plantations now lying idle?"

"Give us the chance, sah!" cried Uncle Phil, with sudden sparkle of eye and lifting of voice. "Give us the opportunity to do what we *can* do, and do it for *ourselves*, sah, and you'll know that free work is better than chained work! All we ask, sah—all I want for my people, sah—is to be rid for ever of—*masterism!*"

From the Pittsburgh Mistery.

Liberty or Death.

The following anecdote was related to us on last Monday, by a gentleman recently from Georgia, now in this city :

George, a slave, belonged to the family of ——— in the State of Georgia, near the Ochmulgee river whom he served faithfully. He was an excellent *mechanic* (!) and during the life of his owners or claimants, (for he never had an *owner*,) they would take no money for him, and, in consequence of his faithfulness to them, at their death, George was will a *freeman*!

Poor George then looked upon himself as one of the lords, even of the accursed soil of Georgia. But George was doomed to disappointment. The unjust heirs broke the will, seized his person, and thrust him into the dark caverns of slavery again! Bound for a new residence, they started down the Ochmulgee. George was on board the steamboat, bound for his destination, but the vicious robbers of his liberty knew not where. George looked sad, and talked but little.

The steamer glided along, with a crowd of guests, unconscious of their weary fellow-passenger. In the night, a splash was heard which awakened the attention of boatmen and passengers; all looked with anxiety, but seeing all appeared to be safe, it was a just conclusion, that this must have been the noise occasioned by the falling in of the bank of the river. Morning came, the *grindstone* of the boat was missed, information was given, and search being made, George was gone, they knew not where.

The river was ordered to be scoured by the eager master, thirsting after the blood of the *mechanic*! it was scoured, and George was found with the *grindstone tied to his neck*! reposing in the depth of the Ochmulgee, preferring as a *man*, *Death* before slavery! George had *tasted* liberty !!!

THROW ME ANYWHERE

Throw me anywhere
    In that ole field
Throw me anywhere, Lord
    In that ole field
Throw me anywhere
    In that ole field
Throw me anywhere, Lord
    In that ole field
Members, you want to die, Lord
    In that ole field
Members, you want to die, Lord
    In that ole field
Members, you want to die, Lord
    In that ole field
Members, you want to die
    In that ole field.

ORIGINAL WORDS OF 'DARLING NELLIE GREY'

Oh my poor Nellie Grey
They have taken her away
And I'll never see my darling any more
I'm sitting by the river
And I'm weeping all the day
For you've gone from the old Kentucky Home.

One night I went to see her
But 'She's gone' the neighbors say
The whiteman has bound her with his chain
They have taken her to Georgia
To wear her life away
As she toils in the cotton and the cane.

Oh my darling Nellie Grey . . .

Written by B. R. Hanby. He
heard it at a concert before he knew
it was published.

The brig William Purington, from Wilmington, N. C., arrived below Boston on Sunday night. On board of her was a colored man, named Pailip Smith, who secreted himself in the Steward's pantry, having made up his mind to try his luck if possible, in a free State. Smith was discovered on the 6th inst., two days after the brig had sailed for her northern port. The captain immediately put about and made for Norfolk, and when within five miles, the wind hauled to the north and blew a gale, forcing the vessel far out to sea. After three days it moderated, and again the captain tried to reach the Southern coast, but again failed, and then abandoned his purpose and put away for Boston. She arrived on Sunday night, and in going up the harbor struck on Lovell's Island, where she remained till the next morning, when Smith jumped overboard and swam for a sloop that was more successful than the brig in keeping in channel way. He was received on board, and in due time arrived up to the city, where he was taken good care of.

While the brig was below she was boarded by a deputy, armed with a writ of *habeas corpus*, to take Smith, and have him ready for the next step. Smith being among the missing, the minister of the law heard the captain's story, including his intention " to blow the nigger's brains out," if any one came on board to molest him, (as it was a *hanging* offense out South to carry off a nigger,) and having informed him that it was a *hanging offense* at the North to blow a nigger's brains out, he started for the city, and reached the wharf some time before daylight the next morning.

Slaves running away

Steal away, steal away, steal away home
I aint got long to stay here.

STEREOTYPE	**FACT**

STEREOTYPE

1. Mulattoes, more aggressive through white blood, were the chief escapees.

2. Field slaves ran; house slaves stayed put because they were well fed, well clothed, and treated like members of the family.

3. Humble, meek, good-humored, inoffensive, cheerful slaves never or rarely ran—industrious ones did not.

4. Runaways sneaked out alone, keeping their guilty secret from their closest associates.

5. Kind masters were not afflicted by runaways.

6. Other slaves never helped runaways.

Black Song, The Forge and the Flame, John Lovell; The Macmillan Company, 1972

FACT

1. The runaway was not predominantly mulatto, but predominantly black. But light-colored slaves forged free papers and went off to jobs in fisheries, on wharves and river boats.

2. All classes ran; domestics, field hands, skilled artisans, house and domestic slaves—all!

3. Typical on this point is the testimony of a Louisiana master who lost three at one time: number one was very industrious, always answered with a smile; number two addressed whites humbly and respectfully; number three was well-disposed and industrious, very timid, and spoke humbly, hat in hand, to whites.

4. Runaways might be single or in groups of two, three, or a dozen; in a few instances, more than fifty; one Maryland case on record, eighty in a group.

5. Masters were often amazed at the runaway's reaction to kind treatment; they called this reaction ingratitude and depravity. One said, "Poor ignorant devils, for what do they run away? They are well clothed, work easy and have all kinds of plantation produce."

6. Other slaves often gave aid to fugitives. The literate wrote passes; when detected, they, too, would go. Slaves took food to runaways; would accept beatings rather than reveal hiding places.

SHE RODE OFF ON A COW

She didn't work in the field. She worked at a loom. She worked so long and so often that once she went to sleep at the loom. Her master's boy saw her and told his mother. His mother told him to take a whip and wear her out. He took a stick and went out to beat her awake. He beat my mother till she woke up. When she woke up, she took a pole out of the loom and beat him nearly to death with it. He hollered, "Don't beat me no more, and I won't let 'em whip you."

She said, "I'm going to kill you. These black titties sucked you, and then you come out here to beat me." And when she left him, he wasn't able to walk.

And that was the last I seen of her until after freedom. She went out and got on an old cow that she used to milk—Dolly, she called it. She rode away from the plantation, because she knew they would kill her if she stayed.

NO MORE OVERSEERS AFTER THAT

Massa never had but one white overseer. He got kilt fighting. The hands was burning logs and trash, and the overseer knocked a old man down and made some of the niggers hold him while he bullwhipped him. The old man got up and knocked the overseer in the head with a big stick and then took a ax and cut off his hands and feet. Massa said he didn't ever want another white overseer, and he made my cousin overlooker after that.

SHE PULLED UP THE STUMP

Early Hurt had an overseer, named Sanders. He tied my sister Crecie to a stump to whip her. Crecie was stout and heavy. She was a grown young woman and big and strong. Sanders had two dogs with him in case he would have trouble with anyone. When he started laying that lash on Crecie's back, she pulled up that stump and whipped him and the dogs both.

Old Early Hurt came up and whipped her hisself. Said, "Oh, you're too bad for the overseer to whip, huh?"

SHE CHOPPED THIS MAN TO A BLOODY DEATH

One day when an old woman was plowing in the field, an overseer came by and reprimanded her for being so slow—she gave him some back talk, he took out a long closely woven whip and lashed her severely. The woman became sore and took her hoe and chopped him right across his head, and, child, you should have seen how she chopped this man to a bloody death.

Too poor in his youth to own slaves, Stonewall Jackson made bargains with the slaves that belonged to his uncle. The servant was to furnish him with pine knots by the light of which he could prepare his lessons for the entrance examination to the military school he had selected. In return he agreed to teach the slave how to read and write. As soon as the black man was confident of his skill to compose, he wrote his own name to a pass and slipped off to the Underground Railroad.

O Canaan, Sweet Canaan
I am bound for the Land of Canaan

Spiritual sung by Henry and John Harris, Sandy Jenkins, Henry Bailey, Charles Roberts and Frederick Augustus Washington Bailey (Frederick Douglass) as they plotted to escape from slavery at St. Michael, Maryland, in 1836.

LITTLE JOE MADE A SONG

The people that owned the plantation near us had lots of slaves. They owned lots of my kinfolks. They master would beat 'em at night when they come from the field and lock 'em up. He'd whup 'em and send 'em to the field. They couldn't visit no slaves, and no slaves was 'lowed to visit 'em. So my cousin Sallie watched him hide the keys. So she moved 'em a little further back so that he had to lean over to reach 'em. That morning soon when he come to let 'em out, she cracked him in the head with the poker and made Little Joe help put his head in the fireplace. That day in the field Little Joe made a song: "If you don't believe Aunt Sallie kilt Marse Jim, the blood is on her underdress." He just hollered it, "Aunt Sallie kilt Marse Jim." They 'zamined Aunt Sallie's underdress, so they put her in jail till the baby come, then they tried her and sentenced her to be hung, and she was.

NO OVERSEER EVER DOWNED HER

My mother had about three masters before she got free. She was a terrible working woman. Her boss went off deer hunting once for a few weeks. While he was gone, the overseer tried to whip her. She knocked him down and tore his face up so that the doctor had to 'tend to him. When Pennington came back, he noticed his face all patched up and asked him what was the matter with it. The overseer told him that he went down in the field to whip the hands and that he just thought he would hit Lucy a few licks to show the slaves that he was impartial, but she jumped on him and like to tore him up. Old Pennington said to him, "Well, if that is the best you could do with her, damned if you won't just have to take it."

Then they sold her to another man, named Jim Bernard. Bernard did a lot of big talk to her one morning. He said, "Look out there and mind you do what you told around here and step lively. If you don't, you'll get that bull whip." She said to him, "Yes, and we'll both be gitting it." He had heard about her; so he sold her to another man named Cleary. He was good to her; so she wasn't sold no more after that.

There wasn't many men could class up with her when it come to working. She could do more work than any two men. There wasn't no use for no one man to try to do nothing with her. No overseer never downed her.

POOR WHITE-TRASH PATEROLLERS

My pappy name Jeff and belong to Marse Joe Woodward. He live on a plantation 'cross the other side of Wateree Crick. My mammy name Phoebe. Pappy have to git a pass to come to see Mammy, before the war. Sometime that crick git up over the bank and I, to this day, 'members one time Pappy come in all wet and drenched with water. Him had made the mule swim the crick. Him stayed over his leave that was writ on the pass. Paterollers come ask for the pass. They say: "The time done out, nigger." Pappy try to explain, but they pay no 'tention to him. Tied him up, pulled down his breeches, and whupped him right before Mammy and us children. . . . Marse Tom and Miss Jane heard the hollering of us all and come to the place they was whupping him and beg them, in the name of God, to stop, that the crick was still up and dangerous to cross, and that they would make it all right with Pappy's master. They say of Pappy: "Jeff swim 'cross. Let him git the mule and swim back." They make Pappy git on the mule and follow him down to the crick and watch him swim that swift muddy crick to the other side.

I often think that the system of paterollers and bloodhounds did more to bring on the war and the wrath of the Lord than anything else. Why the good white folks put up with them poor white-trash paterollers I never can see or understand. You never see classy buckra men a-paterolling. It was always some low-down white men, that never owned a nigger in their life, doing the paterolling and a-stripping the clothes off men like Pappy right before the wives and children and beating the blood out of him. No, sir, good white men never dirty their hands and souls in such work of the devil as that.

THE RED-BONE HOUND

White folks, ... I's gonna tell you a story 'bout a mean overseer and what happened to him during the slavery days. It all commenced when a nigger named Jake Williams got a whupping for staying out after the time on his pass done give out. All the niggers on the place hated the overseer worse than pizen, 'cause he was so mean and used to try to think up things to whup us for.

One morning the slaves was lined up ready to eat their breakfast, and Jake Williams was a-petting his old red-bone hound. 'Bout that time the overseer come up and seed Jake a-petting his hound, and he say: "Nigger, you ain't got time to be a-fooling 'long that dog. Now make him git." Jake tried to make the dog go home, but the dog didn't want to leave Jake. Then the overseer pick up a rock and slam the dog in the back. The dog, he then went a-howling off.

That night Jake, he come to my cabin and he say to me: "Heywood, I is gonna run away to a free state. I ain't a-gonna put up with this treatment no longer. I can't stand much more." I gives him my hand, and I say: "Jake, I hopes you gits there. Maybe I'll see you again sometime."

"Heywood," he says, "I wish you'd look after my hound Belle. Feed her and keep her the best you can. She a mighty good possum and coon dog. I hates to part with her, but I knows that you is the best person I could leave her with." And with that Jake slip out the door, and I seed him a-walking toward the swamp down the long furrows of corn.

It didn't take that overseer long to find out that Jake done run away, and when he did, he got out the bloodhounds and started off after him. It wa'n't long afore Jake heard them hounds a-howling in the distance. Jake, he was too tired to go any further. He circled round and doubled on his tracks so as to confuse the hounds and then he clumb a tree. 'Twa'n't long afore he seed the light of the overseer coming through the woods, and the dogs was a-gitting closer and closer. Finally they smelled the tree that Jake was in, and they started barking round it. The overseer lift his lighted pine knot in the air so's he could see Jake. He say, "Nigger, come on down from there. You done wasted 'nough of our time." But Jake, he never move nor make a sound, and all the time the dogs kept a-howling and the overseer kept a-swearing. "Come on down," he say again. "Iffen you don't I's coming up and knock you outen the tree with a stick." Jake, still he never moved, and the overseer began to climb the tree. When he got where he could almost reach Jake, he swung that stick, and it come down on Jake's leg and hurt him terrible. Jake, he raised his foot and kicked the overseer right in the mouth, and that white man went a-tumbling to the ground. When he hit the earth, them hounds pounced on him. Jake, he then lowered hisself to the bottom limbs so's he could see what had happened. He saw the dogs a-tearing at the man and he holler: "Hold him, Belle! Hold him, gal!" The leader of that pack of hounds, white folks, wa'n't no bloodhound. She was a plain old red-bone possum and coon dog, and the rest done just like she done, tearing at the overseer's throat. All the while, Jake he a-hollering from the tree for the dogs to git him. 'Twa'n't long afore them dogs tore that man all to pieces. He died right under that maple tree that he run Jake up. Jake, he and that coon hound struck off through the woods. The rest of the pack come home.

I seed Jake after us niggers was freed. That's how come I knowed all about it. It musta been six years after they killed the overseer. It was in Kentucky that I run across Jake. He was a-sitting on some steps of a nigger cabin. A hound dog was a-sitting at his side. I tells him how glad I is to see him, and then I look at the dog. "That ain't Belle?" I says. "Naw," Jake answers, "this her puppy." Then he told me the whole story. I always did want to know what happen to 'em.

☞ Queer, isn't it, how sometimes things work in the world. John Brown's daughtor is now keeping a school for negro children in the old mansion of Henry A. Wise, in Virginia.

JOHN BROWN'S INVASION.

FURTHER INTERESTING INCIDENTS OF THE EXECUTION.

From Our Special Correspondent.

CHARLESTOWN, Va., Dec. 3, 1859.

In looking over the note-book of my predecessor just as he was about leaving town, I observed that he had omitted certain matters which are not without considerable interest, and which I will lay before you at this time. Certainly no one who witnessed the scene presented on the field of execution can obliterate it from his memory; for, setting aside the peculiarly memorable event which called it out, the grouping, marching, and deploying of the troops, seen in the bright sunlight, and with so grand a background, would insure its permanency.

The sun arose clear and bright, but was presently lost behind a haze which I thought augured badly for the day. By 9 o'clock, however, almost the entire expanse of the blue heavens was free of clouds, and the thermometer stood so high that, until late in the afternoon, the windows of houses were open, and all the world were sitting on their porches or promenading the streets. I walked out to the field of execution at an early hour to watch all the preliminaries, and secure as good a place as the fears of the military authorities would accord to a peaceful citizen from the North. The timber for the scaffold, all framed ready for erection, was hauled to the ground the evening previous, and at 7 o'clock, the carpenter and his assistants began putting it together. The scaffold was about six feet high from the ground, perhaps twelve feet wide, and fifteen or eighteen long. A hand-rail extended around three sides and down the flight of steps. On the other side, stout uprights, with a cross-beam which was supported by strong braces. In the center of the cross-beam was an iron hook from which the rope was suspended. The trap beneath was arranged to swing on hinges, attached to the platform so slightly, as to break from it when the cord was cut that upheld the trap. The cord, knotted at the end, passed through a hole in the trap, through another hole in the cross-beam, over the corner and down the upright to a hook near the ground, to which it was tied.

John Brown on his way to death by hanging.

It will thus be seen, that the weight of the prisoner being upon it, the sheriff had only to cut the cord near the hook, and the trap would fall at once.

The rope used to strangle Brown was only three feet long. It was of hemp, made in Kentucky, and sent in a box to Sheriff Campbell by a planter for this express purpose. Other ropes had been sent from other sections. One made of South Carolina cotton, in Alexandria, has already been publicly noticed. This would have been preferred beyond all others, because of the eminent fitness of the moral it conveyed for the consideration of all sympathizers with this deluded *Abolitionist!* But Providence willed it otherwise; for it was found on trial unable to sustain a much less weight than that of a man's body. Another, almost as great a pet with our Charlestown friends, was of hemp, made in Missouri by the slaves of Mahala Doyle, and sent by her with a particular request that, for the sake of retributive justice, it might be used to hang the man whom she asserts murdered her husband and two sons. This was tried in the balance, but found wanting also. So the precious gift from Kentucky was applied to the purpose.

The rope was arranged so as to give the body a fall of just eighteen inches—scarcely enough it was thought by some, who expressed a desire that Brown might fall ten feet, so as to insure his death beyond a peradventure.

On Thursday afternoon, a corporal and some of his guard went to to the field with a wagon-load of white flags fixed on short stakes, which were stuck in the ground at twenty paces apart all around the lot, in two rows, the rows twenty paces apart. These were intended to mark the posts of the sentries. Other similar flags showed the positions for the Commander-in-Chief, with his staff, the several companies and troops, and a narrow strip on the town side, where worthy and well qualified citizens who came properly vouched for, should be allotted positions. They need not have gone to this latter trouble, however, for when the time for the execution came, the people had been so warned, and bayonetted, and arrested, and scared, and bamboozled by the military, that they generally remained at home. There were not 400 civilians on the ground, and as to the poor country people, they might have been seen from the scaffold, away off on the roads and in fields, at least a mile off, and all under the watchful supervision of valiant troopers and foot soldiers.

By 9 o'clock the first of the troops came to do their perilous duty. The double line of sentries was arranged, and at the word of command each man in his turn right-faced and forward-marched, and went to pacing up and down his beat, for all the world as if moved by machinery. Cavalry troopers clothed in scarlet jackets sat like statues on their horses at distances of fifty feet from each other, but the lapse of time bringing weariness, they relieved themselves by assuming sundry graceful postures of body, such as hanging a leg over their horse's neck or sitting sidewise like a woman.

Then came an atillery company, with a brass cannon of large size and most approved pattern, which was skillfully pointed so that in the event of an attempted rescue the poor prisoner might be blown into shreds by the heavy charge of grape-shot that lay *perdu* in its cavernous depths. So you see the brave Virginians were determined to vindicate the majesty of the law in any event. This is no joke I assure you. The cannon was actually there, and actually loaded; for I saw it with my own eyes, and felt it with my own hands. This was not the only cannon in question, either, for Capt. Nichols' company had their guns pointed so as to sweep the jail and every approach to it, in case of need; which, considering that the fearful enemy was being quietly hanged at a little distance off, reminded me of dog Noble watching a certain hole after a certain squirrel had run safely from it. I do not speak of the prisoners remaining in jail, for no one feels afraid of them. Brown is the head devil, and almost the only incubus on their breasts.

After the artillery, more cavalry and infantry, and so on until all but the escort were on the ground. The field contains about forty acres, I should say, part of it in corn stubble, but the greater part in grass. The surface is undulating, and a broad hillock near the public road was selected as the site for the gallows, because it would afford the distant spectators a fair view, and place the prisoner so high that if compelled to fire upon him, the soldiers need not shoot each other or the civilians. The field was bounded on the south by the road, on the north by a pretty bit of woodland, and on the remaining two sides by inclosed fields.

The sun shone with great splendor as the prisoner's escort came up, and afar off could be seen the bright-gleaming muskets and bayonets of his body-guard, hedging him in, in close ranks, all about. On the field the several companies glittered with the same sparkle of guns and trappings, and the gay colors of their uniforms, made more intense in the glare, came out into strong relief with the dead tints of sod and woods. Away off to the East and South, the splendid mass of the Blue Ridge loomed against the sky, and shut in the horizon. Over the woods, toward the North-east, long, thin stripes of clouds had gradually accumulated, and foreboded the storm that came in due time; while, looking toward the South, the eye took in an undulating fertile country, stretching out to the distant mountains. All Nature seemed at peace, and the shadow of the approaching solemnity seemed to have been cast over the soldiers, for there was not a sound to be heard as the column came slowly up the road There was no band of musicians to heighten the effect of the scene by playing the march of the dead but with solemn tread the heavy footfalls came, as if those of one man. Thus they passed to their station on the easterly side of the scaffold, and the old man calmly descended from the wagon, mounted the gallows stairs with unfaltering step, and was led to his place on the fatal trap. His unwavering courage is well illustrated in the fact that, when the Sheriff took hold of him to lead him forward under the cross-beam, there was no trembling of body to be noticed, nor anything which would show a weakness, at the very brink of the precipice from which he was about to leap. There he stood, in his dark clothes and blood-red slippers, and with the white hood drawn over his head, for eight minutes, that seemed ages—the cynosure of all eyes on the field and afar off. He, the stone thrown by God into the black and sluggish pool of Slavery; while, ebbing from him, in fast-widening circles of sentries and pickets and mounted scouts that surrounded the place for fifteen miles off, went the ripples that he had caused on its bosom.

The cord cut a finger's depth into Brown's neck, and a considerable distortion of countenance is said to have been produced. This will doubtless decrease as the muscles relax and fall to their natural places again. Brown's hold on life was strong. He did not die easily, judging from appearances, and the testimony of experienced men. The animal heat remained in his body so long, that although it was to have left under escort of a detachment of the Richmond Grays at 5 o'clock, the physicians detained it an hour and a half longer to cool.

Weekly Pendulum.

WE SWING FOR ALL.

Saturday, January 1, 1859

Colored Schools.

Some weeeks since we announced that Mr. Waugh a colored cititizen of Providence, had brought a suit against one of the teachers of that city who had refused, under the direction of the School Committee to receive his son into one of the public schools. Since then, Mr. George T. Downing, now residing in Newport, whose children were excluded there, through his counsel, brought the matter to the attention of the School Commissioner and requested a hearing. The Commissioner returned for answer that if Mr. Downing had any special grievances, he would hear the parties, but it the question was the mooted one of the power of the school authorities to establish separate schools for colored children a hearing would be unnecessary, as he was of opinion there was such a power, and if exercised. it was wholly within the jurisdiction of the local officers. The Commissioner also said that his opinion was fortified by that of Chief Justice Ames. We will not comment on the aspects of the case as affecting these

officers personally, though we must be allowed to say that if His Honor the Chief Justice has ventured his opinion in a case which is in process of adjudication, and is trave ling up to that tribunal over which he presides, he has overstepped the line of judicial propriety.

If such is the law—if the rights and liberties of the citizen are in the hands of the local school officers, the boasted securities of our Constitution are but mockeries. The doctrine that these boards of school officers have the power to set up arbitrary distinctions and make such arbitrary regulations as their several whims and caprices may dictate, smacks strongly of a despotism we have been wont to think could only be found on another continent. The instituting of a caste school is founded on the arbitrary quality of color.— With as much propriety and justice might a School Committee shut out from our public school all red headed children, and establish one for their exclusive attendance. On some other peculiarity might be the basis of their action, as a Roman nose or blue eyes. Th color of the skin is as much of an accidental circumstance or quality as a red head or a Roman nose. When we drop as a motive the great idea of the paternity of God and the brotherhood of the race and govern our action by some arbitrary rule which ig

nores man as such, we have launched on the dark and cheerless ocean of Atheism. We impugn God himself and arraign before our own important selves the work of His hands. There is nothing in the Oracles we all profess to revere and by which we profess to be guided, which can be tortured into a justification for the distinctions set up in certain towns as to the complexion of those who may attend our public schools.

We learn that Mr. Downing intends the coming winter, to appeal personally to the people and vindicate the cause of himself and his colored fellow citizens. He will visit such portions of the State as he may have time to do, setting before the people the views entertained by those who feel they are oppressed by the unrighteous prejudice which denies them equal school privileges and a common participation in the benefits of schools which we boast are free. Mr. Downing wields a ready pen and is also a ready speaker. His abilities are equal to the task he has imposed on himself. He is a sound and logical reasoner, and nerved as he will be by the stimulus of an honest belief that he is combatting oppression and wrong, we anticipate he will vindicate in his own person the right of his brethren to their equal and inalienable rights of " life, liberty and the pursuit of happiness."

PAUL CUFFEE'S BILL.

The House resolved itself into a committee of the whole, Mr. Breckenridge of Va. in the chair, on the bill from the Senate for authorising the President of the United States to permit the departure of Paul Cuffee with a cargo to Sierra Leone; together with the report of the committee of Commerce and Manufactures against the same.

[This bill is predicated on the petition of Paul Cuffee, an African by descent, which our readers will doubtless recollect to have read in our paper some weeks ago, and its object is sufficiently explained by the title of the bill.]

This underwent a discussion of a very diffuse nature, and of no little length, in the course of which the object of the bill was supported by Messrs Wheaton, Grosvenor, Pickering, Taggart, Baylies, Webster, Farrow Duval, and Shipherd, and opposed by Messrs. Newton, Wright, M'Kim, Kerr, Ingham, Fisk, of Vt. and Ingersoll.

This bill was supported on the ground of the excellence of the general character of Mr. Cuffee; the philanthropy of his views; the benefits to humanity and religion generally, of which a success in these views might be productive; the benefits which would result to the U. S. particularly from the establishment of an institution which would invite the emigration of free blacks, a part of our population which we could well spare, &c. &c.

On the other hand, the bill was opposed on various grounds. Whilst the excellence of the general character of Mr. Cuffee was fully credited and generally admitted, it was said that the bill would violate, in favor of a foreign mission, that policy which we had refused to infringe, for the sake even of our coasters and fishermen; that Mr. Cuffee might depart in neutral vessels with his companions, but that it would be improper to permit him to carry out a cargo, which was not at all necessary to his views of propagating the gospel; that his voyage would be contrary to the policy of existing laws, independent of the embargo policy, because Sierra Leone was a British settlement, in the possession of a nation claiming and asserted to be the bulwark of our religion, there was no occasion for cargoes departing from the U. States to enable her to carry her views into effect, &c.

Intermingled in this debate was considerable controversy and something like asperity, as to the character of the British nation for religion and humanity, in which Mr. Pickering of Mass. on the one side, and Mr. Kerr of Va. and Fisk of Vt. on the other, were the principal debaters, and also on the evil which might result from transporting liberated slaves from this country to a British settlement. The question, however, appeared to the reporter to turn on the expediency of permitting, under the existence of the restrictive system, a cargo to go out, which must necessarily sail under British licence, which it was argued would not be granted unless it were considered advantageous to the interest of the enemy, that such trade should be carried on.

The debate having been extended to the usual hour of adjournment, the committee reported the bill to the House with certain amendments, and on the question of the passage of the bill to a third reading, which was decided by Yeas and Nays, the votes was as follows:

For the bill   66
Against it   72

So the bill was rejected,
And the House adjourned.

Negro Colonization.

WASHINGTON, Monday, Sept 1.

The scheme of the President, though abandoned so far as it is contemplated sending out families this fall, has yet produced some interesting results. The publicity of the measure has developed a strong interest in the movement among the negroes themselves, who have heretofore always opposed it. Within two days after the publication of Senator Pomeroy's address, he had applications from over one hundred families. He has since received proposals from a number sufficient to load two vessels. Among them are two sons of Fred Douglass, who has written Senator Pomeroy the following letter:

ROCHESTER, Aug. 26, 1862.

HON. S. S. POMEROY—My Dear Sir: I assent to neither the justice nor the wisdom of colonizing the free colored people in Central America, or elsewhere out of the United States. The American Government could far better employ the energies of this people by stimulating their friendship for the country, and giving them an opportunity, in common with others, to protect and defend its institutions. But I am not now to discuss with you the policy of this colonization scheme. The power and responsibility for the measure belong alike to the Government. Option is yours—necessity ours. It is a hard alternative. To see my children usefully and happily settled in this, the land of their birth and ancestors, has been the hope and ambition of my manhood; but events stronger than any power I can oppose to them, have convinced my son that the chances here are all against him, and he desires to join your colony, and perhaps a younger brother also.

* * * * I have never ceased to remember you and to observe with pleasure and gratitude your fidelity to liberty and humanity in the high position you now occupy. I shall be glad to know that you receive my son Lewis as one of your colony. I shall follow him with my blessing, if I do not follow him personally. *

Sadly and truly yours,
FRED'K DOUGLASS.

Among those offered are twenty two slaves, whose master, resident about eighteen miles from here in Virginia, proposes to manumit them if the Government will send them off. Senator Pomeroy replied that he must consult the negroes in regard to their willingness to go He wished the colored race to consider the movement their own, and is willing to contribute his services as their friend.

The action of Congress in appropriating money for this colonization was intended to result in the removal of the slaves liberated in the District, and the confiscated slaves of rebels.

Half of all the applications made thus far are from Maryland.

The Administration desires Senator Pomeroy to select a sufficient number of men from the applicants, and with them to undertake a trip of exploration, with the view of selecting a suitable region for a colony, and making arrangements with the authorities. His own views are at present favorable to the Valley of the Amazon.—[N. Y. Herald.

"We are opposed to emancipating Negro slaves unless on some plan of colonization, in order that they may not come in contact with the white man's labor."

Resolution passed by the Tammany Hall Young Men's Democratic Committee, March 13, 1862.

This organization was comprised mainly of first-generation Americans whose power rested on corrupt control of an immigrant vote. The attitude expressed in the resolution erupted into the Civil War Draft Riots of 1863 in New York City.

FREDERICK DOUGLASS AGAIN—We see by a card which this notable gentleman in black has published, that he has been accused of having been in a suspicious position with a white lady of Albany, on board of one of our North River steamboats According to the Boston Liberator, the white lady secured for him, in her own name, a state room, to save him from the *desagremens* of his color on board such boats, and, according to his own card, the state-rooms were adjoining, and communicated by a door. Rumor, which is not particular on such occasions, accused him, it seems, of malpractices there, and the white lady of having purposely secured the communicating rooms. Douglass, however, writes:—

"On Monday, May 10th, I was in company with my wife, at Albany, where I went to see my daughter, whom I had not seen for nearly two years. * * * * * I availed myself of the kindness of my friend alluded to, who secured for me a state-room and the adjoining one for herself. On going into mine, in the evening, I found as above stated, that the two rooms communicated with each other by a door. But a thought of its propriety or impropriety never crossed my mind; and, at that time, I did not know but that every state-room on board communicated in a similar manner. Myself and friend conversed together during the evening, when she went to her state-room, and I remained in mine. I neither saw her friend nor I until next morning, when we landed at New York. I then went to her state-room door to assist her with her baggage; and after walking about a full half hour, in the presence of the Captain, while the crowd was pressing on shore, we left the steamer together, without the slightest sign of disapprobation, that I could see, from any quarter. On my return from New York, my friend secured similar state-rooms, as we occupied them, without the least interruption from the captain or any officer, servant, or passenger on board. When we left the steamer in the morning, the captain did utter some filthy remarks, calling me a 'nigger,' &c., and telling me never to take a state-room on board his steamer again. I made no reply, but went off about my business, well knowing that my color was the cause of his brutality, and that, had I been a white man, I might have occupied the state-rooms a dozen times over, without calling forth any foul imputations from himself, or any one else. As to what is alleged to have been said by my friend to the chambermaid, it may or may not be

THE NEGRO TROUBLES IN FAYETTE COUNTY, TENNESSEE.

We find the following account of the recent excitement in Fayette County, Tenn., in the Memphis *Enquirer* :—

LAFAYETTE DEPOT, M. & C. R. R., }
Saturday, Nov. 2, 1856. }

COL. PRYOR—*Dear Sir* : As you have doubtless, like many other persons, had various alarming and conflicting reports in your city in regard to the contemplated servile insurrection in this vicinity, I have concluded to give you, and through you the numerous readers of your paper, the facts as they actually occurred.

On Tuesday morning, a negro girl of Mr. G. W. Vandel, who is engineer at Mr. R. Glenn's steam-mill, three miles below this, informed her mistress that she had been told by one of the negro men at the mill, the night before, that the negroes all intended rising on the day of the election ; and that their plan was to take advantage of the absence of the white men on that day, and while they were all from home at the polls voting, to kill all the women and children, get all the money and arms, and waylay the men on their return home from the election and murder them ; then make for the railroad cars, take them and go to Memphis, where they would find arms and friends from up the river to carry them off to the Free States if they did not succeed in taking this country. Mrs. V. communicated all this to her husband, who said nothing until night, when he and his wife waylaid the cabins, and overhead a similar conversation among the negroes themselves. He next day had them all, some thirty-two in number, arrested and tried, when proof sufficient was adduced for the magistrate to commit twenty-three of them to jail at Somerville, which was accordingly done.

The excitement was very great for several days, but it is now pretty much subsided. We have put out a Vigilant Patrol, and all is now becoming tranquil. Facts were brought to light sufficient to satisfy all present, not only of the guilty intentions of some six or eight of the negroes arrested, but it was made clear to the minds of thinking men present, that the thing was not confined to this particular neighborhood, but that they expected to act in concert with various others in the surrounding counties and States. I simply write you this statement to correct the many false and unjust reports that have been circulated ; such as, that six or eight negroes had been hung by the mob at Lafayette Depot. No such thing. We are law-abiding citizens about here, and as such do not like such reports to get out.

Since writing the above, I have just heard that the patrol company across the river, near Macon, have arrested a white man, who says his name is Williams. He was found, as I understand, in one of the negro cabins, after 12 o'clock at night, and as he had no one who was known to vouch for him, he was also committed to jail. I give this as a report. Further, deponent saith not.

Very respectfully,   W. E. EPPES.

Laura Haviland, a white resident of Adrian, Michigan, was a staunch abolitionist for whom slaveowners offered a reward of $3,000, dead or alive. Despite threats to her life, she harbored fugitive slaves and helped them reach free soil by way of the Underground Railroad. On one occasion she was kidnapped and held captive by slave catchers who ordered her to write a letter to a black fugitive family on her farm and tell them to come to Toledo, Ohio, where "Aunt Laura" Haviland was being held.

"Aunt Laura" wrote to the fugitives, Willis and Elsie Hamilton, and offered them clothing to make the trip, since the couple and their two daughters might not have sufficient clothing. "Tell Elsie," she wrote, "to take for herself my black alpaca dress in the south bedroom and the two pink gingham aprons and striped green dress in the bureau in the west bedroom for the little girls. Take the double team and the farm wagon."

When the letter was delivered and read, Elsie said to her husband, "I shall not stir a step. This is all humbug. Mrs. Haviland does not have a black dress. There is no south bedroom and no bed in the west room; no pink aprons nor any green striped dresses."

Today in Adrian, Michigan, there is a statue of "Aunt Laura" Haviland in one of the public squares.

Captain Jonathan Walker was a white man who made a great sacrifice for blacks in the slavery period. Caught taking fugitive slaves away on his boat, he was sentenced to be branded in his hand with the letters S.S., meaning Slave Stealer; to be jailed and to pay a huge fine. After several months in jail, abolitionists raised the money to free him. He lectured on slavery, but broken health caused him to commit suicide later. John Greenleaf Whittier wrote "The Branded Hand" for him.

The January 26, 1861, issue of *Freedom's Journal* published a revealing letter addressed to the King of Dahomey in West Africa by the African Aid Society of New York. The society pleaded with the king to stop selling African slaves and instead to utilize them to grow cotton and other products to sell to foreign countries. He was also urged to exchange his white slaves for finished products from the countries of their origin. The letter pointed out that in 1860 he sold 10,000 slaves for $50,000 but could earn much more through commerce.

Advertisement.

A Charitable society in England, known by the name of *The Associates of the late Dr. Bray*, hath for a number of years exerted itself in establishing Libraries and Free Negroe Schools in most of the principal cities and towns in England, America, and many of the West-India islands. Under the direction, and at the expence of this society, a negro charity school was instituted and kept up in this city for several years previous to the late war : but this charity was interrupted and discontinued by the intervention of the war. The associates being now desirous of renewing an institution from which so many good effects have been heretofore derived—

Notice is hereby given, That the *Negro Charity School* will be opened on the first Monday in December next, by *Mrs. Ruth Lewis*, in Race street, near Fourth street. Negro children of every religious denomination may be admitted ; boys will be taught to *read*, and girls to *read*, *sew* and *knit*.

The scholars to pay *half a dollar* each for winter's firing, and to find their own books. For admission apply to   FRANCIS HOPKINSON.

Philadelphia, *November 8.*

PARDON. We learn from Jefferson City, that Gov. Edwards has pardoned the Abolitionist, Work, who was sentenced to the Penitentiary about three years since, for assisting in the escape of negroes from Marion County. His punishment was fixed at nine years. There are two others, sentenced at the same time for the same offence, who will probably remain until the expiration of their time. In the case of Work it is stated, that he has manifested proper contrition for his offence, and as he has a wife and several children—one of which he has never seen, public opinion will sanction and justify the clemency of the Governor. It is to be hoped that this act may have its proper influence upon those Abolitionists who are outside of the prison walls, but who, if they persist in their course, deserve places within them.— *St. Louis Rep.*

LATIMER, (a fugitive slave mentioned in the Journal of Saturday before last as confined in Boston jail,) has been freed by his claimant, Mr. Gray of Norfolk, on the payment of $400, raised by subscribers in Boston, and on Latimer's promise not to sue Gray who claimed him, nor Stratton or Coolidge who held him. There has been great excitement on the subject, in Boston and other parts of Massachusetts. A paper has been printed three times a week at the Courier Office, to promote his release : one of the editors is said to be a son of the late Rev. Dr. Channing.

As we commenced an account of the case two weeks ago, and as it is likely to be the last slave case in Boston, we copy a few particulars from a statement made by E. G. Austin, Esq. Mr. Gray's Counsel.

Mr. Austin informs the public that Mr. Coolidge, the Jailor, told him on the 17th Nov. that "a petition was circulating for signatures, to be presented to the Sheriff, praying him to remove him, (Coolidge,) because he was keeping in confinement a person without any legal warrant ; and that he, Coolidge, expected that on the following day he should receive an order from the Sheriff not to confine Latimer any longer in Jail."

To this unexpected announcement Mr. Coolidge said he could make no reply.

Then follows a statement of his endeavours to get as large a sum as possible for the ransom ; $800 being asked, and $400 finally taken,—he then adds the following order from the sheriff to the Jailor :

PAUL CUFFEE'S BILL.

The House resolved itself into a committee of the whole, Mr. Breckenridge of Va. in the chair, on the bill from the Senate for authorising the President of the United States to permit the departure of Paul Cuffee with a cargo to Sierra Leone; together with the report of the committee of Commerce and Manufactures against the same.

[This bill is predicated on the petition of Paul Cuffee, an African by descent, which our readers will doubtless recollect to have read in our paper some weeks ago, and its object is sufficiently explained by the title of the bill.]

This underwent a discussion of a very diffuse nature, and of no little length, in the course of which the object of the bill was supported by Messrs Wheaton, Grosvenor, Pickering, Taggart, Baylies, Webster, Farrow Duval, and Shipherd, and opposed by Messrs. Newton, Wright, M'Kim Kerr, Ingham, Fisk, of Vt. and Ingersoll.

This bill was supported on the ground of the excellence of the general character of Mr. Cuffee; the philanthropy of his views; the benefits to humanity and religion generally, of which a success in these views might be productive; the benefits which would result to the U. S. particularly from the establishment of an institution which would invite the emigration of free blacks, a part of our population which we could well spare, &c. &c.

On the other hand, the bill was opposed on various grounds. Whilst the excellence of the general character of Mr. Cuffee was fully credited and generally admitted, it was said that the bill would violate, in favor of a foreign mission, that policy which we had refused to infringe, for the sake even of our coasters and fishermen; that Mr. Cuffee might depart in neutral vessels with his companions, but that it would be improper to permit him to carry out a cargo, which was not at all necessary to his views of propagating the gospel; that his voyage would be contrary to the policy of existing laws, independent of the embargo policy, because Sierra Leone was a British settlement; in the possession of a nation claiming and asserted to be the bulwark of our religion, there was no occasion for cargoes departing from the U. States to enable her to carry her views into effect, &c.

Intermingled in this debate was considerable controversy and something like asperity, as to the character of the British nation for religion and humanity, in which Mr. Pickering of Mass. on the one side, and Mr. Kerr of Va. and Fisk of Vt. on the other, were the principal debaters; and also on the evil which might result from transporting liberated slaves from this country to a British settlement. The question, however, appeared to the reporter to turn on the expediency of permitting, under the existence of the restrictive system, a cargo to go out, which must necessarily sail under British licence, which it was argued would not be granted unless it were considered advantageous to the interest of the enemy, that such trade should be carried on.

The debate having been extended to the usual hour of adjournment, the committee reported the bill to the House with certain amendments, and on the question of the passage of the bill to a third reading, which was decided by Yeas and Nays, the votes was as follows:

For the bill 66
Against it 72
So the bill was rejected,
And the House adjourned.

Negro Colonization.

WASHINGTON, Monday, Sept 1.

The scheme of the President, though abandoned so far as it is contemplated sending out families this fall, has yet produced some interesting results. The publicity of the measure has developed a strong interest in the movement among the negroes themselves, who have heretofore always opposed it. Within two days after the publication of Senator Pomeroy's address, he had applications from over one hundred families. He has since received proposals from a number sufficient to load two vessels. Among them are two sons of Fred Douglass, who has written Senator Pomeroy the following letter:

ROCHESTER, Aug. 26, 1862.

HON. S. S. POMEROY—My Dear Sir: I assent to neither the justice nor the wisdom of colonizing the free colored people in Central America, or elsewhere out of the United States. The American Government could far better employ the energies of this people by stimulating their friendship for the country, and giving them an opportunity, in common with others, to protect and defend its institutions. But I am not now to discuss with you the policy of this colonization scheme. The power and responsibility for the measure belong alike to the Government. Option is yours—necessity ours. It is a hard alternative. To see my children usefully and happily settled in this, the land of their birth and ancestors, has been the hope and ambition of my manhood; but events stronger than any power I can oppose to them, have convinced my son that the chances here are all against him, and he desires to join your colony, and perhaps a younger brother also. * * * * I have never ceased to remember you and to observe with pleasure and gratitude your fidelity to liberty and humanity in the high position you now occupy. I shall be glad to know that you receive my son Lewis as one of your colony. I shall follow him with my blessing, if I do not follow him personally. *

Sadly and truly yours,
FRED'K DOUGLASS.

Among those offered are twenty two slaves, whose master, resident about eighteen miles from here in Virginia, proposes to manumit them if the Government will send them off. Senator Pomeroy replied that he must consult the negroes in regard to their willingness to go He wished the colored race to consider the movement their own, and is willing to contribute his services as their friend.

The action of Congress in appropriating money for this colonization was intended to result in the removal of the slaves liberated in the District, and the confiscated slaves of rebels.

Half of all the applications made thus far are from Maryland.

The Administration desires Senator Pomeroy to select a sufficient number of men from the applicants, and with them to undertake a trip of exploration, with the view of selecting a suitable region for a colony, and making arrangements with the authorities. His own views are at present favorable to the Valley of the Amazon.—[N. Y. Herald.

"We are opposed to emancipating Negro slaves unless on some plan of colonization, in order that they may not come in contact with the white man's labor."

Resolution passed by the Tammany Hall Young Men's Democratic Committee, March 13, 1862.

This organization was comprised mainly of first-generation Americans whose power rested on corrupt control of an immigrant vote. The attitude expressed in the resolution erupted into the Civil War Draft Riots of 1863 in New York City.

FREDERICK DOUGLASS AGAIN—We see by a card which this notable gentleman in black has published, that he has been accused of having been in a suspicious position with a white lady of Albany, on board of one of our North River steamboats According to the Boston Liberator, the white lady secured for him, in her own name, a state room, to save him from the desagremens of his color on board such boats, and, according to his own card, the state-rooms were adjoining, and communicated by a door. Rumor, which is not particular on such occasions, accused him, it seems, of malpractices there, and the white lady of having purposely secured the communicating rooms. Douglass, however, writes:—

"On Monday, May 10th, I was in company with my wife, at Albany, where I went to see my daughter, whom I had not seen for nearly two years. * * * * * I availed myself of the kindness of my friend alluded to, who secured for me a state-room and the adjoining one for herself. On going into mine, in the evening, I found as above stated, that the two rooms communicated with each other by a door. But a thought of its propriety or impropriety never crossed my mind; and, at that time, I did not know but that every state-room on board communicated in a similar manner. Myself and friend conversed together during the evening, when she went to her state-room, and I remained in mine. I neither saw nor heard my friend till next morning, when we landed at New York. I then went to her state-room door to assist her with her baggage; and after walking about a full half hour, in the presence of the Captain, while the crowd was pressing on shore, we left the steamer together, without the slightest sign of disapprobation, that I could see, from any quarter. On my return from New York, my friend secured similar state-rooms, an we occupied them, without the least interruption from the captain or any officer, servant, or passenger on board. When we left the steamer in the morning, the captain did utter some filthy remarks, calling me a 'nigger,' &c., and telling me never to take a state-room on board his steamer again. I made no reply, but went off about my business, well knowing that my color was the cause of his brutality, and that, had I been a white man, I might have occupied the state-rooms a dozen times over, without calling forth any foul imputations from himself, or any one else. As to what is alleged to have been said by my friend to the chambermaid, it may or may not be

Washington D.C. Jan. 28.

May Please Your Honor.

I am charged with the high crime of marrying a lady a few shades lighter in complexion than myself: Pardon me, I pray, and do not think me a hardened wretch if I boldly declare before your honor, that I am I am not in the least ashamed of this crime. But what business has any man to trouble himself about the color of any other man's wife? Does it not appear prilently impertinent this intermeddling. Every man ought to try to be content with the form and color of his own wife. And stop at that. Thanks Dear Ruffin for your congratulation. It is a word in season

Yours truly always

Fredk Douglass

Birth records of slaves owned by Blacks.

ue; and, true or false, it is a small matter. We needed either bolts, bars, nor locks, to keep us in the path of virtue and rectitude."

The "Liberator" endorses the rectitude of all concerned, it properly censures Douglass for stealthily violating the ws of the boat, and thus subjecting himself and the lady malevolent suspicions. The very appearance of evil, it isely says, should be shunned.

We presume that we shall hear more of this, for rumor has een very busy with the facts, the week past. If Douglass onducted himself decently, nobody would care about his olor,—but he will soon learn that the United States is not treat Britain, where all classes, more or less, used him to tarm this country.

BLACK SLAVEOWNERS

In 1862, Congress abolished slavery in the District of Columbia and paid cash compensation to owners of freed slaves who established claims within a specified time limit. Under that act, seven colored residents in the nation's capital received a total of $5,978.20 in return for 26 slaves. Largest among black slaveholders were Robert Gunnell who owned ten slaves and Gabriel Coakley, owner of eight slaves.

The Case of the Wanderer.

Savannah, Dec. 30.—The Wanderer case was continued to-day. Capt Christy was recalled, and testified that on Dec. 24 he went from Brunswick to Jekyl Island, and saw negroes landed by unknown white men. He supposed the number was about 300—some of them were put on his steamer and conveyed 14 miles above Savannah. Other witnesses were sworn, but the testimony was unimportant. The case was then adjourned in consequence of the illness of one of the prisoners.

The Wanderer's negroes are in the hands of speculators, and they are "the combination of the first families in Georgia and South Carolina," that have received them, taken them into their auction pens, "purely from patriotic motives."

Capture and Escape of one of the Wanderer's Negroes.—Savannah, Dec. 27.—The United States officers caught one young wild African at Jekyl Island last week, and brought him here on Saturday. The negro has since absquatulated, and the officials are engaged in searching for him, while scores have been transported by railroad and steamer throughout the South. The United States Marshal has been requested to resign, but refuses to do so. He will probably, though, be generally thought blameless.

Fragments of records kept in family Bible of slaves owned by a black man, John C. Stanley. Stanley lived in New Bern, North Carolina. Birth dates are noted here and data concerning their frequent manumission.

THE NEGRO TROUBLES IN FAYETTE COUNTY, TENNESSEE.

We find the following account of the recent excitement in Fayette County, Tenn., in the Memphis *Enquirer* :—

LAFAYETTE DEPOT, M. & C. R. R.,
Saturday, Nov. 2, 1856.

COL. PRYOR—*Dear Sir :* As you have doubtless, like many other persons, had various alarming and conflicting reports in your city in regard to the contemplated servile insurrection in this vicinity, I have concluded to give you, and through you the numerous readers of your paper, the facts as they actually occurred.

On Tuesday morning, a negro girl of Mr. G. W. Vandel, who is engineer at Mr. R. Glenn's steam-mill, three miles below this, informed her mistress that she had been told by one of the negro men at the mill, the night before, that the negroes all intended rising on the day of the election ; and that their plan was to take advantage of the absence of the white men on that day, and while they were all from home at the polls voting, to kill all the women and children, get all the money and arms, and waylay the men on their return home from the election and murder them ; then make for the railroad cars, take them and go to Memphis, where they would find arms and friends from up the river to carry them off to the Free States if they did not succeed in taking this country. Mrs. V. communicated all this to her husband, who said nothing until night, when he and his wife waylaid the cabins, and overhead a similar conversation among the negroes themselves. He next day had them all, some thirty-two in number, arrested and tried, when proof sufficient was adduced for the magistrate to commit twenty-three of them to jail at Somerville, which was accordingly done.

The excitement was very great for several days, but it is now pretty much subsided. We have put out a Vigilant Patrol, and all is now becoming tranquil. Facts were brought to light sufficient to satisfy all present, not only of the guilty intentions of some six or eight of the negroes arrested, but it was made clear to the minds of thinking men present, that the thing was not confined to this particular neighborhood, but that they expected to act in concert with various others in the surrounding counties and States. I simply write you this statement to correct the many false and unjust reports that have been circulated ; such as, that six or eight negroes had been hung by the mob at Lafayette Depot. No such thing. We are law-abiding citizens about here, and as such do not like such reports to get out.

Since writing the above, I have just heard that the patrol company across the river, near Macon, have arrested a white man, who says his name is Williams. He was found, as I understand, in one of the negro cabins, after 12 o'clock at night, and as he had no one who was known to vouch for him, he was also committed to jail. I give this as a report. Further, deponent saith not.

Very respectfully,   W. E. EPPES.

Laura Haviland, a white resident of Adrian, Michigan, was a staunch abolitionist for whom slaveowners offered a reward of $3,000, dead or alive. Despite threats to her life, she harbored fugitive slaves and helped them reach free soil by way of the Underground Railroad. On one occasion she was kidnapped and held captive by slave catchers who ordered her to write a letter to a black fugitive family on her farm and tell them to come to Toledo, Ohio, where "Aunt Laura" Haviland was being held.

"Aunt Laura" wrote to the fugitives, Willis and Elsie Hamilton, and offered them clothing to make the trip, since the couple and their two daughters might not have sufficient clothing. "Tell Elsie," she wrote, "to take for herself my black alpaca dress in the south bedroom and the two pink gingham aprons and striped green dress in the bureau in the west bedroom for the little girls. Take the double team and the farm wagon."

When the letter was delivered and read, Elsie said to her husband, "I shall not stir a step. This is all humbug. Mrs. Haviland does not have a black dress. There is no south bedroom and no bed in the west room; no pink aprons nor any green striped dresses."

Today in Adrian, Michigan, there is a statue of "Aunt Laura" Haviland in one of the public squares.

Captain Jonathan Walker was a white man who made a great sacrifice for blacks in the slavery period. Caught taking fugitive slaves away on his boat, he was sentenced to be branded in his hand with the letters S.S., meaning Slave Stealer; to be jailed and to pay a huge fine. After several months in jail, abolitionists raised the money to free him. He lectured on slavery, but broken health caused him to commit suicide later. John Greenleaf Whittier wrote "The Branded Hand" for him.

The January 26, 1861, issue of *Freedom's Journal* published a revealing letter addressed to the King of Dahomey in West Africa by the African Aid Society of New York. The society pleaded with the king to stop selling African slaves and instead to utilize them to grow cotton and other products to sell to foreign countries. He was also urged to exchange his white slaves for finished products from the countries of their origin. The letter pointed out that in 1860 he sold 10,000 slaves for $50,000 but could earn much more through commerce.

Advertisement.

PARDON. We learn from Jefferson City, that Gov. Edwards has pardoned the Abolitionist, Work, who was sentenced to the Penitentiary about three years since, for assisting in the escape of negroes from Marion County. His punishment was fixed at nine years. There are two others, sentenced at the same time for the same offence, who will probably remain until the expiration of their time. In the case of Work it is stated, that he has manifested proper contrition for his offence, and as he has a wife and several children—one of which he has never seen, public opinion will sanction and justify the clemency of the Governor. It is to be hoped that this act may have its proper influence upon those Abolitionists who are outside of the prison walls, but who, if they persist in their course, deserve places within them.—*St. Louis Rep.*

LATIMER, (a fugitive slave mentioned in the Journal of Saturday before last as confined in Boston jail,) has been freed by his claimant, Mr. Gray of Norfolk, on the payment of $400, raised by subscribers in Boston, and on Latimer's promise not to sue Gray who claimed him, nor Stratton or Coolidge who held him. There has been great excitement on the subject, in Boston and other parts of Massachusetts. A paper has been printed three times a week at the Courier Office, to promote his release : one of the editors is said to be a son of the late Rev. Dr. Channing.

As we commenced an account of the case two weeks ago, and as it is likely to be the last slave case in Boston, we copy a few particulars from a statement made by E. G. Austin, Esq. Mr. Gray's Counsel.

Mr. Austin informs the public that Mr. Coolidge, the Jailor, told him on the 17th Nov. that "a petition was circulating for signatures, to be presented to the Sheriff, praying him to remove him, (Coolidge,) because he was keeping in confinement a person without any legal warrant ; and that he, Coolidge, expected that on the following day he should receive an order from the Sheriff not to confine Latimer any longer in Jail."

To this unexpected announcement Mr. Coolidge said he could make no reply.

Then follows a statement of his endeavours to get as large a sum as possible for the ransom ; $800 being asked, and $400 finally taken,—he then adds the following order from the sheriff to the Jailor :

"SHERIFF'S OFFICE,
Boston, Nov. 17th, 1842

In conformity to advice given me by distinguished Counsel whom I have consulted in relation to the subject, and in accordance with the views which I have always maintained in conversations with you, touching the confinement of George Latimer in the Jail in this county by you, as Agent of one James B. Gray, (who claims said latimer as a fugitive slave,) and not as my Deputy Keeper of the Jail, and without any legal warrant or mittimus emanating from competent judicial authority, I do direct you to remove said Latimer from said Jail at or before 12 o'clock, noon, to-morrow. And I further order and direct you not to receive and confine in said Jail any person claimed as a slave, "or a person held to service" in another State, without a warrant or mittimus from competent Judicial authority of this Commonwealth or of the United States. This order you will place on file in the office of the Jail, and consider it as applicable to all future cases of this character.

JOSEPH EVELETH,
Sheriff of the county of Suffolk.
Mr. NATH'L. COOLIDGE, Deputy Jail Keeper."

At about 10 o'clock on that night $400 dollars was paid to Mr. Coolidge, and Latimer was made a free man.

By the order of the Sheriff to the Jailer, no fugitive slave can ever be detained in and removed from Boston under the present provisions of the laws of the United States. So far then, this case is highly important in its results.

Gray did not come here to sell this man. He came here under the mistaken belief that the laws of the United States were sufficiently explicit to enable him to obtain, in a legal manner, that which, by the Constitution of the United States, is made property.

Mr. Austin adds,—that he has acted in this matter throughout in a professional capacity. He has no more favourable opinion of the institution of slavery, than the most ardent of those who seek its immediate abolishment—and no feeling of regret that Latimer is a free man. He could have wished however that his e-mancipation had been effected in a different manner.

It is manifest from Mr. Austin's statement, that no further efforts will be made to recover fugitive slaves in Boston—and that the existing laws of the United States are not sufficient to reclaim a slave there.

PROGRESS BACKWARD IN MISSISSIPPI.

From the Chicago Tribune.

ADVICES from Mississippi are as unsatisfactory as they could well be. But one member of the convention has yet spoken who uttered anything that would pass at the North for Unionism. We refer to Mr. Crawford, from the county known as the "State of Jones," which seceded from the State and set up for itself on the passage by Mississippi of the ordinance of secession in 1861. That county, from some unexplained reason, though located in the very heart of Southern Mississippi, is almost destitute of slaves, and has maintained its Union-ism throughout the war—organizing a Union army, and defeating the minions of Jeff. Davis that were sent to subdue them. He opposed the withdrawal of the negro troops, "in order to let secessionists loose again on the Union people, as they had been the last four years," and said that he spoke for Union people, and that "the time for boasting and bluster had passed."

While the few Unionists of the "State of Jones" are thus bearding the spirit of secession in its den, Gov. Sharkey, representing heretofore the conservative rebel element, has taken a step of startling significance, and which, if not forthwith overruled from Washington, will be fraught with great trouble hereafter. In furtherance of the policy of expelling the black Federal troops from Mississippi, Gov. Sharkey has issued a proclamation calling on the people to form two companies in each county, one of cavalry and the other of infantry, "*for the purpose of restoring order* and putting a stop to the frequent murders and robberies." This means the reorganization of the rebel army in Mississippi to supersede the Union army now there, and to enforce that system of peonage which the Mississippi Convention authorizes any future legislature to establish ostensibly for the "protection and security of the persons and property of the freedmen of the State, and to guard them and the State against any evil that may arise from their sudden emancipation.

CAUTION!!

COLORED PEOPLE

OF BOSTON, ONE & ALL,

You are hereby respectfully CAUTIONED and advised, to avoid conversing with the

Watchmen and Police Officers of Boston,

For since the recent ORDER OF THE MAYOR & ALDERMEN, they are empowered to act as

KIDNAPPERS

AND

Slave Catchers,

And they have already been actually employed in KIDNAPPING, CATCHING, AND KEEPING SLAVES. Therefore, if you value your LIBERTY, and the *Welfare of the Fugitives* among you, Shun them in every possible manner, as so many *HOUNDS* on the track of the most unfortunate of your race.

Keep a Sharp Look Out for KIDNAPPERS, and have TOP EYE open.

APRIL 24, 1851.

THEODORE PARKER'S PLACARD.

Placed and written by Theodore Parker and printed and posted by the Vigilance Committee of Boston after the rendition of Thomas Sims to slavery in April 1851.

Lunatic Hospital, Williamsburg.

NOTICE is hereby given that all the cells in this institution are occupied, and that no more patients will be received until some of the said cells are vacant; due notice of which will be given. By order of the Court of Directors.

May 26.   5—tf   LEO: HENLEY, c.c.d.

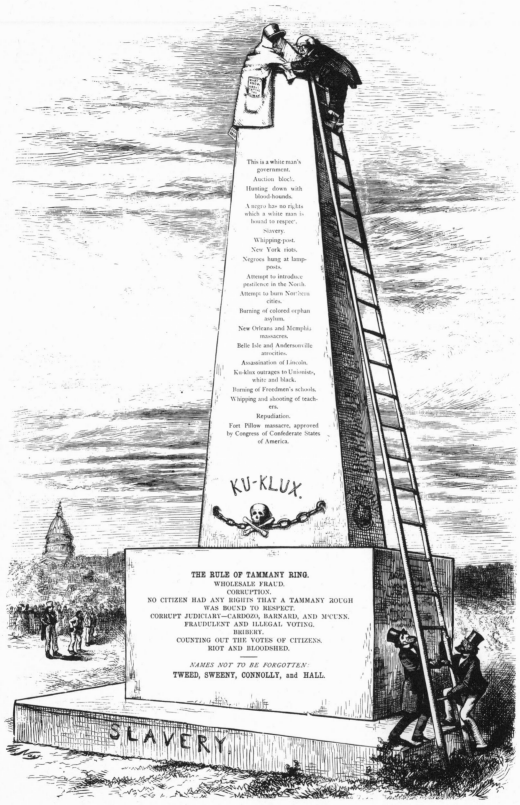

THE WHITED SEPULCHRE.
COVERING THE MONUMENT OF INFAMY WITH HIS WHITE HAT AND COAT.

All the way from Africa to Georgia
I carried my sorrow songs.
I made ragtime.

—Langston Hughes

There is a theory that the plantation cakewalk originated when colored servants imitated others doing the minuet. Whether or not that's true, the cakewalk gravitated right back to white folks by way of minstrel shows. Even high society behind their cloistered doors "kicked up high" for fun without the incentive of a simple cake for a prize. A high spot of one society season came when Bert Williams sent a formal letter to Cornelius Vanderbilt which contained a challenge to a contest to determine precisely who was the best cakewalker in New York City. The contest never came off and the matter now will never be settled.

BERT WILLIAMS.

To Mr. William K. Vanderbilt
Corner of 52 and Fifth Avenue
New York

Dear Sir:

In view of the fact that you have made a success as a cakewalker and having appeared in a semi-public exhibition and having posed as an authority in that capacity, we, the undersigned, the world-renowned cake-walkers, believing that the attention of the world has been distracted from us on account of the tremendous hit which you have made, hereby challenge you to compete with us in a cakewalk match, which will decide which of us deserve the title of Champion Cakewalker of the World.

Yours very truly,
Williams & Walker

Juba, *jubilant* and *jubilee*. The Juba was a plantation dance in slavery time and there was always a jubilee on New Year's Day on plantations where any consideration was given to the servants. Such handmade gifts as the slaves were able to make were exchanged. There would be much eating and drinking and then the dancing to the accompaniment of hand-clapping, rattling bones and often a banjo or a violin.

It was the minstrel men who took the Juba dance off the plantation, smoothed it up and introduced it all over America and Europe. The man who deserves the most credit for the popularity of the Juba as entertainment acquired the name "Mr. Juba." His true name was William Henry Lane, freeborn in Providence, Rhode Island. He was living in the Five Points district of Manhattan in the 1840's when minstrel shows were popular, but most often they were all-white casts in blackface cork.

Lane had a reputation as a "jig" dancer, so when big-time minstrel shows took on mixed casts, he worked with the best and soon had top billing as "Mr. Juba." He had a sense of artistry that enabled him to blend the wild African frenzy with the more mellow steps of Old World folk dances. Soon he was called "the king" of dancers and it was a great loss to the entertainment world when William "Mr. Juba" Lane died at age twenty-nine in London

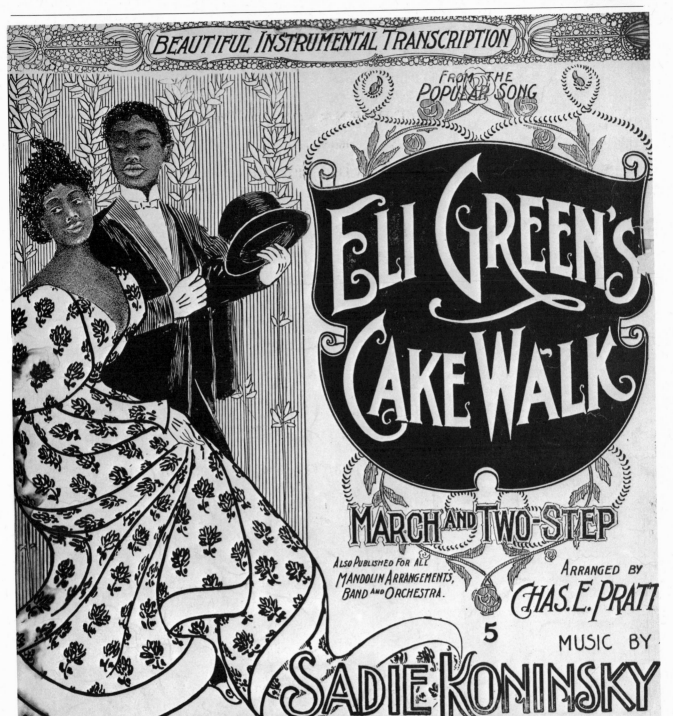

in 1852. He would certainly have enjoyed competing on Labor Day in 1897 when the Old Georgia Plantation Company held the world championship cakewalk contest at old Madison Square Garden.

Blue Tail Fly

When I was young I use to wait
On Master and give him his plate,
And pass the bottle when he got dry,
And brush away the blue tail fly.

Chorus:
Jimmy Crack corn and I don't care,
Jimmy crack corn and I don't care,
Jimmy crack corn and I don't care,
  My master's gone away.

When he ride in the afternoon,
I follow him with a hickory broom;
The pony being rather shy
When bitten by a blue tail fly.

One day he ride around the farm,
The flies so numerous they did swarm;
One chanced to bite him on the thigh—
The devil take the blue tail fly.

The pony run, he jump, he pitch;
He tumble Master in the ditch.
He died and the jury wondered why—
The verdict was the blue tail fly.

They laid him under a simmon tree;
His epitaph is there to see:
"Beneath this stone I'm forced to lie,
A victim of the blue tail fly."

Old Master's gone, now let him rest,
They say all things are for the best;
I'll never forget, till the day I die,
Old Master and that blue tail fly.

"Blue Tail Fly," also known as "Jimmy Crack Corn," probably originated with the blackface minstrels, but it was taken up by slaves and became widely popular among them. It tells of the delight, only half hidden, with which a slave might view the untimely death of his master.

CASEY JONES

John Jones, was the engineer of a famous steam locomotive train. He got the nickname "Casey" from a town in Tennessee named "Cayce." Wallace Saunders, a black man, was the engine wiper on that line, and another black, named Sim Webb, was the fireman.

On April 30, 1900, Casey's train was wrecked in a head-on collision. Casey ordered Sim Webb to jump but refused to do likewise. When his body was finally extricated, one hand was on the whistle and the other was on the airbrake lever. Wallace Saunders, who idolized Casey, made up a song about him simply for his own consolation and the enjoyment of friends. That song, "Casey Jones," became widely popular in the hands of others and made a lot of money for its "owners" but none for Saunders.

The first French horn brought to America was played by a colored man, Adrastus Lew of Dracut (now Pawtucketsville), Massachusetts. He was a businessman of the town by occupation, but a musician at heart. For over fifty years he sang in the choir of the Congregational Church of Dracut and was a member of the celebrated Lowell Cornet Band. In addition to French horn and cornet, he played the violin and flageolet.

Adrastus Lew came by his musical talent naturally, as his grandfather, Barzillai Lew, had a family band that is said to have played at Washington's inauguration. "Bar" Lew was a veteran of the French-Indian and Revolutionary Wars. Fanset's *For Freeman* says of "Bar" Lew: "During the attacks of the British (at Bunker Hill), the Negro fifer, Barzellai Lew, kept up the spirits of his comrades playing the inspiring strains of the song 'There's Nothing Makes the British Run Like Yankee Doodle Dandy . . .'"

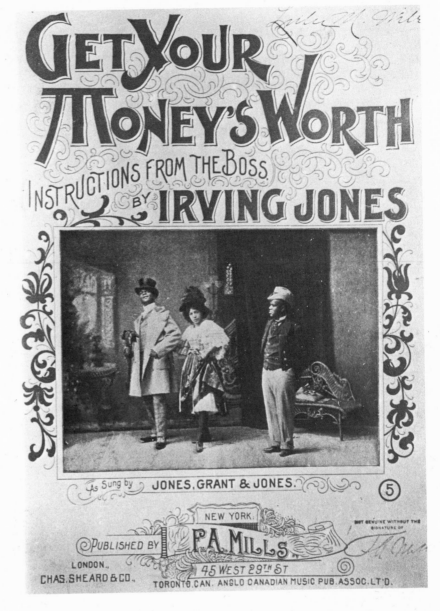

Prof. Handy is well versed in every department of music. For many years he has enjoyed the distinction of being one of the leading band masters of America, having been for seven years in charge of Mahara's Famous Minstrel Band. Also, he had the honor of training bands in Evansville, Henderson, Clarksdale, and Memphis. For three years he was at the head of the Department of Music at Prof. Council's school, Normal, Ala. As a solo cornetist he has few equals and no superiors. He has gained a substantial reputation as an arranger and composer of music, and some of his productions rank with the best in the country. He does the arranging of music for one of the most prominent music houses of Memphis, and his work has proven highly satisfactory. He is well acquainted with the laws of harmony and his productions are always founded upon correct musical principles. All Memphians take great pride in the fact that in Prof. Handy the city of Memphis has, as one of its citizens, one of the greatest musicians in the country, irrespective of race. He is one of America's leading musical virtuosos, and as a cornetist he is one of the great masters. He is a man of class, both socially and musically, and bears the impress of a high-toned gentleman.

The Old Flag Never Touched the Ground

40

Words by
J. W. JOHNSON and
BOB COLE

Music by
ROSAMOND JOHNSON
Arranged by Claude G. Garreau

Sgt. William Carney, heroic flag bearer of the 54th Massachusetts U.S. Colored Troops, was immortalized in song by James Weldon Johnson, his brother, J. Rosamond Johnson, and Bob Cole.

SUNG WITH GREAT SUCCESS BY ALMA GLUCK

CARRY ME BACK TO OLD VIRGINNY

BY

JAMES A. BLAND

SONG AND CHORUS .50   PIANO SOLO .50

BOSTON: OLIVER DITSON COMPANY

NEW YORK: CHAS. H. DITSON & CO.   CHICAGO: LYON & HEALY

The composer, James Bland, was a black man.

FAMOUS CANADIAN JUBILEE SINGERS

MALE QUARTETTE,
PLANTATION LULLABIES.

After giving their first concert in 1871, the original Fisk Jubilee Singers went around the world and gathered fame as a singing group. What ever happened to them as individuals later? Few had any prior vocal training and most had either been born in slavery or were first-generation freedmen.

So far as is known, only one of the original group continued on the concert stage for a livelihood. She was Patti Malone, who must have possessed a beautiful voice. Frederick Loudin selected her when he formed his group that traveled throughout the world in concert for eighteen years. He was a member of the Fisk Jubilee Singers when they made their second tour but quit to form his own group. After they disbanded, Patti Malone went to Europe, where she changed her name to Desireo Plato and continued to sing on the concert stage. The place and date of her passing are unknown.

FOR HIRE: either for the remainder of the year or by the month, week or job, the celebrated musician and fiddler, George Walker. All persons desiring the services of George Walker are notified that they must contract for them with us, and in no case pay to him or any other person the amount of his hire without a written order from us. George Walker is admitted by common consent, to be the best leader of a band in all eastern and middle Virginia.

[*Richmond Daily Enquirer*, June 27, 1853]

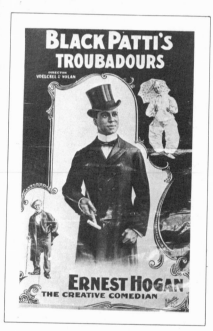

It is a question whether Tom Turpin or Scott Joplin should be called the "father" of ragtime music. Turpin was a fine pianist, but for him music was more an avocation, while to Scott Joplin (1868–1917) it was life itself. He was born into a musical family in Texas and learned to play piano at an early age. Soon he was an itinerant musician hearing all the sounds a musical ear picks up in little town and big cities among people of color. He never stopped studying music and he composed continually, but it was not until 1899 that he was first published—a group of songs entitled "Original Rags."

The "Maple Leaf Rag" was his first real hit that made money for him. Other "ragtime" songs were published and Joplin turned to an effort at composing ragtime operas. *Treemonisha*, the one he thought a masterpiece, failed to catch on. His heart was broken and his intellectual motors ran down, and Joplin died a sad and lonely man. In 1970, *Treemonisha* was rediscovered and has been put on with moderate success by groups in several large cities.

Once in New York City, an elderly man with failing eyesight sat and hoped that delayed lightning would strike again so that some of his composer-father's operettas would be played for appreciative audiences. The man was Valdo Freeman and his father was H. Lawrence Freeman, who was a native of Cleveland, Ohio, and a thoroughly trained composer and conductor. In Cleveland, where he had the honor of conducting the city symphony at the turn of the century, Harry Freeman was referred to in awe as "the black Wagner." However, like Joplin, Freeman could find neither the musicians nor the public for his work.

When Sophie Tucker was belting out songs in her inimitable manner, her theme song was "Some of These Days," which was written by a black man who was quite an entertainer himself on the big-time vaudeville circuit.

Benny Benjamin lived it up on royalties from his song hits, and one of his best was "I Don't Want to Set the World On Fire."

Chris Smith's most famous tune was "Ballin' the Jack." The song was put into the *Ziegfeld Follies* along with a dance by that name. The title came from an old railroad expression. "Jack" was a Negro folk name for a locomotive and "balling" referred to a train running on the tracks. Going at a high rate of speed, a train would be "high balling." "Ballin' the Jack" was a fast, good time song with a catchy tune that made listeners jump and sway to these words:

First you put your two knees close
    up tight,
Then you sway'em to the left, then
    you sway 'em to the right.
Step around the floor kind of nice
    and light,
Then you twist around, twist around
    with all your might.
Stretch your lovin' arms straight out
    in space,
Then you do the Eagle Rock with
    style and grace.
Swing your foot way round, then
    bring it back
Now that's what I call "Ballin the
    Jack."

When Bessie Smith was eight years old, her brother, Clarence, entered her in an amateur contest at the Star Theatre. She won one dollar which she put away toward the purchase of a pair of ball bearing roller skates. With ten cents of every dollar she won at amateur contests, she paid for a daily rental of skates from local merchants. Adults in the community often watched her performing intricate tap steps with the skates on; more often this was done in exhibition to a tune from her brother's guitar.

By the age of nine she was making professional appearances at the Ivory Theatre in Chattanooga for which she was paid nine dollars. She spent her first pay on the very best pair of ball bearing roller skates she could buy. Bessie Smith became so talented and skillful on her skates that she went on to win the Tennessee roller skating championship in Chattanooga.

Among the contemporaries and competitors of Bessie Smith were nine other Smiths:

Mamie Smith—the first Negro to record. Her "Crazy Blues" played an important part in making the blues a commercial success in the phonograph industry.

Trixie Smith—she won the first blues-singing contest.

Laura Smith—she recorded with Oheh Records.

Hazel Smith—she recorded with King Oliver in 1928.

Ada "Bricktop" Smith—she became a Parisian nightclub hostess.

Elizabeth Smith—she recorded with King Oliver.

Bessie Mae Smith—nicknamed Blue Belle—thought by patrons in St. Louis to be the original.

Ruby Smith—Bessie's niece—recorded in the 30's.

Clara Smith—the most serious threat to Bessie—known as "Queen of the Mooners"—the only one of the Smith's to be invited to record with Bessie ("Far Away Blues" and "I'm Going Back to My Used To Be").

They took my joy, my
ragtime
my own true sound...
and sold it...too

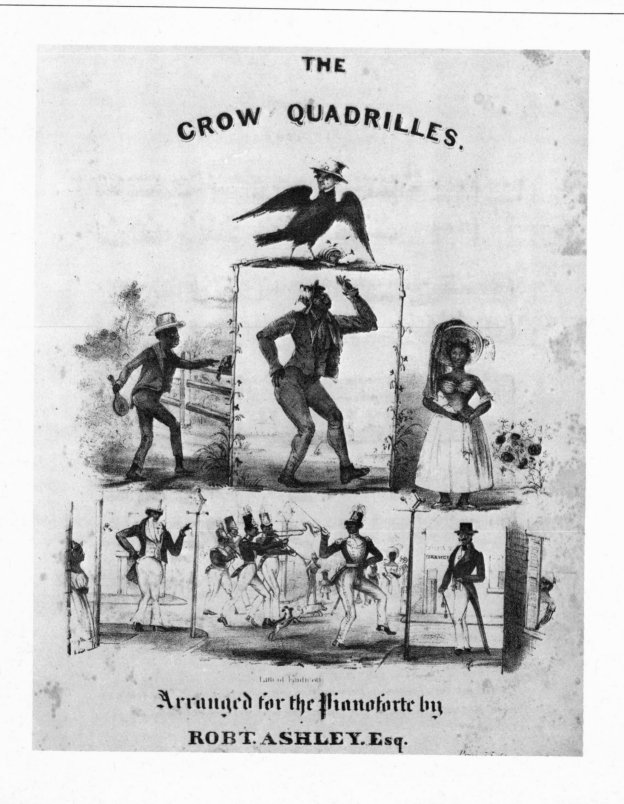

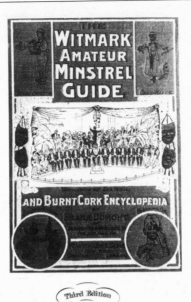

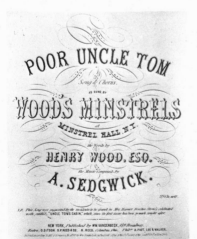

NEGROES OF THE 1800's AS SEEN BY OTHERS

SMOKY MOKES

ERNEST R. SMITH
c/o PORT JERRY
ON LAKE GEORGE
BOLTON LANDING, N. Y. - 12814

PHOTO BY HALL. N.Y.

COPYRIGHT 1899 BY FEIST & FRANKENTHALER.

CAKEWALK AND TWO-STEP

COMPOSED BY A. HOLZMANN

NEW YORK
C. H. DITSON & CO.

CHICAGO, ILL.
LYON & HEALY.

TORONTO, CAN.

PUBLISHED BY
FEIST AND FRANKENTHALER.

1227 BROADWAY,
42 W. 30TH ST. NEW YORK.

SAN FRANCISCO, CAL.
SHERMAN, CLAY & CO.

CHICAGO, ILL.
NATIONAL MUSIC CO.

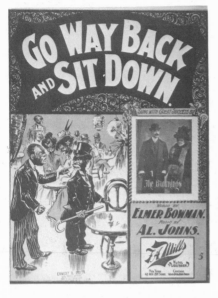

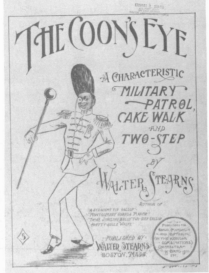

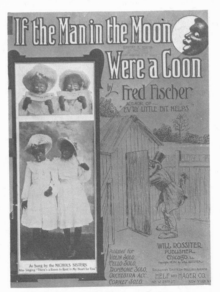

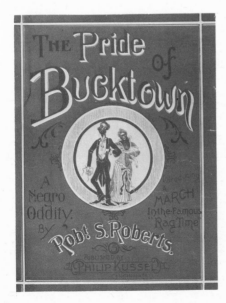

Rare photo shows James Reese Europe and part of his Clef Club orchestra that made musical history. On May 2, 1912, at Carnegie Hall in New York City, he led the band in the first jazz concert performance at that citadel of music. It was a full quarter century later before Paul Whiteman and Benny Goodman followed suit. Critics raved:

In the Clef Club, N.Y. possesses one of the most remarkable orchestras in the world. This orchestra was splendid in its swing, rhythm, power and the singing of its gifted members . . . This club should be heard regularly every winter. Its aim is the preservation of the music of the Colored race, the only musical production of American soil.—*New York Sun*, May 2, 1912

The work of the Clef Club orchestra last night at Carnegie Hall was a marvel of daring and temperament. The concertgoers will, or should, look backward with pride to remember that they were present at the beginning of an innovation in music which will doubtless grow to be a power and which should have been inaugurated long ago.—*Brooklyn Eagle*, May 2, 1912.

We was mostly 'bout survival 'Bout living anyhow

Tourists who visit Oklahoma City, Oklahoma, can see the memorial to black cowboy Bill Pickett in the Cowboy Hall of Fame. Known as "the Dusky Demon," Pickett is credited with inventing the sport of bulldogging and was a star of the 101 Ranch show. Bill Miller, owner of the 101 Ranch, considered Pickett the best cowhand he ever knew. Pickett died in 1932.

The Goodnight Trail was the route by which huge herds of steer owned by Charles Goodnight were taken. It led from Texas through New Mexico to the railroad centers in Colorado. The cowboy that Mr Goodnight depended on most to get his herd to market was Boise Ikard, a black man. Ikard not only saved Goodnight's life, but almost single-handedly saved an entire crew of cowboys from a stampeding herd. When Ikard died in 1929, Goodnight erected a memorial over the grave of his friend.

In 1860, the Pony Express was started to enable the mails to go West as far as San Francisco. Letters from the Eastern U.S. went as far as the railroad could carry them, to St. Joseph, Missouri. From that point, a series of expert riders carried the mail by relays all the way to Sacramento, California. Each rider went about seventy-five miles and both horse and rider had to have great endurance.

From Merced to Marysosa, California, the mail was carried by one of the black Pony Express riders. His name was George Monroe. Another black rider was William Robinson, whose run was from Stockton to the gold-mining area. One can be certain that the sight of a black or white man with mail from home was a welcome sight in all parts of the West.

Private George Washington of the famous all-black 10th Calvary was deputized to join in the capture of Billy the Kid. Washington persuaded Billy the Kid to meet with Lew Wallace.

Willis Meade, a black rancher of Meade, Kansas, gained local fame when he tracked down and killed "Two Toes," a wolf that had killed many cattle in that area.

GOBO FANGO

This account of the life of Gobo Fango has come from combined reminiscences of three surviving grandchildren of Edward Hunter, plus information found in a section of the Negro Pioneer, in OUR PIONEER HERITAGE compiled by Kate B. Carter and published in 1965 by Daughters of Utah Pioneers.

Gobo Fango came to Utah in about 1861 from South Africa with a family named Talbot. The story has been told that on the trek west, the group encountered Confederate officers who were searching wagon trains for escaping slaves, shooting them on sight, and that one of the women took the young boy, Gobo, and hid him in the folds of her skirt and apron until the danger was past.

Gobo Fango came to Grantsville as a young boy when Mary Ann Whitesides Hunter wrote to her brother, Lewis Whitesides, in Kaysville, Utah, and asked him to find her a young man to help herd her sheep. At this time Mary Ann's daughters, Elizabeth and Margaret, were herding sheep between Grantsville and Tooele, the sons in the family being too young to trust with this work. Mary Ann began to worry that these girls were having no opportunity to learn skills in running a home well.

Mary Ann drove her wagon to Kaysville and brought Gobo home with her. Her husband, Edward Hunter, paid the "owner" thirty dollars a month. Gobo had been made to sleep in a woodshed in cold weather at some time and was suffering from frozen feet. Mary Ann doctored his feet as best she could, but he limped all his life. He lived with the Hunter family for several years, helping with farm chores and herding sheep.

When slavery was abolished, Edward Hunter stopped paying the thirty dollars to Gobo's "owner"

and began paying it to Gobo. The owner sued Mr. Hunter on this matter but was not able to change this.

In about 1880 Lewis and Billy Hunter and Gobo Fango took Edward Hunter's sheep to the Oakley, Idaho, area to run them on shares. A sheep and cattleman's war developed over grazing rights, and Gobo was shot by a man named Bedky, who rode up pretending to be a friend. Gobo managed to crawl to the home of Walt Matthews, but died there a few days later. Before he died he wrote a will leaving some money for Mary Ann Whitesides Hunter and her youngest daughter, Etta Neilson, and $500.00 to the Grantsville Relief Society. Mary Ann was president of that organization for twenty-two years.

A few of the older people in Grantsville remember Gobo Fango. One granddaughter of the Hunters says he visited often in their home when she was young. She remembers him as a kind and friendly person, always bringing candy for the children.

(This information furnished by John Paul Millward, great great grandson of Edward and Mary Ann Whitesides Hunter)

Early in the Colonial period, with the British soldiers on Macinac Island, there was a half-French half-black servant Jean Bonga. He fled in 1794 and went into the wilderness of what was an area of contention between Great Britain, France and America. After the Louisiana Purchase the dispute narrowed down to the U.S. and England. Pierre Bonga married an Indian woman by whom he had children. Like their father they became great hunters, trappers and watermen. Pierre's grandson was George Bonga, strong, black and wealthy from the fur business. Like the Bongas before him, George married an Indian woman and considered the Bongas the "first white men" in that area. George Bonga was a government interpreter for General Cass and other officials who had treaty business with Indians.

He was known far and wide for his hospitality to persons who passed his way.

The first, and probably the most important, exploring expedition by Americans, was the Lewis and Clark Expedition which charted the territory acquired by the Louisiana Purchase in 1803. The leaders of the expedition kept a journal, which was later published, and in addition, other books have been written about that expedition. Each account gives slight mention to York, the black manservant of Captain William Clark. Aside from his great strength and other skills that were utilized, it appears that York smoothed the way in dealings with Indians. York was unable to write, and since he was a slave, probably would not have been allowed to publish an account of the three-year journey. After the expedition ended, Clark stayed out West; York was freed and returned to Richmond, Virginia, to live out his life.

Beckwourth Pass through the Sierra Nevada Mountains was discovered and named for Jim Beckwourth, a legendary Negro guide, trader and trapper who was a pioneer of the Old West. The pass is on U.S. alternate Road 40 just east of the junction with U.S. Road 395.

In Central City, Colorado, there is a chair in the Opera House which is dedicated to a black woman who lived there from 1859 until her death in 1877 at age eighty-five. Her name was Clara Brown and she was born a slave in Missouri but was freed by the will of her master. In Central City she operated a laundry and tried to acquire enough money to purchase freedom for her husband and children. Her many acts of charity in Central City caused the dedication of the Opera House chair in her memory.

In the days when the West was young and wild, Independence, Missouri, was well known because it was there that black Hiram Young built the Conestoga wagons upon which travelers depended to carry them through the wilderness. Young employed 50 men who operated the 25 forges in his smithy and he had the reputation for building the best wagons in the region.

A mural by the famous artist Thomas Hart Benton includes the figure of the famous wagon builder. As many of the Conestoga wagon drivers smoked big black cigars, the cigars were nicknamed "stogies."

Edward Booth was a pioneer miner in the gold fields of Alaska. Born free, he went to the West Indies, where he heard about the gold strike in California. He mined successfully for a year and soon had a stake sufficient to go back East and bring his family to California. When he learned about a gold strike in Alaska, he arranged to try his luck in the Klondike fields. He died a wealthy man in Alaska.

As the result of Edwin McCabe's encouragement of black men to go West, several all-Negro towns were founded in Oklahoma: Boley, Langston, Summit and Verson among them.

A Negro slave, born in Virginia, was a pioneer settler in the state of Washington. His name was George Washington and he owned the land on which the town of Centralia was built.

With his foster parents he migrated to the Oregon Territory, which at that time consisted of land which was eventually made into two states: Oregon and Washington.

George Washington homesteaded in a beautiful part of the Northwest and dreamed of having a town built on his property. He attracted settlers by offering free lots and moving services to all newcomers.

Blacks can be members of the Mormon Church but they cannot become priests nor do they go to the Mormon heaven. The Book of Mormons, II Nephi, chapter 5, verses 21–23, tells that because of a curse upon them some whites were turned to black people, and whites who mix with them suffer the same dreadful fate.

Yet there were a few blacks who accompanied the pioneer Mormons on their cross-country trek. One was Abel Burns, a servant to the Mormon leader, Joseph Smith. According to Mormon tradition, because of his loyalty to Smith, Abel Burns is the only black man in the Mormon heaven. When his nephew, Eugene Burns, died, that "sad" fact was announced at Eugene's funeral by a Mormon patriarch.

Bronco Sam, famous in the sport of bull dogging.

1. **Nat Love, famous cowboy**
2. **Bob Leavitt ran this saloon in Miles City, Montana, calling it after his nickname "Nigger Bob"**
3. **Bertoli Saloon, Freeland, Colorado, 1890's**
4. **Isom Dart, Colorado cowboy and outlaw**
5. **Special invitation sent out to guests for a Montana hanging**
6. **Eugene Tyler, a "bad" man of the West who robbed the Los Baños Stage May 7, 1877, with Dan Mc Carty**
7. **Louis Sheridan Leary**
8. **Dangerfield Newby**

— underneath its clouds of sin,
  The heart of man retaineth yet
Gleams of its holy origin;
  And half-quenched stars that never set,
Dim colors of its faded bow,
  And early beauty, linger there,
And o'er its wasted desert blow
  Faint breathings of its morning air,
O, never yet upon the scroll
Of the sin-stained, but priceless soul,
Hath Heaven inscribed " DESPAIR ! "

Mr. *Frank Adkins*
You are invited to witness the execution of William Gay and William Biggerstaf on Friday, December 20, 1895, at 10 o'clock A. M., at the Lewis and Clarke County Jail.
Respectfully,
H. Henry Jurgens
Sheriff of Lewis and Clarke County.

4

6

7

8

Matt Henson accompanied Admiral Perry to the North Pole

Negro miner in Auburn Ravine, 1852, during the California Gold Rush

I've been a victim
The Belgians cut off my hands
in the Congo
They lynched me in Texas.

—Langston Hughes

THE WEATHER

For Coatesville, Chester county and vicinity: Generally fair tonight and Tuesday; light to moderate variable winds.

COATESVIL

VOL. 3, NO. 258

COATESVILLE, PA., MO

ANGRY MOB BURNS
COLORED MAN
POLICE C

Masked Men Break Into Hospital and Drag Zachariah Walker to Newlin Farm Where Fire is Kindled With Fence Rails

NEGRO HAD ATTEMPTED TO COMMIT SUICIDE

Surrounded Yesterday Afternoon While Treed in Robert Faddis' Woods Near Youngsburg He Placed Revolver to His Head But Failed to Blow Out His Brains

SHERIFF IN CHARGE OF POLICE ALL BARS IN TOWN CLOSE

Rigid Investigation Being Made and Many Arrests Likely to Follow. Thousands Visited Seen of Burning Last Night and This Morning

Having shot in cold blood and instantly killed Special Police Officer Edgar Rice of the Worth Brothers' force about nine o'clock Saturday night, Zachariah Walker, the murderer, was taken from the Coates-ville Hospital by an angry mob just 24 hours later and burned at the stake.

After a search lasting all Saturday night and until nearly three o'clock Sunday afternoon Walker

was found hiding up a tree in the woods of Robert Faddis, in East Fallowfield Township, and seeing that capture was inevitable, he turned the revolver upon himself, but failed to inflict a mortal wound. He was brought to the lockup in Coatesville, quickly revived and when removed to the hospital an hour later made a full confession of his crime.

For the sake of Coatesville it is well to say right here that the entire tragic scene, the shooting, the lynching and all the details thereto took place in East Fallowfield township, outside the borders of the borough.

It was just 9.12 according to Police Officer Stanley Howe on guard at the Hospital, that about 15 men gained entrance by forcing one of the large front windows near the Main doorway. The window was first broken, sash and all, by a large stone being smashed against it and Howe, who had rushed to the window-dowdow as soon as he saw the attack being made at that point was struck on the back with the rock as he was bracing his weight against the sash to block the entrance.

From the ground to the window is about ten feet, but the crowd forcing entrance had first rushed to the porchway and standing on the bannister railing around this they were easily able to leap through the window after it had been forced in.

This gave them entrance to the main hallway or lobby of the hospital. All wore white handkerchiefs knotted around their faces and shielding them completely from the eyes to below the chin.

Howe was at once rushed into a corner and pinned there, with the closed hand of a man placed over his eyes so he could not see. Walker was confined in a private room n

the first floor in the building. the foot of the only as a preca from escaping, being taken ou by a mob.

Howe was at the room in wh was confined, bu ter a quick gla ward and assuri there was no d men quickly so of the building ed man tugging trying to jump was then asked key with which were bound to formed them th possession of C police station.

Took Part

It was then d foot of the bed oner and this wa and unhooked fr this time both th the front and re been opened wid en men siezing shoulders pulled doorway and stra race leading to t

Word of the a tal had spread so time the murder fully 2,000 peop the institution ar from Main street with people hur

From the hos farmhouse in fro murderer was bu mile and Walker this distance wi bed dangling fro the way he was

E RECORD

GREATEST ADVERTISING
MEDIUM IN THE REAL
BUSINESS CENTRE
OF CHESTER COUNTY

, AUGUST 14, 1911.

ONE CENT

T STAKE
HO MURDERED
FICER EDGAR RICE

rth wing of hackled to dstead, not keep him revent his institution

ed to reveal colored man used and af- the public patients that o them, the e other end d the color-hackles and bed. Howe liver up the rderer's legs , but he in- was in the sted at the

Along
to take the ith the pris- ly lifted up position. By e doors of trance had half a doz- er by the ut the front own the ter-verville road. n the hospi- y that by the s taken out, surrounded rode avenue was black to the scene. o the Newlin which the s a good half dragged all foot of the heels. All with stones,

and beaten with sticks though every precaution was taken by those hav- ing him in charge to prevent him from receiving a wound which would make him insensible to the flames when the fire had been kind- led.

Where He Was Burned
The point at which the mob had decided to burn the murderer at the stake is a field on the Sarah Jane Newlin farm just to the right of the road and almost directly op- posite the farm house. A lane leads down from the house and right near the road a small wooden bridge spans the creek. On the opposite side of the road is a grass field ris- ing to a little knoll and hemmed in by a post and rail fence leading down to the road. A spot about fifty feet from the road and direct- ly along the fence was chosen for the burning. Straw was taken from the Newlin barn to kindle the flam- es and then dry chestnut rails were slipped out of the fence broken in- to bits and placed on top of the burning straw In less than three minutes from the time the match was applied the flames had reached a height of ten feet or more. The murderer was then asked if he had anything to say and making no re- ply was immediately thrown on the burning pile.

Tried to Escape Flames
As the flames licked his clothing and seared his flesh he gave a mighty leap and dragging the foot of the bedstead with him jumped over the fence and was instantly siezed, a rope place around his neck and thrown back on the flames.
Twice more he attempted to get away from the seething furnce and each time he was beaten back with fence rails until all was still and only the sickening smell of burning flesh remained.

The fire was lighted about 9.30 and within an hour ntohing but the charred bones of the murderer re- mained although the crowd still watced the fire on past midnight and well into the morning.
CONTINUD ... ...

Removed Their Masks
The men who had dragged Walk- er from the hospital, left the fire the instant they were satisfied life was extinct and running up over the hill removed their masks under the cover of darkness.
By this time thousands of people were gathering from every direction the entire countryside for miles around having received word in the mysterious way news travels so quickly, and with the great crowds rushing to the scene of the burning it was easy for those who had taken the murderer to his doom to return unnoticed.
Everything was quiet and orderly around the fire if such a thing can be said of a lynching. There was no loud talking, no profanity, and the utmost deference shown to the hundreds of women who came to the scene. Men stepped back as the women came forward and led them to points of vantage where they could obtain the best view of the burning negro.
A thick grey fog coming up from the creek enveloped everything like a pall. Lights from the autos shone a sickly yellow through the mist and the spirit of death seemed to be in the very air.
Then the crowds dispersed and wended their way to their homes, awed and silent and the last sput- tering sparks crackled over all that remained of the man who just 24 hours before had committed the most awful crime in Coatesville's history.

Leading Up To The Burning
The events leading up to the burning fo Walker at the stake were uneventful and little portrayed the awful vengeance that was to over- take the murderer. A large crowd surrounded the lockup when the prisoner was brought in, but it re- mained outside, quiet and orderly, and no open threats of any kind were heard. This was perhaps due to the first report that Walker had died shortly after being found in the Faddis woods, and then the lat- er report that while not dead from his self inflicted shot he was expect- ed to die at any time.
When he was removed from the police station on a stretcher to the patrol and thence to the Hospital the crowd stepped back and made way for the men who carried out the wounded man.

Crowd Around Hospital
It was only when the news be- came general that his wound was not dangerous and that he had made full confession of the murder that mutterings of taking the law in their own hands were heard from the friends of the dead officer. Even then no one thought for a moment that an attack on the Hospital would be made although hundreds had surrounded it from the time the prisoner was taken there about four o'clock in the afternoon. In this crowd were many women and children attracted mostly by idle curiosity. The crowd grew in numbers until by eight o'clock pro- bably 2000 persons had surrounded the Hospital or were on Strode av- enue nearby.

The First Serious Note
The first intimation of the ser- iousness of the situation was given when Dr. E. A. Graves with the am- bulance conveyed an accident case to the Hospital from the Pennsyl-

SOUTHERN DISTURBANCES.

Six Negroes Lynched at Trenton, Tenn.

Whites and Blacks in the Vicinity Said to Be Arming.

Negro Criminals Lynched at Brookhaven, Miss.

NASHVILLE, Tenn., Aug. 26.—The negroes at Pickettsville, Gibson County, 6 miles from Humboldt, last Saturday and Sunday, threatened a riot on account of some supposed wrong done to them, and manifested a strong desire to kill two or three citizens, and fire and sack the town.

Yesterday sixteen of the ringleaders were arrested and taken to Trenton and placed in jail for safe-keeping.

About 1 o'clock this morning, between seventy-five and 100 masked men entered the town, rode up to the jail and compelled the Sheriff to deliver the keys to them. They then

TOOK THE SIX NEGROES FROM THE JAIL.

Four were killed and two mortally wounded at the edge of town. The masked men then rode off with the other ten, and are supposed to have killed them. Nothing has been heard from them since they left. Considerable excitement exists among the negroes there, and the whites are taking defensive steps in case of any outbreak.

A special to the *Union and American* from McKenzie, Tenn., reports as follows:

TRENTON, Aug. 26—3 p. m.—Armed men are pouring in from the country to find all quiet. Scouts say they cannot find an armed negro. Two of the negroes found shot last night are still alive.

HUMBOLDT, Aug. 26—5 p. m.—All quiet.

PICKETTSVILLE, Aug. 26—6 p. m.—The men are resting on their arms. All rumors of armed negro bands, and fighting in the country, are believed to be false.

MEMPHIS, Aug. 26.—The *Appeal's* special from Humboldt to-night says the excitement in Gibson County is subsiding. No further bloodshed is anticipated. Women and children have been coming in there during the day, and the wildest excitement existed throughout the county through rumors of negroes marching in strong force on Pickettsville, and rumors of their having murdered two women. On the other hand, the negroes were terribly alarmed, and many fled to the woods, fearing the fate of those taken from Trenton jail last night.

The origin of the troubles there occurred at a barbecue near Pickettsville five weeks since, in a difficulty between a white man named J. Hale and Josh Webb, colored, about the payment of half a dollar, since when the negroes had made numerous threats of violence. On Saturday night last, while two young men, named Morgan and James, were riding along the road, 3 miles from Pickettsville, they were

FIRED UPON BY THIRTY OR FORTY NEGROES

hid in the woods. The young men abandoned their horses, took to the woods, and escaped to town, the citizens in which had become alarmed at the firing, in view of the reports that the negroes were organizing armed companies. Suspecting a negro named Ben Walker of complicity in the shooting, a constable, with a posse, proceeded to his house, where they captured a negro named Ben Ballard, who confessed that they had met on Saturday night and organized to protect Col. Webb, colored, from the Ku-Klux, and after that to kill Bassel Butler for divulging their plans to the whites, but after meeting and firing on Morgan and Warren, they

separated. He also gave the names of a large number engaged in the plot for assassination and murder. When Ballard's confession was made public, the greatest excitement spread throughout the country, and the citizens gathered at Pickettsville, and a meeting was called, at which Squire Burnett presided. It was decided to summon a posse, and arrest the following negroes, who, according to Ballard, were the ringleaders: George Green, Steve Bryant, Dan Williams, Bob Love, Dick Shaw, Dug Jamison, Hays Peebles, Parret Burrows, Alfred Williams, and Nick Joey; which was done, and they were brought to Picketsville. On Sunday night a band of masked men rode into town and demanded the prisoners, but Marshall Dungan refused to give them up, and the maskers left. On Monday they were arraigned before three Justice's of the Peace on a charge of shooting with intent to kill, and inciting a riot. One of them, Jarrett Burrows, turned State's evidence, and related the story of the cause, origin, purposes, and expectations of an extensive organization among the negroes of Gibson County, which was corroborated by Nelson McGhee, colored, who also said it was rumored for some time past that President Grant would back the negroes in whatever course they took against the whites, and, acting on this belief, the colored people had determined

TO EXTIRPATE THE WHITES

so as to obtain the lands, &c., but had not agreed upon the time for the outbreak. This measure for the murder of the whites was agreed to by all except Burrell Butler, of Pickettsville, and because of his opposition they intended to kill him on Saturday night, for fear he would tell the whites. Burrows also gave the names of several other persons who were to be killed on Saturday night, and told where the negroes met in the railroad cut and organized by electing Wesley Shields Captain, until they reached Col. Webb's house, who was then to take command. They expected to meet a company from Humboldt, under charge of John Regan, which failed to come. Their object in organizing thoroughly was to shoot the KuKlux, who they understood were raiding the country to persecute the negroes.

After the examination they were committed to jail at Trenton, and the result has been already announced. The lynching of the prisoners causes much indignation here.

ANOTHER DISPATCH.

MEMPHIS, Aug. 26.—A special from Trenton to the *Avalanche* gives the following additional particulars regarding the slaughter of the colored prisoners:

After the maskers, numbering about 100, had obtained possession of the prisoners, they tied them together and marched off on the Huntington road half a mile from town. Six of the number were cut loose and ordered to escape, and, as soon as that command was given, a full volley was fired upon them, killing four and wounding the other two,—one mortally. The remainder were carried up the river 2 miles and killed. Their remains were collected, and are being taken care of.

The Circuit Court was in session at this place. On the assembling of the Court this morning, several speeches were made by members of the Bar denouncing the conduct of the disguised men, who were from the country, and urging upon the Judge to give the Grand Jury an extra charge ordering them to send out for witnesses all along the road from here to Pickettsville in order to arrest and punish the criminals. While the charge was being delivered runners arrived in hot haste with a report that

A LARGE BODY OF NEGROES,

well armed, were marching to Trenton, which caused the adjournment of the Court. Scouts were sent out, and returned reporting all quiet.

There is no mistake but that the negroes are well organized in this county, and ready for action at a moment's warning. Two companies from Union City have arrived here. Other dispatches report everybody under arms.

Lynch Law in Mississippi.

BROOKHAVEN, Miss., Aug. 23.—The three negroes, Dick Cooper, Anthony Grant, and Silas Johnson, who at 3 o'clock on Sunday morning last forcibly entered the residence of Mrs.

Burnley, were taken from the jail at 4 o'clock on Saturday and hung by the citizens, about 1,000 of whom were present. Johnson was captured on Sunday. The other two were taken at Canton, brought here Saturday morning, and lodged in jail. They all confessed their guilt on the gallows.

The Chicago Daily Tribune, August 27, 1874.

MARSHALL COUNTY.

A letter from Marshall County of the 1st ult. gives a fearful account of the resurrected rebels in that district:

MARSHALL Co., July 1.—We have gathered some further particulars about the cruel inflictions of those infamous wretches, the Ku-Klux, or resurrected rebels as they call themselves. On the night of the 15th of July those infamous wretches went to the house of Mr. Lewis Strikally and abused him; as we learn their calculations were to serve in a like manner the person of Berryman Scales, Mr. Willis, and also R. Royster for the sole cause of boarding the teacher at his house. They expressed an intention to hang Mr. Jenkins for his habit of reading the Bible to those of his own race, thereby making them as wise as the white men, as they allege.

It is impossible at this time to give the number of murders up to the 1st of July. The reports of the Sub-Assistant Commissioners of the Freedmen's Bureau for June have not all come in yet, and complete reports of outrages in that month will not be made until the first of August. But from the few reports received, and from other authentic sources, we have collected 96 additional homicides, so that the statistics of homicides committed in Texas during the three years since the conclusion of the rebellion stand thus:

Killed in 1865,	47 whites,	51 freedmen........ 98
Killed in 1866,	75 whites,	95 freedmen........170
Killed in 1867,	173 whites,	174 freedmen........347
Killed in 1868,	182 whites,	147 freedmen........319
Year unknown,	32 whites,	29 freedmen........ 61
Race unknown,	–	– 40
Total........., 509	486	1,035

We have thus a grand total of 1,035 homicides in three years, or 345 per year; and estimating our population since 1865, at 800,000, we have one person killed out of every 2,026 of the whole population per year. We doubt very much if such a record of blood can be exhibited in any Christian or civilized State in the world in a time of peace. It has been stated in the papers that the homicides in New York during the year 1867, numbered 47. If this be correct, there was one person killed out of every 80,000 of her population, and then in that year there were *forty times* as many homicides in Texas as in New York, according to the population of each. The eighth census of the United States for the year 1860, reports for that year 37 homicides and murders in New York, making one person killed out of every 104,000 of her whole population, so that Texas has averaged per year since the war, *forty-five times* more homicides than New York did in 1860. We note, also, that for 14 murders in New York there were three executions in 1860, while for the 1,000 in Texas since the war there has been but one execution.

It should be remembered that in New York and other States in the North, every murder is accurately reported, while the figures here presented come far short of representing the actual number of murders in Texas during the time specified. We have kept scrupulously within the number presented to us, of which fact any candid man can satisfy himself by patiently examining all the data. We assert, too, that the reports usually relied on do not present all the homicides committed in the

section described by them. For example, from the ordinary sources of information we had reported only three homicides in Washington County since the 1st of December, 1867; but when a full report is obtained from that county it gives 16 in that time. Through the usual channels only two murders are reported in Tarrant County, whereas a more complete account gives 15, and so it is with other counties. Now, when it is remembered that we have full reports from about 30 of the 137 organized counties of the State, it becomes very evident that we have information only of a portion of the murders committed. It is proper to state further that the reports which we call full do not profess to give full accounts of the murders in the counties represented by them. Many of them positively state that they do not report all, and witnesses tell us of men disappearing mysteriously, and of dead bodies being hid away in ravines, or floating down streams, of which cases no history is given.

National Anti-Slavery Standard, August 15, 1869

FREE NEGROES IN ARKANSAS. The Arkansas papers contain an address from a Committee appointed by the citizens of Little Rock, to the people of that State, upon the subject of the removal of free negroes from its limits. The address sets forth the undesirableness of that class of population in a slave-holding community, suggests that the necessary laws be passed by the Legislature to remove them from Arkansas, and forbid their return forever afterwards. The question was mooted two years ago, but failed.

The Liberator, September 3, 1858

AN OUTRAGE.—We learn from a friend, who had his facts from a resident of Belbucle, on the Chattanooga Railroad, that Mrs. Long, the wife of Dr. Long of that place, a few days since, whipped a negro woman so severely that she died within an hour or two after the infliction. The coroner's verdict was in accordance with this statement. The woman and her husband, we learn, have fled from the country.— *Nashville Daily News.*

SLAVES REMANDED TO THEIR MASTERS. CINCINNATI, Aug. 27.—Two fugitive slaves belonging to Robert W. Ingraham, who escaped in March from Kentucky, were arrested last night and taken before Commissioner Newhall, who remanded them to their master; whereupon they were taken to Covington. The arrest was made quietly.

A REIGN OF MIDNIGHT TERROR

KU KLUX DEVILS INCARNATE

NEGROES HIDING IN THE SWAMPS OF LOUISIANA.

Harper's Weekly, May 10, 1873

THE LOUISIANA MURDERS.

THE official report of Colonels WILLIAM WRIGHT and T. W. DE KLYNE, of General LONGSTREET'S staff, who were sent to Grant Parish, Louisiana, to investigate the late massacre of colored people there, shows that the first reports of that atrocity were not exaggerated. Between one hundred and fifty and two hundred colored men had been killed by the whites. The former had intrenched themselves about the court-house at Colfax, inclosing a space of about 200 yards square with a slight earth-work, with ditch inside. This ditch was from ten to eighteen inches in depth, and the breastwork in front of it from twenty to thirty inches in height, and was protected in front by two-and-a-half-inch planking. On the lower side of the court-house the greater portion of the breastwork was composed of planking alone, laid in zigzags, and without ditches. They were poorly armed, and had rigged up a couple of guns by fastening lengths of gas-pipe on rafter timbers, blocking up one end with a pine plug, and drilling a

touch-hole. One of these was burst while trying it, some days before the fight, and the other has not the appearance of having been used. The attacking party had in their possession a small cannon, taken from a steamboat in the river, with which they bombarded the court-house.

During the fight the negroes were driven from their breastworks into the court-house, one end of which was without windows, nor had the besieged prepared loop-holes. The leader of the whites, a man named NASH, caused the court-house to be fired, and the negroes "were shot down like dogs" as they fled from the burning building. The report, describing the atrocities of the massacre, says:

"Many were shot in the back of the head and neck. One man still lay with his hands clasped in supplication; the face of another was completely flattened by blows from a broken stock of a double-barreled gun, lying on the ground near him; another had been cut across the stomach with a knife after being shot; and almost all had from three to a dozen wounds. Many of them had their brains literally blown out. It is asserted by the colored people that after the fight thirty-four prisoners who were taken before the burning of

the court-house were taken to the river-bank two by two, executed, and hurled into the river. We caused to be buried in the ditch near the ruins of the court-house the remains of fifty-four colored men, three of whom were so badly burned as to be unrecognizable. There were inside the court-house the charred bones of one other, and five bodies we gave to their friends for interment elsewhere. We saw also twelve wounded colored men, two of whom will certainly die, and others of whom are very unlikely to recover. We are informed that since the fight parties of armed men have been scouring the country surrounding Colfax, taking the mules and other property of the colored people."

Near the court-house the commissioners met a party of colored men and women carrying away a wounded colored man upon a sled. At a little distance in the field were the dead bodies of two colored men. About two hundred yards nearer the court-house were three dead bodies of colored men, and from that point to the court-house and its vicinity the ground was thickly strewn with dead. A general feeling of insecurity prevails among the colored people of Louisiana, and hundreds are seeking safety in the swamps and forests.

PERSECUTION OF NEGROES IN THE CAPITOL— ASTOUNDING REVELATIONS.

UNDER the heading of "Secrets of the Prison House," we last week alluded to the revelations which have recently been made in Washington, of the confinement of negroes in that city, for no other cause than their color, under the authority of municipal laws derogatory of the spirit of the age, in violation of the precepts of Christianity, and pre-eminently disgraceful to the fame of the National Capitol. The matter, as we have said, was brought before Congress by Senator Wilson, and referred to the Senate Committee on the District of Columbia, with instructions to make it a subject of inquiry, and to report what legislation is necessary to remedy the abuse. In the interval, Mr. Seward has issued an order to General McClellan to arrest all persons who may attempt to imprison negroes on the ground of their being fugitives. It seems that a law has existed for many years in the District of Columbia, authorizing the constables and police magistrates to arrest and confine negroes, fugitives from labor, or unable to produce free papers. Under this law they have lately arrested and confined considerable numbers, without any investigation and without using any efforts to have justice done. Some of the victims were no doubt runaway slaves, others slaves of secessionists, living in the adjoining counties of Virginia and Maryland; others free colored men of the North, who came to Washington in company with the three months' regiments, in the capacity of servants to the officers, and while visiting the city upon a necessary errand, were taken into custody. Others inhabitants of Washington, living peaceably at home, without any intention of departing, who were captured, in some cases merely from a spirit of malice or tyranny, and locked up in the city prison.

The motive alleged for the capture of these negroes is a desire to have them kept in prison for a certain space of time—we think a year—and then have them sold for the purpose of paying their costs. While we think it hardly possible that a motive so base could actuate men occupying responsible positions, and administering justice, yet the evidence in the case, collected by Mr. Detective Allen, and reported by him to Provost-Marshal Porter, seems to prove the fact. In his report this officer draws a fearful picture of the sufferings of the poor captives. He says:

"I find incarcerated in the city jail in this city, in the midst of filth, vermin and contagious diseases, on a cold stone floor, many without shoes, nearly all without sufficient clothing, bedding or fire, and all in a half-starving condition, 60 colored persons, male and female, confined because—in the language of their commitments—they were suspected of being runaways, and no proofs had been adduced that they were not runaways."

Our Artist in Washington has visited the city prison, and has drawn the revolting scenes there presented before him with photographic accuracy. His pictures, which we this week present, speak with a powerful although silent truth and rhetoric, and will contribute their share towards rousing the people against the abuse practised in their name, in the capitol of the nation.

Frank Leslie's Illustrated Newspaper, December 28, 1861

MURDER OF THE REV. B. F. RANDOLPH.

ONE of the most satisfactory results of General GRANT's accession to the Presidency will be peace in the South, involving protection to life as well as property, and a toleration by each political party of the opinions of the other. It is not chiefly the fact that GRANT has been elected President which will secure this result, but rather the utter defeat which that election brings upon them in the South who as a habit intimidate their political opponents and slay all whom they can not intimidate. It is now settled that the national law means Liberty and Equal Rights, and that those who violate that law must be punished as law-breakers. We give on this page a portrait of the Rev. B. F. RANDOLPH, a Methodist clergyman of South Carolina, and a Senator of that State, who, on the 17th of last month, fell a victim to assassination for his political opinions. Shortly after the murder the Charleston *Christian Advocate* published the following account:

"We are called upon to record one of the most daring and cold-blooded murders that ever darkened the pages of history, committed upon the person of one of the members of our Conference. The Rev. B. F. RANDOLPH was, on the 17th inst., assassinated, in open day, while traveling by public conveyance. He was upon a lecturing tour in one of the upper counties of the State. He lectured at Abbeville on the 15th inst., and left on Friday morning to go to Anderson, where he was to lecture in the evening. When he got upon the Greenville train at Hodge's station he put his carpet-bag and shawl on a seat, and then returned to the platform of the car to speak to a colored man. While engaged in conversation with this

THE LATE REV. B. F. RANDOLPH, OF SOUTH CAROLINA.—Assassinated Oct. 17, 1868.
[PHOTOGRAPHED BY N. A. COOLEY.]

person he was shot from behind by three ruffians, simultaneously, and fell dead, the shots taking effect in his head, lungs, and bowels. These murderers came to the dépôt on horseback, and immediately after committing the deed remounted their horses and rode quietly away. The report is that they are un-

known and can not be identified. This speaks for itself, when it is remembered that the deed was committed in open day, with the usual throng of passengers on the cars and around the dépôt. No one starts in pursuit, and all seem to concede that it is useless to make any effort to identify or arrest the murderers. Brother RANDOLPH's remains were taken on the following day to Columbia and interred on Sabbath, the 18th inst., with appropriate religious services, a vast concourse of people following them to the grave. Mr. RANDOLPH was born in Kentucky, and was educated at Oberlin, enjoying the advantages of the classical department. He was duly licensed and ordained as a minister in the Old School Presbyterian Church. Having received the appointment of chaplain in the army, and assigned to a colored regiment in that capacity, the fortunes of war brought him to our State. After the organization of the South Carolina Conference, he felt that the field opened by the Methodist Episcopal Church in this section would afford him a greater opportunity for usefulness than he could enjoy in continuing his connection with the Presbyterian Church. He consequently solicited admittance to the Methodist Episcopal Church, and was duly received and admitted on trial at the session of our Conference in the spring of 1867. His first appointment was in connection with the Freedmen's Bureau as Assistant Superintendent of Education in this State. His next appointment by the Conference was to Columbia. Although he was connected with our Conference, he received no fund from our Missionary Society. When the Charleston *Advocate* was started he held to it the relation of an assistant editor, in which he was continued until the resignation of the entire editorial corps in anticipation of the appointment of an editor, as arranged by the last General Conference. At the time of his death Mr. RANDOLPH was a member of the State Senate and Chairman of the Republican State Central Committee. In these official positions he was doing good service for his race and the cause of human rights. He took the position which he occupied in connection with the political interests of the State from a sense of duty which he could not well resist from the peculiar state of political affairs here."

Harper's Weekly,
November 21, 1868

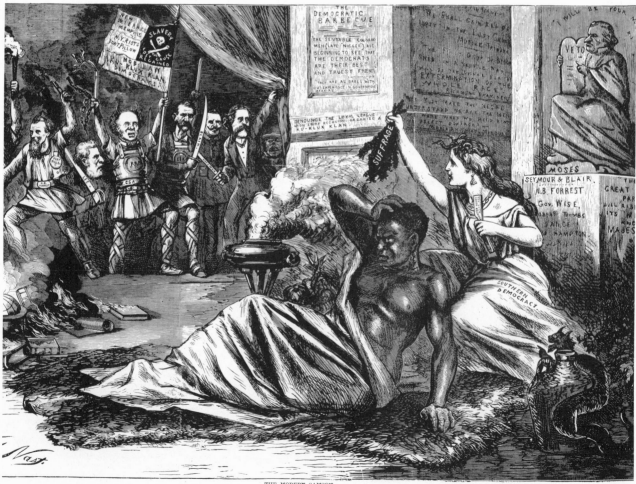

THE MODERN SAMSON.

THE MOBILE RIOT.

The Mobile *Tribune* of the 15th inst. gives the following account of the origin of the riot in that city on the night of the 14th. The riot, as will be remembered, commenced while Judge Kelley of Philadelphia was addressing a large assemblage of negroes and some few whites in front of the old court house in that city. The *Tribune* says:

The speaker had spoken about three-quarters of an hour when the difficulty commenced, which at the time it was the general impression originated in the attempt of the Chief of Police to arrest Mr. David J. Files, a well known and respectable citizen of Mobile, who it is alleged had made some remarks which in the judgment of Captain Charpentier were calculated to provoke disorder in the excited state of the crowd.

Mr. Files objected to the arrest, and stated that he had no intention of creating any disturbance whatever. This led to some movement on the part of the crowd, and the clattering of a cab over the stones on Government street a short distance above the meeting induced many to believe that a fight had commenced, and a panic seized upon them and the whole crowd broke and rushed frantically down Royal street and up Government street. Numerous pistol shots were fired on Royal street, near the Municipal Building, but strange to say, but few were hurt at that time and none seriously. The Council was in session in the Municipal Building at the time the disturbance occurred. The negroes, who had rushed away pell mell in a moment of panic, rallied and returned to the spot, where, finding that there was no disposition in interfere with them, they became very boisterous and brandished their clubs and pistols in a threatening manner, declaring that "they were now ready," "wade in you—of—," and other like remarks.

Captain Jack Petty, of the night police, who was standing on the corner, having been engaged in using every effort to quell the disturbance was seen by some of these negroes, who immediately rushed upon him, swinging their clubs and firing their pistols at him. Captain Petty was forced to retreat, and sought refuge in the Corporation Building. Faithful old Frank being at the gate, which had been barred in case of an assault, opened it for him. The negroes rushed up against the gate and tried to break through, demanding admittance and crying, "kill the — of a —." Several shots were fired through the railings, and the marks can now be seen on the walls and panels of the doors at the stairs. After clamoring for some time they left and commenced roaming through the streets.

The community will bear in mind that this attack on Captain Petty occurred after the crowd had been dispersed and there was no disturbance on the street.

The general alarm was rung and hundreds of people turned out, the city remaining in a fever of excitement during the entire night. After whooping and yelling around the scene of the late meeting the negroes dispersed in small squads and attacked nearly every white man they met. With the exception of three or four persons who were shot and stricken with clubs when the difficulty commenced and in the immediate vicinity of the place of meeting, the other parties were all injured at points several squares distant and over a half hour after the first dispersion.

Gabriel Olsen, a shoemaker, living at 204 Dauphin street, was passing along Water street in the vicinity of Church when he was attacked by a squad of negroes and brutally murdered.

Captain Sedberry, a well known citizen, was wounded slightly with a pistol shot.

Mr. James Risk was badly beaten over the head and shoulders with a club, and is now suffering severely.

A young man named James Burns was also shot, but it not supposed to be in a dangerous condition.

Policeman Taylor, who was striving to maintain order, received a severe wound in the wrist with a pistol ball.

Another policeman, whose name we have been unable to learn, was also injured by being beaten with clubs.

A gentleman by the name of Goldsmith was also injured, but not seriously.

A white man, named J. Gough, who was wounded in the affray, is reported dead.

A negro boy, shot in the head, was found dead on Cedar street, near Dauphin. It is supposed that he was shot at the original disturbance, and was running home when he fell dead.

We have heard of several negroes who were injured but none others are reported dead.

The negroes continued to prowl through the streets in the upper portion of town, some of whom had muskets, and interfering with every white man passing.

The Baltimore Gazette, May 21, 1867

The Galveston Riot.

The Galveston *News* of the 16th instant gives the following account of the riot in that city at a negro meeting the night before. It says:

About five hundred negroes assembled last night on the lot in front of Turner Hall. The band played the Star Spangled Banner, after which Dr. R. K. Smith, of United States direct tax notoriety, nominated O. F. Hunsacker President of the meeting. After several speeches by white Radical orators Stephen Paschal, negro, was introduced and commenced speaking, addressing himself to the whites, stated that if he had had the same opportunity they possessed he would have been one of the smartest men under the heavens. "The colored man was the smartest man on the globe." [Voice in the crowd—"You're a liar."] Cries here arose of "put him out," "put him out." Paschal said, "Yes, put him out." Several women made for the party who had interrupted the speaker. The confusion became general and about fifty pistol shots were fired, which caused the crowd to disperse in all directions, even to the speakers on the stand. The greater, together with the lesser lights, ignominiously fled the field. We saw a medical gentleman, with a plug hat and eye glasses, under a bench alongside of a negro woman, each trying to get as close to the floor as they possibly could. Such confusion, such excitement, we never saw before. The man who cried out "You're a liar" was a United States soldier. This the negroes all agree in stating, as well as a gentleman well known in the city, who was standing by him and not only saw the man, but heard him cry out. There were only two persons injured, one negro shot in the thumb and one white man shot in the shoulder. The firing was mostly in the air and done entirely by negroes; this we saw ourself; are willing to swear to it.

THE SOUTH.

EXCITEMENT IN LOUISIANA.

GOV. WARMOUTH'S CALL FOR AID.

DISORDER reigns in Louisiana. Gov. Warmouth's requisition on the President for a military force to secure aid in maintaining the peace in Louisiana, has arrived at Washington. Accompanying documents give details of rebellious outrages in the State, and estimate that ONE HUNDRED AND FIFTY UNION MEN have been murdered in the last six weeks. A secret organization to keep down the colored race is in existence.

The Governor wants three regiments and a battery of artillery.

NEW ORLEANS, August 10.—In support of Gov. Warmouth's assertion that 150 murders were committed last month in this District, and half of them in this State, yesterday's *Republican* contained two columns of extracts from and references to letters in Gov. Warmouth's possession, detailing outrages in the country parishes, from March last to date. These extracts do not show that either the civil or military authorities, or Freedmen's Bureau, took cognizance of any of these affairs.

THE KU-KLUX.

MURDERS, ROBBERIES, AND OUTRAGES BY THE KLAN —SCHOOL TEACHING AND BIBLE READING PROSCRIBED.

[From the Nashville Press, July 9.]

ACCOUNTS reach us from Giles, Marshall, Hamilton and Bedford Counties, of fresh outrages perpetrated by the Ku-Klux on colored people. The horrors practiced by these wretches grow more intensely black every day. They roam through the country and perpetrate their crimes with apparent impunity, and a satanic determination and disregard of consequences perfectly appalling.

From Giles County a dozen or more colored men arrived yesterday morning, by way of the Alabama railway. Their narrative of suffering is heartrending. They all have families depending on them, are farmers who cultivated pieces of land, and were just housing their crops. They had from thirty to fifty acres each under cultivation, beside other little property in the way of stock. They are men rugged and knotted up with ceaseless toil in an up-hill struggle, not only to make a little for future contingencies, but even to make bread whereon to live. Honest laborers, out in the fields from early dawn to dewy eve, earning as they simply express it, "meat and clothes for their little ones." They all lived in the neighborhood of Cornersville, about twelve miles from Pulaski, in Giles County.

The young scoundrels of the Klan having grown bold of late by reason of the impunity with which many of their order have been allowed to roam over the country, whipping and robbing, determined to be ahead of every other place in the persecuting spirit and hostile demonstrations

TEXAS.

ANOTHER OFFICIAL REPORT ON THE LAWLESSNESS IN THAT STATE—LARGE NUMBER OF MURDERS.

SOME time ago we printed a report to the Constitutional Convention of Texas, showing the lawlessness of the Rebels of that State. We now lay before our readers a supplementary report to the same body, which confirms all that we presented at first:

COMMITTEE ROOMS, Austin, **Texas, July** 21st 1868. *Hon. E. J. Davis, President of the Convention*:

Sir: The Special Committee on **Law**lessness and Violence respectfully present the following supplementary report:

It is, perhaps, due to ourselves to state that in collecting evidence no reference has been had to the political opinions of witnesses. The Committee issued a circular summons to all the members of the Convention, so that all, without distinction of party, were requested to report on the lawlessness in their several districts, and it is for those who failed to obey the summons to explain why they failed. They are certainly stopped from all rights to denounce the labor of the Committee as partisan in its character. We take pleasure in saying, however, that Conservatives have testified before the Committee, and some of the most flagrant outrages embodied in our report were furnished by them.

In our report of the 30th ultimo, it was stated that Milton Biggs, a loyal man, was murdered in Blanco County last year. Subsequent investigation shows that Claiborne Biggs, the son, was murdered as described, that circumstances point to certain rebel outlaws as the murderers, and that the father and other members of the family understand that their lives are in danger, and have left the county for safety.

It was also stated in said report that the District Clerk of Hunt County had been driven away on account of his loyalty. It is the Clerk of the County Court who has been thus exiled. The present Clerk of the District Court of that county is not a loyal man, and was not compelled to leave.

In the Counties of Collins and Hunt, five men, well known as sterling loyalists, were brutally murdered within the last two weeks by some rebel desperadoes. The Hon. A. O. Cooley, a worthy citizen of Gillespie County, and a prominent Republican, was shot and wounded on the 10th inst. at home by an assassin from a distant county. We also learn that W. H. Upton, a Union man, was hung by a mob on the 3d inst. in Brazoria County. Here, then, are six well known Unionists murdered, and the life of another attempted—all in the present month. Some time ago, the Rev. Joshua Johnson, an excellent citizen of Titus County, and against whom nothing can be said by anybody, unless it be that he has always been true to his country, was driven from his home and the State by rebel intolerance. It is now a matter of general notoriety that loyal men in various parts of the State are receiving notices to leave, threatening them with death and the burning of their homes if they do not fly. It is equally notorious that great alarm prevails among the Union men in many localities, and many of them are abandoning their homes for their lives. We also state that it is a fact that many honorable members of this body are in receipt of letters from those that love them, from wives and children, informing them of threats to take their lives and imploring them not to return home. And we say further that the families of at least two delegates on this floor have been forced away from their homes by rebel proscription since the meeting of this Convention.

Now these are all undeniable facts, and they certainly justify the affirmation that many of the persons killed in Texas are killed for their loyalty. It is an easy matter, when a Union man is murdered, to start the cry of "thief," or "Indians," and to get credulous people to believe it; but this hypocrisy only serves to expose the guilt to the minds of reflecting men, and cannot change the fact that loyal men are murdered by rebels.

And we are constrained to add that it is by no means significant of good, that while Union men are falling at the hands of paroled prisoners of war, there are those who do not only deny the fact, but accuse those as slanderers who attempt to reveal and arrest this alarming march of crime. Certainly the first step toward providing a remedy is to ascertain the extent and the nature of the evil, and we cannot understand how any friend of mankind or of Texas can oppose an examination into the abounding violence in the State, or attempt to conceal the same from public view. It is, doubtless true that a ventilation of the social disorder in Texas will deter many good people in other States and countries from coming here. But this is already the case. Capital and emigration turn away from our State as a land of violence, while good and loyal citizens are forsaking us in large numbers. We have evidence that between 800 and 900 families within a territory of 25 or 30 counties are now leaving the State on account of the persecutions they have suffered from lawless men. Texas is to-day undergoing a process of depopulation, at least as to her truest and best citizens. And while this is going on, the lawless and outlawed in other States are flocking within our limits.

National Anti-Slavery Standard,
August 16, 1868

THE LOUISIANA MURDERS—GATHERING THE DEAD AND WOUNDED.

Slave and Friend

All the Pretty Little Horses

Hushaby, don't you cry,
Go to sleepy, little baby.
When you wake, you shall have
    cake,
And all the pretty little horses.
Blacks and bays, dapples and grays,
Coach and six-a little horses.

Way down yonder in the meadow,
There's a poor little lambie;
The bees and the butterflies
    pickin' out his eyes,
The poor little thing cries,
    "Mammy."

Hushaby, don't you cry,
Go to sleepy, little baby.

"All the Pretty Little Horses" is an authentic slave lullaby; it reveals the bitter feelings of Negro mothers who had to watch over their white charges while neglecting their own children.

☞ **The late Arkansas legislature passed a law to take effect January 1st, 1860, prohibiting the employment of free colored persons on water-craft navigating the rivers of that State, under heavy penalties.**

NEGROES EXCLUDED FROM THE PUBLIC LANDS. The Pittsburg *Gazette* says that about a month ago a company of colored people in that city desired to form a party to emigrate westward, and settle upon and preempt public lands. Their counsel communicated with the Land Department at Washington, and received in reply the following flat refusal:

GENERAL LAND OFFICE, March 7, '59.
John M. Kirkpatrick, Pittsburg, Penn.:

Sir—In reply to your letter of the 24th ult., I have to state, that under the now settled ruling of this office, which has been sanctioned by the Secretary, colored persons are not citizens of the United States as contemplated by the preemption law of September, 1841, and are, therefore, not legally entitled to preempt public lands.

Very respectfully, your ob't serv't,
J. S. Wilson, Acting Commissioner.

HOW THE FIRST FAMILIES OF VIRGINIA MAKE THEIR MONEY.—A writer from Virginia gives some idea of the profits of negro raising. One man engaged in this business told the correspondent of a woman he owns, named Fanny. She was just sixteen when he bought her, and had a boy child soon after. She is hired out at $6 per month. Her first child is now five years old, and in fifteen years will be worth $1,000 to $2,000. The owner goes on with his story:

I am thus paid for the trouble of raising him, about $100 a year; and I have no trouble either, for the mother takes care of him until he is old enough to hire, and then he will begin to bring me wages. She has had a child every spring since, and now she sends me word not to hire her for May, for she expects to have another! That will be five in a little over five years, and in twenty-five years from this time, if they all live, which they are very likely to do, the youngest will be twenty years old, and, if a man, worth at least $1,500. There are now two boys and two girls, and they will be worth at least $5,000 in the aggregate at that time, to say nothing of the one that's coming. And the mother will not stop there; she will have a good many more. If she keeps on as she has done, and has as many boys and girls, she will bring me $20,000 worth of niggers before she stops.

New York Tribune, 1859

COLORED AMERICANS IN CALIFORNIA.

FRIEND GARRISON:—

The infamous attempt to prevent the emigration of colored persons into California was defeated in the Legislature, by a vote of 32 to 30—mainly through the exertions of Hon. G. A. Hall, in grateful recognition of which, the colored citizens of the various localities have united in the presentation of an appropriate testimonial.

But, as will be seen by the following protest from an enterprising business firm, colored citizens in California are daily victims of TAXATION WITHOUT REPRESENTATION.

Boston, June, 1857.   W. C. N.

THE POLL-TAX VS. COLORED MEN.

During a residence of seven years in California, we, with hundreds of other colored men, have cheerfully paid city, State and county taxes on real estate and merchandise, as well as licenses to carry on business, and every other species of tax that has been levied from time to time for the support of the government, save only the 'poll-tax'—that we have persistently refused. On the day before yesterday, the Tax Collector called on us, and seized and lugged off twenty or thirty dollars' worth of goods, in payment, as he said, of this tax.

Now, while we cannot understand how a 'white' man can refuse to pay each and every tax for the support of government, under which he enjoys every privilege—from the right to rob a negro up to that of being Governor of the State—we can perceive and feel the flagrant injustice of compelling 'colored men' to pay a special tax for the enjoyment of a special privilege, and then break their heads if they attempt to exercise it. We believe that every voter should pay poll-tax, or every male resident who has the privilege of becoming a voter; but regard it as low and despicable, the very quintessence of meanness, to compel colored men to pay it, situated as they are politically. However, if there is no redress, the great State of California may come around annually, and rob us of twenty or thirty dollars' worth of goods, as we will never willingly pay three dollars as poll-tax as long as we remain disfranchised, oath-denied, outlawed colored Americans.

LESTER & GIBBS,
184 Clay street.

*The Liberator,
July 3, 1857*

☞ PLACE WANTED.—A colored lad, between 14 and 15 years of age, wants a place in a good family in the country. He is used to the care of a horse, &c. Apply to SAMUEL MAY, Jr., 21 Cornhill.

PENNSYLVANIA.—WAR OF RACES IN THE CITY OF BROTHERLY LOVE—COLORED WASHERWOMEN BERATING CHINESE LAUNDRYMEN.—DRAWN BY RÉGAMEY.

ASSIST COLORED YOUTH.

A colored Lad of 16 years, who has enjoyed academic facilities, and studied book-keeping, is a ready penman, and can produce the best testimonials of character and disposition, desires some suitable situation.

Also—Two others desire to learn trades—one of them the upholsterer's.

Apply to   WM. C. NELL, 21 Cornhill.

Frank Leslie's Illustrated Newspaper, May 29, 1875

NEGRO MECHANICS.

There is much that is worthy of consideration in the following remarks of the Centreville *Enquirer*, which first met our eye in the Pennsylvania *Observer* :—

'We believe the Legislatures of all slaveholding States should pass an act prohibiting the owners of slaves from making mechanics of them. The rice, corn and cotton field is the proper place for the negro—and not the workshop. That should be kept for the white man exclusively. There are thousands of industrious, enterprising young men, who are driven from the mechanical trades, rather than work all day side by side with the negro. Their pride revolts at it, and we think very properly; all cannot be professional men, their inclinations do not lead in that way, but necessity drives them to business of some kind, and they rush into the learned professions without one single qualification. And why do they do this? Because they do not like to be thrown into daily intercourse with the negro mechanics. See how many young lawyers and physicians are starving, because the country is overrun with them, and their pride forbids them from following trades. But exclude the negro race from the mechanical arts, and you at once ennoble the business. Men who are now ashamed to acknowledge themselves mechanics, would take pride in it, and there would be but few drones in society.

All parents are not able to give their children education sufficient to be a professional character, and how far superior is the respectable artisan to the quack doctor or the jack-leg lawyer, the one scarcely able to distinguish chill from fever, and the other incompetent to make a speech in a magistrate's court. We hope the Legislatures of the different States will take this matter into consideration. We are aware that men will say we have the right to do as we please with our negroes, and convert them to any use we think proper; but it is not so. The rich have no right to build up fortunes at the expense of the poor, and this is done whenever you degrade the mechanic to the level of the slave. The only trade entirely excluded from the negro is the printer—he may defy them, for the States have wisely prohibited them from education.'

No one will pretend that a master who owns a skilful mechanic ought to be or can be deprived of half of his value by a law forbidding such mechanic from working at a trade which he has been taught at much expense and loss of time. The master, beyond dispute, has a vested right in the enhanced productiveness of the mechanic slave's labor at a trade wherein skill, training and intelligence are as important elements as physical strength.

Nor is it certain that a law, which should permit negroes who have already acquired mechanic arts to work at them, but which should prohibit any others from being taught and employed at such trades, would be quite equitable and just to the owners of intelligent negroes, whose services would be doubled in value by being so instructed and employed.

If the proposal to exclude negroes from the mechanic arts were merely a question of competition between white mechanics and the few owners of negro mechanics, a satisfactory solution of it might be reached by legislation. But laws, if just, are not made for classes, but for the whole people. We are to guard with lynx-eyed vigilance against all that can endanger even remotely our vital institution. It is much to be feared that any hasty and unnecessary tampering with the limits wherein slave labor may be employed may become a precedent for a greater mischief hereafter.—*N. O. Cour.*

The Liberator, September 3, 1858

I rode a railroad that had no track.

Camden, Del., March 23d, 1857

Dear Sir;—I tak my pen in hand to write you, to inform you what we have had to go throw for the last two weaks. Thir wir six men and two woman was betraid on the tenth of this month, thea had them in prison but thea got out was conveyed by a black man, he told them he wood bring them to my hows as he wos told, he had ben ther Befor, he has com with Harrett, a woman that stops at my hous when she pases two and throw yau. You don't no me I supos, the Rev. Thomas K. Kennard dos, or Peter Lowis. He road Camden Circuit, this man led them in dover prisin and left them with a whit man but tha tour out the winders and jump out, so cum back to Camden. We put them throug, we hav to carry them 19 mils and cum back the sam night wich maks 38 mils. It is tou much for our littl horses. We must do the bes we can ther is much Bisness dun on this Road. We hav to go throw dover. and smerny, the two wors places this sid of mary land lin. If you have herd or sean them ples let me no. I will Com to Phila be for long and then I wil call and se you. There is much to do her. Ples to wright, I Remain your frend,

William Brinkly

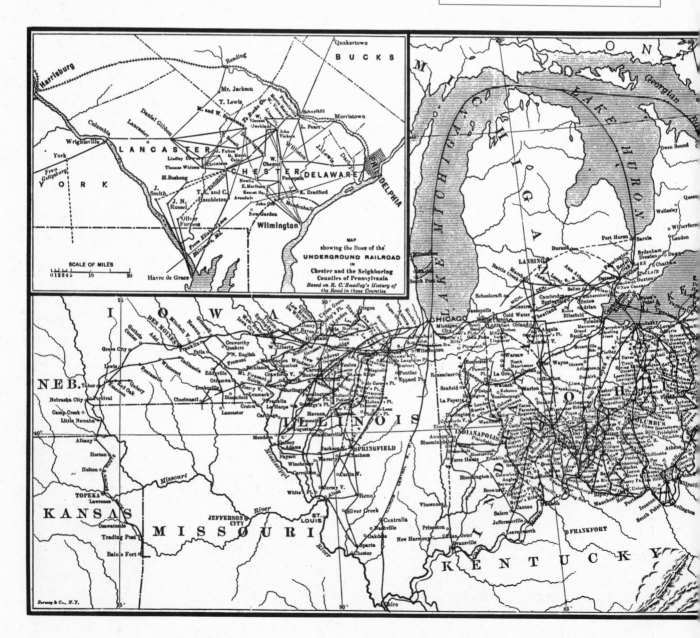

The resurrection of Henry Box Brown at Philadelphia, who escaped from Richmond, Va. in a box 3 feet long, 2½ feet deep and 2 feet wide.

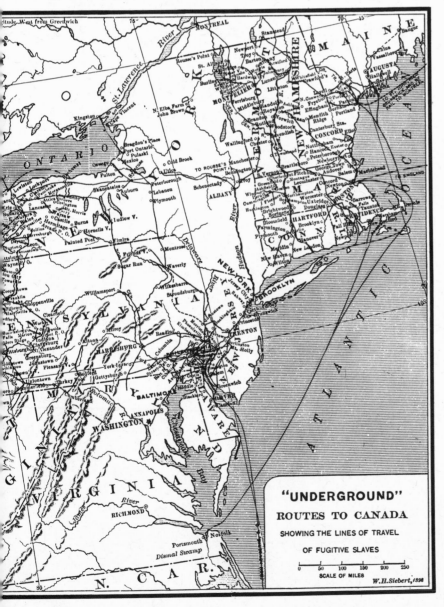

"UNDERGROUND" ROUTES TO CANADA

SHOWING THE LINES OF TRAVEL

OF FUGITIVE SLAVES

SCALE OF MILES
0   50   100   150   200   250

W. H. Siebert, 1896.

Three Pounds Reward.

RAN AWAY, from the Subscriber, a NEGRO MAN, named TOM, African-born, about 32 Years of Age, about Five Feet Six Inches high, square made, and has a Cast in one of his Eyes. I know of no other Clothes he has with him but two Oznaburg Shirts, and a Pair of Tow-Linen Trousers. FORTY SHILLINGS Reward will be given for taking him up, if in the County, and THREE POUNDS, if out of the County, and reasonable Charges for bringing him Home, by   JAMES CHESTON.

West-River, Ann-Arundel County, July 15, 1790.

Forty Dollars Reward.

WHEREAS a certain CHARLES TRAVIS, on the 11th Ult. ran away with FRANCES DE BAPTIST, lawful Wife of JOHN DE BAPTIST, of Fredericksburg, Virginia, and stole, from said Baptist, a Sky-blue superfine Broadcloth Coat with double-gilt Buttons, a Pair of black Velvet Breeches with Basket Buttons of the same Colour, and rode away a large roan Horse : Whoever apprehends the said CHARLES TRAVIS, and brings him to this Town, or lodges him in any Gaol of the United States, shall, in Addition to the Rewards offered in the Virginia Herald, and Maryland Journal, receive FORTY DOLLARS, and all reasonable Expenses, paid by   JOHN BOYES.

Fredericksburg, Virginia, July 6, 1790.

Twenty Dollars Reward.

ABSCONDED, from his Master's Service, about Six Weeks ago, a MULATTO MAN, named WILL ; he is about 35 Years of Age, short in Stature, bow-legged, but otherwise well made ; he is addicted to Drunkenness, and, when sober, his Eyes have the Appearance of his being in Liquor ; his Address is awkward, and attended with a considerable trembling of his Hands : He formerly belonged to the late Mr. JONATHAN HUDSON, and used to attend at his Table and travel with him ; from which Circumstances, he is, probably, well known in the State—he has lived with me a few Years. Whoever will deliver him to the Subscriber, shall receive a Reward of TWENTY DOLLARS, including what the Law allows.   HARRY DORSEY GOUGH.

Perry-Hall, June 29, 1790.

L O S T,

Four Dollars Reward.

RAN AWAY, from the Subscriber, living in Abbet's-Town, York County, on the 8th of May last, a SERVANT BOY, named DAVID BURNSIDES, a Country-born, about 4 Feet 6 or 7 Inches high, supposed to be about 20 Years of Age, short fair Hair, has a remarkably large Mouth, a small Scar near one of his Eyes, very small Feet, and is of a fair Complexion : Had on, and took with him, an old Felt Hat, a dirty yellow Hunting-Shirt, brown Cloth Overalls, and Two Tow Shirts ; he was at Mr. LEAMON's, his former Master, on the 17th or 18th of May last, whom he informed that he was a Freeman, and, after remaining there Two or Three Days, he stole a Plush Vest and other Clothing : He says his Father lives near the Blue-Ball-Tavern. Whoever secures the said Servant, so that his Master may get him again, shall receive the above Reward, and reasonable Charges.   WILLIAM MACKEY.

July 8, 1790.

Twenty Dollars Reward.

RAN AWAY, on the 13th Instant, from the Subscriber, living on Elk-Ridge in Ann-Arundel County, a NEGRO MAN, named HARRY, about 40 Years of Age, near 6 Feet high, has Knots on his left Leg, which is larger than his right, and on his great Toes, and has red Eyes : Had on, and took with him, a Tow-Linen Shirt and Trousers, brown Cloth Coat, brown Corduroy Jacket and Breeches, Two Pair of Yarn Stockings, one white and the other blue mixed, a white Shirt, Felt Hat, and red Silk Handkerchief. Whoever takes up said Negro, and secures him in Gaol, so that his Master may get him again, shall receive, if 20 Miles from Home, Eight Dollars ; if 40 Miles, Sixteen Dollars ; and, if out of the State, the above Reward, including legal Fees, and reasonable Charges, if brought Home.   NICHOLAS DORSEY.

July 19, 1790.

I jump around and spin around
And do just so
But every time I turn around
I jump Jim Crow.

BLOOD IN SAVANNAH.

The Street-Car Riots--Black vs. Whites.

Terrible Fight Between Rival Factions of Grantites, at a Public Meeting.

THE STREET-CAR RIOTS.
From the Savannah (Ga.) News, July 30.

It becomes our painful duty this morning to chronicle a series of outrageous acts, resulting in serious injury, probably loss of life, and disgrace to our fair city. We mentioned in our previous issue the various disturbances that had occurred on Saturday and Sunday, occasioned by the attempt of certain colored men to ride in the street cars reserved for the whites. The object of this movement was plainly set forth: it was shown to be nothing more than a mere electioneering scheme of the Radicals; and, being desirous of thwarting them in their plans, we earnestly advised caution, prudence, and non-interference, feeling assured that much evil, and no possible good, could result from a recourse to violence. In this position we are sustained by the intelligent, respectable, and law-abiding portion of the community. Yet certain irresponsible parties, representing in no manner the sentiments and views of the citizens of Savannah, by their imprudent and unjustifiable course, yesterday inaugurated a scene of riot and bloodshed in our streets, fraught with untold horror and distress, and the end of which we may not yet have seen.

We are unable to discover any reason or justification on the part of a few young men in creating riot and discord in this community on account of some silly negroes riding in the cars which had been set apart for other purposes.

During the morning several negroes amused themselves by riding up and down in the various cars, without interfence; very few, if any, white persons travelling at that time. About half-past 1 o'clock, however, as a number of young men were returning to dinner, a negro entered the car on Whitaker street, near Broughton, and here commenced the trouble. Some remark was made to him by one of the party in a pleasant manner, to which he made a surly reply. This led to further words, when the negro became very impudent and insulting. He was threatened with expulsion from the car, when he answered very defiantly, and with an oath, that no one could do it. In the next instant he was kicked into the street with a damaged head, and the car rolled on.

Subsequent to this we learn that the notorious Jim Simms, negro preacher and agitator, was ejected from one of the cars.

About 5 o'clock in the afternoon crowds of negroes commenced to assemble at the different corners on Whitaker street, and it was evident some mischief was brewing. Their presence attracted similar crowds of white, and at one time there was probably nor less than 1,000 persons in line, extending from South Broad street to Bryan, on Whitaker street. The excitement was intense, and a serious row was expected as a car came down the street. It, however, passed through the crowd, but on its return was boarded by two or three negroes. There was a number of young men on the car, and in a few minutes we saw the colored persons pushed off, and the car proceed. These scenes were repeated at different intervals throughout the afternoon, every succeeding one only serving to increase the excitement.

About 6 o'clock a drunken negro shoemaker, by the name of Thomas Bolling, came staggering through the crowd in company with a comrade, cursing and howling. He was ordered off by a policeman, when he immediately became very abusive, for which he recived a knock under the chin, and was taken to the barracks. This little incident revived the spirits of the negroes, and kept them agitated until the next car came along. Lieutenant Howard, of the police force, with two Sergeants, was present, and prevented any outbreak at that time.

About a quarter past 6 o'clock the Union Lincoln Guards, the colored troops, turned the corner of South Broad street, into Whitaker, and immediately the cry arose, "Here comes the 'Linkum' Guards," and the excitable negroes fairly jumped. Fortunately this command were unarmed, and marched quietly down the street to Broughton, which they rounded, and were followed by many of the negroes. Had they been armed, it is very likely a disturbance would have commenced just then.

By 7 o'clock, however, the excitement had subsided somewhat, and but few negroes remained on the street. An hour later they began to assemble in force, men, women, and children, principally on Whitaker street, in the vicinity of South Broad. The women were particularly excited, and endeavored strenuously to encourage the negro men to take some violent course. Shortly afterward a negro boarded a car passing, and was almost instantly thrown from the platform. The car being monopolized by a party of young men. Matters remained in *statu quo* until probably a quarter past 8 o'clock, when suddenly a volley of musketry greeted the ears of the excited people, from the direction of the park, on Whitaker street.

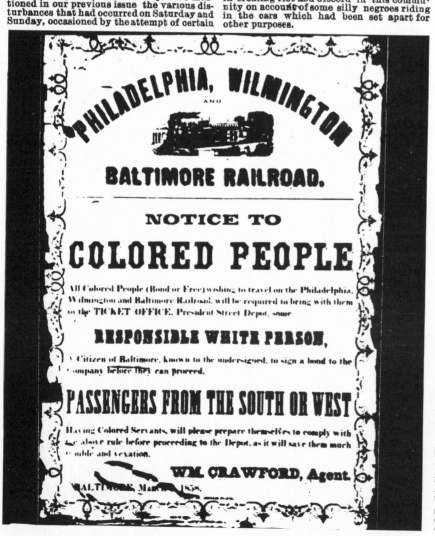

PHILADELPHIA, WILMINGTON AND BALTIMORE RAILROAD.

NOTICE TO COLORED PEOPLE

All Colored People (Bond or Free) wishing to travel on the Philadelphia, Wilmington and Baltimore Railroad, will be required to bring with them to the TICKET OFFICE, President Street Depot, some

RESPONSIBLE WHITE PERSON,

A Citizen of Baltimore, known to the undersigned, to sign a bond to the Company before they can proceed.

PASSENGERS FROM THE SOUTH OR WEST

Having Colored Servants, will please prepare themselves to comply with the above rule before proceeding to the Depot, as it will save them much trouble and vexation.

WM. CRAWFORD, Agent.

BALTIMORE, MARCH, 185?.

Chicago Tribune, August 7, 1872

COLORED PEOPLE AND THE CARS

To the Editor of the North American and U.S. Gazette

SIR: As a colored man, and constant reader of your paper, allow me a brief corner in your columns to make a few remarks on the sore grievance of genteel colored people in being excluded from the city passenger railway cars, except they choose to "stand on the front platform with the driver."

However long the distance they may have to go, or great their hurry —however unwell or aged, genteel or neatly attired—however hot, cold or stormy the weather however few in the cars, as the masses of the colored people now understand it, they are unceremoniously excluded.

Of course my own humble opinion will weigh but little with yourself and readers (being, as I am, of the proscribed class) as to whether it is reasonable or unreasonable, just or unjust, as to whether it is a loss or a gain to railroad companies, thus to exclude colored people. Nevertheless, pardon me for saying that this severe proscription, for some unaccountable reason, is carried to an extent in Philadelphia unparalled in any of the leading cities of this Union. This is not imagination or an exaggerated assertion.

In New Orleans, colored people— slaves as well as free—ride in all the city cars and omnibuses. In Cincinnati, colored women are accommodated in the city omnibuses, but colored men are proscribed to a certain extent. In Chicago it may be safely said that not the slightest proscription exists in the public conveyances of that flourishing city. In New York, Brooklyn, &c. (except on one or two of the New York city passenger lines), there is not the slightest barrier to any persons riding, on account of complexion. There is no obstruction in the way of colored persons riding in any of the Boston cars or omnibuses.

I need not allude to cities of minor importance, whether favorable or unfavorable, North or South. Sufficient are the facts in the examples of the cities already alluded to to make

it a very painfully serious inquiry with intelligent colored people, why it is so in Philadelphia, the city of "Brotherly Love," so noted as the bulwark of the "Religious Society of Friends, commonly called Quakers," so noted as one of the leading cities in the Union in great religious and benevolent enterprises, so preeminently favorable to elevating the heathen in Africa, while forgetful of those in their very precincts—those who are taxed to support the very highways that they are rejected from.

NEGRO EXPULSION FROM RAILWAY CAR, PHILADELPHIA.

SHALL COLORED PEOPLE RIDE IN THE CITY PASSENGER RAILWAY CARS?

Yesterday was set apart as one of the days in which this question was to be tested. Accordingly, the conductors of most of the cars running through the city in different directions had placed in their possession printed slips, by which the will of the passengers was to be made known. The conductors in most cases collected the fares from the passengers first, then handed them the slips on which to write their answers.

In most instances those who received the tickets carefully folded them in their porte-monnaies, commenced to discuss the questions which they were expected to answer. In this way much exciting debate was kept up throughout the day in the cars.

The prevailing opinion appears to be in favor of colored persons riding, and in order to make them as comfortable as possible, that separate

cars should be set apart for their use, and that these cars should be driven by colored drivers and supplied with colored conductors.

Some went further than this, and suggested that in order to make the thing more complete, the cars should be drawn by colored horses.

There were many who were in favor of colored persons riding in the cars with white persons. This class took decided ground against separate cars being provided and said they would rather ride with respectable colored ladies than with mechanics and working people who had just left their places of labor.

One gentleman who rode some distance by the side of a colored lady, said on leaving the car, that it was not so bad, after all, and that he would have no objection to ride all day by the side of a respectable lady of color. A gentleman who got on one of the Sixth Street cars, before entering, asked if there were any of the gentlemen of color inside, stating at the same time, that he would not stay there if any of that complexion were admitted. The conductor told him that he should have his own way in the matter, and need not remain longer than he saw fit. Others looked upon the thing as a first-class joke, immediately jotted down their "yes" or "nay" and handed the ticket, neatly folded, back to the conductor. Some few declined to vote at all; they were perfectly non-committal, and expressed a willingness to abide by the decision of the majority.

A few of the tickets voted were very odd, and contained many additions written in lead pencil. One of them was signed J. R. M-----n, who was against the proposition "decidedly" (this word being added to the ticket). He had also written upon the bottom of the ticket "rides four times per day."

Another individual, who also contended that he patronized a car four times per diem, was in favor of the proposition. One negative ticket had written upon it "in favor of every third car for people of color." Another, in favor of the proposition, "equal rights the world over." Another, "all men are born free and equal," and a third, "one man is as good as another." Some of the votes are very decided, as for instance, one ticket, at the bottom of which were the words, "never! never! never!"

Some few wags had a fine opportunity for displaying their wit. One ticket read, "Gold down, niggers up." The vote up to the hour of closing the trips last night was largely in favor of white persons riding inside the cars and the exclusion of the blacks. The vote on one of the lines at noon yesterday stood four thousand opposed and one hundred and sixty in favor of the question. Votes will continue to be deposited during the present week that all may have an opportunity of depositing their vote as their feelings may dictate.

1926. Chapter 569. It shall be the duty of any person, firm or institution conducting any public hall, theatre, motion picture, show, or any place of public entertainment or assemblage which is attended by both white and colored persons, to separate the white race and the colored race, and to set apart and designate in each public place of public entertainment or assemblage, certain seats to be occupied by white persons and certain by colored persons. Failure to comply is a misdemeanor and the one guilty may be fined from $100.00 to $500.00 for each offense. The one who fails to take the seat assigned is also guilty of a misdemeanor and may be ejected from the place, and if admission has been paid, he shall not be entitled to a return.

1930. Chapter 128. All passenger motor vehicles shall separate white and colored passengers in their motor busses and set apart in each bus a portion thereof or certain seats to be occupied by white passengers and certain by colored passengers. Failure to comply is a misdemeanor.

There shall be no difference or discrimination in the quality or convenience of the accommodation provided for the two races.

Drivers shall be special policemen and have all the powers of conservators of the peace in the enforcement of this act. Persons who fail to occupy the seats assigned are guilty of a misdemeanor and may be ejected and shall not be entitled to the return of any part of their fare.

From *Black Laws of Virginia*, June Purcell Guild, LL.M., Whittet & Shepperson, Virginia, 1936.

THE CIVIL WAR DRAFT RIOTS

There was an element of great unfairness in the Draft Act for the Civil War. Persons able to pay $300 toward a substitute were not drafted; black men were not taken into the army at that time in New York, so were ineligible for the draft. The poor laboring class of men could not afford to pay a substitute and a high proportion of those drafted were poor Irish, many of them recent immigrants who had fled the potato famine and English repression of Ireland. In America they were engaged mainly in menial jobs, but if they had to go into the army it meant that their competitors, the blacks, would get their jobs by default. What was anger inspired by the draft turned into a murderous and savage assault by mobs upon innocent blacks and whatever white persons sought to stop the bloody assaults.

The riots lasted four days, July 13 through 16, 1863, before the mob was brought under control. Dead and wounded numbered approximately 1,000, mainly blacks, and property damage approximated two million dollars.

Sixty-six inquests on white persons killed during the riots revealed

that forty-four were Irish; eight were Germans; eight were Americans; one was English; one was Danish; origin of four was unknown. Of the whites killed, four were boys under twelve years of age who were throwing rocks at police, and four were Irish females who were throwing Irish confetti (rocks) at policemen. The police force, like the mob itself, was almost all Irish.

During the riots a white bartender, Henry Simons, was knocked off

his wagon, and while he was insensible, the rioters drove off with his horse and wagon.

A colored man, John Martin of Madison Street, was so terrified by the drunken mob approaching his house during the Draft Riots that he first cut his throat and then hanged himself.

Similar riots by draft opponents in cities outside New York resulted in great property damage and loss of life and limb. In Boston alone,

Scenes from Civil War Draft Riots

*Frank Leslie's Illustrated
Newspaper, August 1, 1863*

twenty persons were killed and wounded. The mob attacked an armory in an attempt to obtain weapons but were beaten back and scattered by a round of canister shot from a six-pounder.

The Jewish Hospital became a sanctuary for the wounded during the New York draft riots.

In Troy, New York, the mob stormed and released all prisoners held in the jail. A ship with black waiters on board turned back because feeling against blacks was so high.

Not one life was lost at the colored orphanage in New York City during the riots, thanks to the white staff and to the bravery of Fire Chief Becker. The orphanage itself was burned to the ground. The only thing saved was the Bible which a little girl ran back and brought out of the burning building. The children were temporarily housed on Blackwell's Island.

One black man, who along with his family escaped bodily harm by going over rooftops to escape the mob, was Albro Lyons, who owned a seamen's boarding house on Pearl Street. He was a retired seaman, a well-educated man and highly respected by all who knew him. More fortunate than many others who became victims of the mob, Albro had relatives in Providence, Rhode Island, who took the Lyons family in. Lyons soon opened a small factory for making ice cream, and prospered. Before long he was a respected member of the community and was appointed a justice of the peace. Eventually he returned to New York City and died in Brooklyn.

they failed to ask my name, and called me negro

—Henry Dumas

. . . the British Government was beginning to find out that hanging men for petty theft was a serious mistake. Anyhow hanging did no good. Transportation (of British criminals) was tried and the great dominion of Australia was founded. The simple fact of the matter is that the penal laws of England at that time and for seventy years after were a black disgrace to civilization. Women and children were hanged for shoplifting to the value of a pocket-handkerchief. Black Monday opposite the Debtors Door at New-gate will not bear description.

. . . The British government began to think it just as well if some of them took their flight to Australia. The Americans having got their independence refused any more white labor. A philanthropic pro-posal to hand criminals over to the slave-holders of Morocco was made in a Christian country and rejected. Consignments were sent to the fever-coast of Africa where they died like sheep under the lash. So the Penal Settlements of New South Wales were founded, and the "Suc-cess" and her fellow floating torture-chambers were brought into being.

An official communication dated from Whitehall, August 18, 1786, informed the Lord Commissioners of the treasure that the gaols were crowded and that it would be neces-sary to ship the prisoners off some-where. The revolt of America was a serious bore to my lords of the Treasure for they had for some time past been adding a yearly sume of $250,000 to the revenue by selling offenders as white labor to thē (American) planters. Now the mar-ket was closed and the article be-came a drug to the purveyor's hands . . . Humane men looked into the question in the light of their environment and in the spirit of the country and of the age. They em-bodied their results in a series of pro-posals that might curdle the blood with horror. The most merciful was one suggesting transportation to Botany Bay.

—from The History of the Convict Ship "Success" (undated).

Records with names of convicts transported to the colonies in America were destroyed by England to avoid embarrassing the descendants.

ANNO DOM: 1642.

Marvilous it may be to see and consider how some kind of wicknes did grow & breake forth here, in a land wher the same was so much witnesed against, and so narrowly looked unto, & severly punished when it was knowne; as in no place more, or so much, that I have known or heard of; insomuch as they have been somewhat censured, even by moderate and good men, for their severitie in punishments. And yet all this could not suppress ye breaking out of sundrie notorious sins, (as this year, besids other, gives us too many sad presidents and instances,) es-petially drunkennes and unclainnes; not only incontinencie betweene

persons unmaried, for which many both men & women have been punished sharply enough, but some maried persons allso. But that which is worse, even sodomie and bugerie, (things fearfull to name), have broak forth in this land, oftener then once. I say it may justly be marveled at, and cause us to fear & tremble at the consideration of our corrupte na-tures, which are so hardly bridled, subdued, & mortified; nay, cannot by any other means but ye powerfull worke & grace of Gods spirite.

—from Bradford's History Of Plimoth Plantation

IS THE NEGRO A BEAST?

A REPLY TO
CHAS. CARROLL'S BOOK
ENTITLED
"THE NEGRO A BEAST."

Proving that the Negro is Human from Biblical, Scientific, and Historical Standpoints.

BY
WM. G. SCHELL,
Author of "Biblical Trace of the Church," "The Better Testa-ment," "The Ordinances of the New Testament," etc.

MOUNDSVILLE, W. VA., U. S. A.
GOSPEL TRUMPET PUBLISHING COMPANY.
1901.

Court of Criminal Correction.

Michael Lamb, petit larceny; three months in the Work House.

William Drefenbrook, petit larceny; dis-charged.

Mary Ann McGee, James McGee and Mary Sewell, grand larceny; first defendant dis-charged and the other two held in $800 bond.

N. H. Andrews, grand larceny; nolle prossed.

John J. Gier, grand larceny; bond for-feited.

Edward Morsely, forgery third degree; waived examination, held in bond of $800.

Patrick Brennan, assault to kill; dis-charged.

New Accusations.

Rafe Washington, stealing a $50 spring wagon from John F. Lay.

Dr. Stark and R. C. Stark, assaulting John W. Menagh.

Charles Foley, assaulting Josephine Welp-ley.

Tony Wilmus, petit larceny.

John C. Cramer, stealing a silver watch and a pocketbook containing $5 from Charles Hopper.

Louise Boley, stealing $10 from Wm. Hub-elman.

Wm. Burleigh, stealing a gold watch and chain from George B. Lee.

St. Louis Daily Globe Democrat,
August 15, 1876

WORSE THAN A BRUTE.

Charge Against an Unnatural Father in the Court of Criminal Correction.

A hellish and most disgusting case of incest has come to light, an Italian lemon peddler, named Chas. Manca, being the guilty party, as alleged. From the preliminary statements taken down by Col. Babcock, in the Court of Criminal Correction, it appears that Manca has systematically outraged the person of his eleven-year-old daughter, Angelina Manca. Some time ago he had warrants made out against a man for committing rape upon the girl, but a compromise was made, and then the brutal father himself became the offender. Several days ago the child took sick, and Manca sold out all the furniture, and locking in little Angelina, left for another part of the city. The neighbors handed her food through the windows, and when it was discovered that the father did not mean to return, an entrance was effected into the house, and a charitable lady took the unfortunate child under her protection, an order being had from the authorities to restrain the father from claiming possession, if he so took it into his head. The mother died several months ago, and left $4,000 to be divided among her three children, one boy and two girls. Manca clutched the money for himself, and his children have seen ne'er a nickle. It is charged against Manca that he outraged the second daughter, and was the means of her becoming a girl of the town. She reformed, however, and is now living an honest and decent life. The complaint is made by the son, a young man of about eighteen.

St. Louis Daily Globe Democrat, August 15, 1876

Priscilla Wharfield, of Westfield, for adultery with a negro man, while her husband was in the army, to set one hour on the gallows with a rope about her neck, be severely whipped 20 stripes in the way from the gallows to the goal, and forever after to wear a capital A two inches long, and of proportionable bigness, cut out in cloth of a contrary colour to her cloaths, sowed upon her upper garment of her back, in open view, and pay costs.

Ebenezer Briggs, of Pelham, for uttering counterfeit dollars, knowingly, to pay a fine of 25l. and costs.

Pennsylvania Packet, December 14, 1885

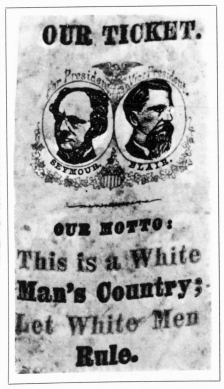

OUR TICKET.

For President / Vice President

SEYMOUR. BLAIR.

OUR MOTTO:

This is a White Man's Country; Let White Men Rule.

1792. Chapter 41. No Negro or mulatto, bond or free, shall lift his hand in opposition to any person not being a Negro, under penalty of not exceeding thirty lashes on the bare back, well laid on, except when it shall appear that such Negro was wantonly assaulted and lifted his hand in self defense.

Slaves may not be castrated, except a slave who is convicted of an attempt to ravish a white woman.

WESTERN ELOQUENCE. Eloquence has not entirely died out. The following is given as a verbatim report in the Illinois House:
"Mr. Speaker—I think sheep is paramount to dogs, and our laws hadn't oughter be so that dogs can commit ravages on sheep. Mr Speaker, I represent sheep on this floor. [Laughter, and cries of that's so] Up where I live, sheep is of more account than dogs; and although you may tell me that dogs is useful, still I say, on the other hand, that sheep is usefuller; and show me the man that represents dogs on this floor, and that thinks dogs is more important than sheep, and I will show you a man that is tantamount to a know nothing. Mr. Speaker, I am through."

THE NEGROES AND NEWSPAPERS.

A North Carolina correspondent of the Washington *Chronicle* says, that the greatest hallucination prevails among the old slaveholders as to their ability to control the vote of the freedmen. He adds:

What is required and that forthwith, is that loyal presses be established at every available point. The colored people to-day, strange as it may seem, rely more upon newspapers for information than the whites at the South. True, a large portion of the blacks cannot yet read, but a baker's dozen cannot be found without one of the number possessing the accomplishment, and I know of no sight more interesting than to see a group of these benighted ones listening eagerly to catch every word that falls from the lips of some one reading the news of the day to them.

National Anti-Slavery Standard, June 24, 1865

THE FREEDOM OF THE PRESS.

"Every citizen may freely speak, write, and publish hi sentiments on all subjects, being responsible for the abuse of that right ; and no law shall be passed to restrain or abridge the liberty of speech or of the press."—*Constitution of the State of New York, Art. I., Sec. 8.*

"Were it left to me to decide whether we should have a *government without newspapers, or newspapers without government,* I should not hesitate a moment to prefer the latter.* But I should mean that every man should receive those papers and be capable of reading them."—*Jefferson*

"UNDER NO POSSIBLE EMERGENCY, NOT EVEN IN INSUR-RECTION, OR AMID THE THROES OF CIVIL WAR, can this Government justify official interference with the freedom of speech or of the press, ANY MORE THAN IT CAN WITH THE FREEDOM OF THE BALLOT. The licentiousness of the tongue and of the pen is A MINOR EVIL COMPARED WITH THE LICENTIOUSNESS OF ARBITRARY POWER."—*F. P. Blair, senior*

New-York

" I hold that this Government was made on the WHITE BASIS, by WHITE MEN,

VOL. II.   NEW YORK, SATUR

THE GREAT CIVIL WAR.

SPEECH

OF

Hon. C. L. Vallandigham,

OF OHIO,

IN THE HOUSE OF REPRESENTATIVES,

JANUARY 14, 1863.

MR. VALLANDIGHAM—Mr. Speaker, indorsed at the recent election within the same district for which I still hold a seat on this floor, by a majority four times greater than ever before, I speak to-day in the name and by the authority of the people who, for six years, have intrusted me with the office of a representative. Loyal, in the true and highest sense of the word, to the Constitution and the Union, they have proved themselves devotedly attached to and worthy of the liberties to secure which the Union and the Constitution were established. With candor and freedom, therefore, as their representative, and with much plainness of speech, but with the dignity and decency due to this presence, I propose to consider the STATE OF THE UNION to-day, and to inquire what the duty is of every public man and every citizen in this the very crisis of the Great Revolution.

[Mr. Vallandigham here reviews at some length the question as to how the civil war was inaugurated, and also defines his own position. —EDS.]

COERCION IS WAR.

Now, sir, on the 14th of April, I believed that coercion would bring on war, and war disunion. More than that, I believed, what you all in your hearts believe to-day, that the South could never be conquered—never. And not that only, but I was satisfied—and you of the abolition party have now proved it to the world—that the secret but real purpose of the war was to abolish slavery in the States. In any event, I did

not doubt that whatever might be the momentary impulses of those in power, and whatever pledges they might make in the midst of the fury for the Constitution, the Union, and the flag, yet the natural and inexorable logic of revolutions would, sooner or later, drive them into that policy, and with it to its final but inevitable result, the change of our present democratic form of government into an imperial despotism.

These were my convictions on the 14th of April. Had I changed them on the 15th, when I read the President's proclamation, and become convinced that I had been wrong all my life, and that all history was a fable, and all human nature false in its development from the beginning of time, I would have changed my public conduct also. But my convictions did not change. I thought that if war was disunion on the 14th of April, it was equally disunion the 15th, and at all times. Believing this, I could not, as an honest man, a Union man and a patriot, lend an active support to the war ; and I did not. I had rather my right arm were plucked from its socket, and cast into eternal burnings, than, with my convictions, to have thus defiled my soul with the guilt of moral perjury. Sir, I was not taught in that school which proclaims that "all is fair in politics." I loathe, abhor, and detest the execrable maxim. I stamp upon it. No State can endure a single generation whose public men practice it. Whoever teaches it is a corrupter of youth. What we most want in these times, and at all times, is honest and independent public men. *That man who is dishonest in politics is not honest, at heart, in anything ; and sometimes moral cowardice is dishonesty.* Do right ; and trust to God, and Truth, and the People. I did not support the war ; and to-day I bless God that not the smell of so much as one drop of its blood is upon my garments. Sir, I censure no brave man who rushed patriotically into this war ; neither will I quarrel with any one, here or elsewhere, who gave to it an honest support. Had their convictions been mine, I, too, would doubtless have done as they did. With my convictions I could not.

THE STATE OF THE UNION.

And now, sir, I recur to the state of the Union to-day. What is it ? Sir, twenty months have elapsed, but the rebellion is not crushed out ; its military power has not been broken ; the insurgents have not dispersed. The Union is not restored ; nor the Constitution maintained ; nor the laws enforced. Twenty, sixty, ninety, three hundred, six hundred days have passed ; a thousand millions been expended ; and three hundred thousand lives lost or bodies mangled ; and to-day the Confederate flag is still near the Potomac and the Ohio, and the Confederate government stronger, many times, than at the beginning. Not a State has been restored, not any part of any State has voluntarily returned to the Union. And has anything been wanting that Congress, or the States, or the people in their most generous enthusiasm, their most impassioned patriotism, could bestow ? Was it power ? And did

not the party of the Executive control the entire Federal Government, every State government, every county, every city, town and village in the North and West ? Was it patronage ? All belonged to it. Was it influence ? What more ? Did not the school, the college, the church, the press, the secret orders, the municipality, the corporation, railroads, telegraphs, express companies, the voluntary associations, all, all yield to the utmost ? Was it unanimity ? Never was an Administration so supported in England or America. Five men and half a score of newspapers made up the opposition. Was it enthusiasm ? The enthusiasm was fanatical. There has been nothing like it since the Crusades. Was it confidence ? Sir, the faith of the people exceeded that of the patriarch. They gave you Constitution, law, right, liberty, all at your demand for arbitrary power that the rebellion might, as you promised, be crushed out in three months and the Union restored. Was credit needed ? You took control of a country, young, vigorous and inexhaustible in wealth and resources, and of a government almost free from public debt, and whose good faith had never been tarnished. Your great national loan bubble failed miserably ; as it deserved to fail ; but the bankers and merchants of Philadelphia, New York and Boston lent you more than their entire banking capital. And when that failed too, you forced credit by declaring your paper promises to pay a legal tender for all debts. Was money wanted ? You had all the revenues of the United States, diminished indeed, but still in gold. The whole wealth of the country, to the last dollar, lay at your feet. Private individuals, municipal corporations, the State governments, all in their frenzy gave you money or means with reckless prodigality. The great eastern cities lent you $150,000,000. Congress voted first, the sum of $250,000,000, and next $500,000,000 more in loans ; and then, first, $50,000,000, then $10,000,000, next $90,000,000, and, in July last, $150,000,000 in Treasury notes ; and the Secretary has issued also a "paper postage currency," in sums as low as five cents, limited in amount only by its discretion. Nay, more ; already since the 4th of July, 1861, this House has appropriated $2,000,000,000, almost every dollar without debate, and without a recorded vote. A thousand millions have been expended since the 15th of April, 1861, and a public debt or liability of $1,500,000,000 already incurred. And to support all this stupendous outlay and indebtedness, a system of taxation, direct and indirect, has been inaugurated, the most onerous and unjust ever imposed upon any but a conquered people.

Money and credit, then, you have had in prodigal profusion. And were men wanted ? More than a million rushed to arms ! Seventy-five thousand first, (and the country stood aghast at the multitude,) then eighty-three thousand more were demanded ; and three hundred and ten thousand responded to the call. The President next asked for four hundred thousand, and Congress, in its generous confidence, gave him five hundred thousand and, not to be outdone, he took six hundred and thirty-seven thousand. Half of these melted away in their first campaign ; and the President demanded three hundred thousand more for the war, and then drafted yet another three hundred thousand for nine months. The fabled hosts of Xerxes have been outnumbered. And yet victory strangely follows the standards of the foe. From Great Bethel to Vicksburg, the battle has not been to the strong.

Caucasian.

THE NEW YORK WEEKLY CAUCASIAN
CITY EDITION,
Is published EVERY FRIDAY MORNING, at
No. 162 NASSAU STREET,

and can be obtained, by out of town dealers, through all City News Agents. It is for sale at the principal News Stands in New York and Brooklyn.

It will also be served by carriers in New York, Brooklyn and Jersey City, for THREE CENTS per week, by sending address to the office, or at $1 50 per year, payable in advance.

☞ The WEEKLY CAUCASIAN (country edition) is published every Saturday morning, at $1 50 per year, and sent by mail as follows:—Single copies, $1 50; ten copies for $12; twenty copies, $20.

he Benefit of WHITE MEN and THEIR POSTERITY FOREVER."—[*S. A. Douglas.*

AY, JANUARY 24, 1863.   **NO. 17.**   **SINGLE COPIES, 3 CTS.**

---

t every disaster, except the last, has been followed by a call for more troops, and every time far they have been promptly furnished. rom the beginning the war has been conducted like a political campaign, and it has been e folly of the party in power that they have sumed that numbers alone would win the ld in a contest not with ballots but with muskets and sword. But numbers you have had most without number—the largest, best appointed, best armed, best fed, and clad host of ave men, well organized and well disciplined, er marshaled. A navy, too, not the most rmidable perhaps, but the most numerous d gallant, and the costliest in the world, and gainst a foe almost without a navy at all. wenty million people, and every element of rength and force at command—power, patronage, influence, unanimity, enthusiasm, fidence, credit, money, men, an Army and Navy the largest and the noblest ever seen the field or afloat upon the sea; with the apport, almost servile, of every State, county, d municipality in the North and West; with Congress swift to do the bidding of the Executive; without opposition anywhere at home, nd with an arbitrary power which neither the zar of Russia nor the Emperor of Austria are exercise; yet after nearly two years of ore vigorous prosecution of war than ever corded in history; after more skirmishes, ombats and battles than Alexander, Cæsar, r the first Napoleon ever fought in any five ears of their military career, you have utterly, signally, disastrously—I will not say ignoiniously—failed to subdue ten millions "reels," whom you had taught the people of the orth and West not only to hate but to despise. ebels, did I say? Yes, your fathers were rebels, or your grandfathers. He now who looks own so sadly upon us, the false, degenerate, and imbecile guardians of the reat Republic which he founded, was rebel. And yet we, cradled ourselves n rebellion, and who have fostered and aternized with every insurrection in the nineteenth century everywhere throughout the lobe, would now forsooth make the word "rebel" a reproach! Rebels certainly they are, ut all the persistent and stupendous efforts of he most gigantic warfare of modern times ave, through your incompetency and folly, availed nothing to crush them out, cut off though they have been by your blockade from all the world, and dependent only upon their own courage and resources. And yet they were to be utterly conquered and subdued in six weeks, or three months! Sir, my judgment was made up and expressed from the first. I learned it from Chatham: "My lords, you cannot conquer in America." And you have not conquered the South. *You never will.* It is not in the nature of things possible; much less under your auspices. But money you have expended without limit, and blood poured out like water. Defeat, debt, taxation, sepulchres, these are your trophies. In vain the people gave you treasure and the soldier yielded up his life. "Fight, tax, emancipate, let these," said the gentleman from Maine, [Mr. Pike,] at the last session, "be the trinity of our salvation." Sir, they have become the trinity of your deep damnation. The war for the Union is, in your hands, a most bloody and costly failure. The President confessed it on the 22d of September, solemnly, officially, and under the broad seal of the United States. And he has now repeated the confession. The priests and rabbis of abolition taught him that God

would not prosper such a cause. War for the Union was abandoned; war for the negro openly begun, and with stronger battalions than before. With what success? Let the dead at Fredericksburg and Vicksburg answer.

CAN THE WAR CONTINUE?

And now, sir, can this war continue? Whence the money to carry it on? Where the men? Can you borrow? From whom? Can you tax more? Will the people bear it? Wait till you have collected what is already levied. How many millions more of "legal tender"—to-day forty-seven per cent below the par of gold—can you float? Will men enlist now at any price? Ah, sir, it is easier to die at home. I beg pardon; but I trust I am not "discouraging enlistments." If I am, then first arrest Lincoln, Stanton, and Halleck, and some of your other generals; and I will retract; yes, I will recant. But can you draft again? Ask New England—New York. Ask Massachusetts. Where are the nine hundred thousand? Ask not Ohio—the Northwest. She thought you were in earnest, and gave you all, all—more than you demanded.

"The wife whose babe first smiled that day,
The fair, fond bride of yester eve,
And aged sire and matron gray,
Saw the loved warriors haste away,
And deemed it sin to grieve."

Sir, in blood she has atoned for her credulity; and now there is mourning in every house, and distress and sadness in every heart. Shall she give you any more?

But ought this war to continue? I answer, NO—NOT A DAY, NOT AN HOUR. What then? Shall we separate? Again I answer, NO, NO, NO! What then? And now, sir, I come to the grandest and most solemn problem of statesmanship from the beginning of time; and to the God of Heaven, Illuminer of hearts and minds, I would humbly appeal for some measure, at least, of light and wisdom and strength to explode and reveal the dark but possible future of this land.

CAN THE UNION OF THESE STATES BE RESTORED?
HOW SHALL IT BE DONE?

And why not? Is it historically impossible? Sir, the frequent civil wars and conflicts between the States of Greece did not prevent their cordial union to resist the Persian invasion; nor did even the thirty years Peloponnesian war, springing, in part, from the abduction of slaves, and embittered and disastrous as it was—let Taucidides speak—wholly destroy the fellowship of those States. The wise Romans ended the three years social war after many bloody battles, and much atrocity, by admitting the States of Italy to all the rights and privileges of Roman citizenship—the very object to secure which these States had taken up arms.— The border wars between Scotland and England, running through centuries, did not prevent the final union, in peace and by adjustment, of the two kingdoms under one monarch. Compromise did at last when ages of coercion and attempted conquest had failed to effect. England kept the crown, while Scotland gave the king to wear it; and the memories of Wallace and the Bruce of Bannockburn, became part of the glories of British history. I pass by the union of Ireland with England—a union of force, which God and just men abhor; and yet precisely "the Union as it should be" of the Abolitionists of America. Sir, the rivalries of the

houses of York and Lancaster filled all England with cruelty and slaughter, yet compromise and intermarriage ended the strife at last, and the white rose and red were blended in one. Who dreamed a month before the death of Cromwell that in two years the people of England, after twenty years of civil war and usurpation, would, with great unanimity, restore the house of Stewart in the person of its most worthless prince, whose father but eleven years before they had beheaded? And who could have foretold in the beginning of 1812, that within some three years, Napoleon would be in exile upon a desert island, and the Bourbons restored? Armed foreign intervention did it; but it is a strange history. Or who then expected to see a nephew of Napoleon, thirty-five years later, with the consent of the people, supplant the Bourbon and reign Emperor of France? Sir, many States and people, once separate, have become united in the course of ages through natural causes and without conquest; but I remember a single instance only in history of States or people once united, and speaking the same language, who have been forced permanently asunder by civil strife or war, unless they were separated by distance or vast natural boundaries. The secession of the Ten Tribes is the exce—— these parted without actual war; and the subsequent history is not encouraging to secession. But when Moses, the greatest of all statesmen, would secure a distinct nationality and government to the Hebrews, he led them and established his people in a different country. In modern times, the Netherlands, three centuries ago, won their independence by the sword; but France and the English channel separated them from Spain. So did our Thirteen Colonies; but the Atlantic ocean divorced us from England. So did Mexico, and other Spanish colonies in America; but the same ocean divided them from Spain. Cuba and the Canadas still adhere to the parent Government. And who now, North or South, in Europe or America, looking into history, shall presumptuously say that because of civil war the reunion of these States is impossible? War, indeed, while it lasts, is disunion, and, if it lasts long enough, will be final, eternal separation first, and anarchy and despotism afterward. Hence I would hasten peace now, to-day, by every honorable appliance.

WHAT IS THE DIRECT CAUSE OF THE WAR?

What, then, I ask, is the immediate, direct cause of disunion and this civil war? Slavery, it is answered. Sir, that is the philosophy of the rustic in the play—"that a great cause of the night, is lack of the sun." Certainly slavery was in one sense—very obscure indeed—the cause of the war. Had there been no slavery here, this particular war about slavery would never have been waged. In a like sense, the Holy Sepulchre was the cause of the war of the Crusades; and had Troy or Carthage never existed, there never would have been Trojan or Carthaginian war, and no such personages as Hector and Hannibal; and no Iliad or Æneid would ever have been written. But far better say that the negro is the cause of the war, for had there been no negro here, there would be no war just now. What then? Exterminate him? Who demands it? Colonize him? How? Where? At whose cost? Sir, let us have an end of this folly.

In 1833, England abolished slavery in the West Indies. Soon regiments of black West Indian troops were raised to garrison and suppress Ireland and to help subdue India. Influential Indians were "bought" to help bring India's millions of people under British control for exploitation akin to the slavery abolished by Britain in the West Indies. An opium industry was begun and the drug was exported to corrupt the peasants of China. When Chinese rulers protested, Britain opened the "Opium War," which resulted in humiliating defeat for China and a century of exploitation by European nations and America.

The Opium Trade in India.

The opium manufacture in India, whatever may be its moral aspects, is financially of great importance to the British Government. It is said that between 12,000,000 and 13,000,000 pounds of poppy juice, or upwards of 5,000 tons, are gathered yearly in Bengal. This yields to the Indian Government a gross revenue of £6,500,000. The poppy is grown in the broad valley of the Ganges, and principally in the districts near Patna and Benares. The crude opium is carried from the country in earthen pans to the examining headquarters at Patna, where it is thoroughly tested; it is then thrown into vats and stirred until it becomes a homogeneous paste, after which it is made into balls. These balls are rolled into poppy petals, then dried and stacked before being packed in boxes for Calcutta, *en route* to China. A number of boys are constantly engaged in stacking, turning, airing and examining the balls. To clear them of mildew, moth or insects, they are rubbed with dried and crushed poppy petal dust. Our illustration shows an opium fleet of native boats, conveying the drug to Calcutta. The fleet is passing the Monghyr Hills, and is preceded by small canoes, the crews of which sound the depth of water, and warn all boats out of the channel by beat of drum, as the Government boats claim precedence over all other craft. The timber raft shown in the sketch has been floated down from the Nepal forests, and will be used in making packing-cases for the opium.

Frank Leslie's Illustrated Newspaper, July 22, 1882

One day, while hauling dirt with a fractious horse, the animal manifested an unwillingness ·to perform his duty satisfactorily. At this procedure the master charged George with provoking the beast to do wickedly, and in a rage he collared George and bade him accompany him "up stairs" (of the soap house). Not daring to resist, George went along with him. Ropes being tied around both his wrists, the block and tackle were fastened thereto, and George soon found himself hoisted on tip-toe with his feet almost clear of the floor.

The "kind-hearted master" then tore all the poor fellow's old shirt off his back, and addressed him thus: "You son of a b—h, I will give you pouting around me; stay there till I go up town for my cowhide."

Our tobacco they plant, our cotton they pick,
And our rice they can harvest and thrash
They feed us in health, and they nurse us when sick
And they earn—while we pocket—our cash
They lead us when young, and they help us when old
And their toil loads our tables and shelves
But they're "niggers" and therefore (the truth must be told)
They cannot take care of themselves!

Rev. John Pierpont (J. Pierpont Morgon)

A white and a black man were condemned to be hanged. The white man asked not to be hanged on the same gallows as the black man.

A Convention of delegates in favor of using dynamite in order to obtain Irish independence will meet in Chicago next month.

—Leslie's Illustrated Weekly, July 22, 1882.

THE GREAT SUNDAY-SCHOOL CONVENTION.

THE meeting of the delegates to the International Sunday-school Convention that took place during the month of April at Atlanta, Georgia, was characterized by unusual interest and enthusiasm, one incident only having occurred that might in any way cast a shadow upon the general harmony of the occasion. This was the exclusion of the colored brother whose portrait accompanies the present article. The Rev. B. W. ARNETT is the pastor of a church in Ohio, and was regularly commissioned by the Sunday-school Union of that State to attend the Atlanta Convention as a delegate. Objection was, however, made to his presence, it having been decided by the officers of the Convention that the time was not yet arrived when such action might be taken without detriment to the cause of religion in the South. It is to be regretted that such is the condition of affairs, for certainly a religious body should be the last to insist upon distinctions of race that are not recognized by the State. The exhibition of feeling contained in the request that their single delegate should not attend the Convention, on account of his color, can not fail to impress the African Methodists with a sense of injury received at the hands of their white brethren.

The Convention was held in the First Baptist Church, as offering the best accommodation of any religious edifice in the city, and the tasteful decorations proved the interest taken by ladies of the congregation in preparing for the reception of the delegates. Conspicuous above the main entrance was the word "Welcome," arranged in large letters of cedar twigs, while on either side the doorway were shrubs and plants, many of them bearing a wealth of blossoms. Over the central aisle were the words, in gilt, "Our Text, the Scriptures; our Trophy, the Soul." Above, over the pillars of the gallery, in large letters, was inscribed, "Truth, Prayer, Sympathy." The gallery was beautifully festooned with flowers, and the walls were hung with wreaths and rich draperies of nature's floral wealth. The platform was almost covered with flowers in vases, bouquets, and other attractive shapes. The high arch above was adorned with long lines of cedar interspersed

with lilies and roses. At the head of the arch were the words, "Our Sufficiency is of God." The recess back of the pulpit was adorned with varied flowers. Above them were the words, "Our Story, Jesus and His Love—Peace be unto you." All through the church were the names of the various States represented, designating the seats of delegates.

The Convention, which was large and influential, included representatives from the Baptist, Presbyterian, Congregational, and Methodist denominations from every State of the Union and from the British Provinces; and while its main object was to afford an opportunity for an interchange of views on the subject of Sunday-schools and the best method of religious training for the young, it can not be doubted that the fraternal intercourse of so many of the leading minds from all sections of the country will tend to promote a true and lasting harmony that will pervade all

classes of society, and obliterate the traces of bitterness that still survive the war. The addresses, whether by clergymen or laymen, breathed the spirit of genuine harmony, and were highly significant of the gradual fading out of sectional feeling. With the exception of the exclusion of the worthy colored clergyman, alluded to previously, there was no feature of the Convention to which exception could be taken. The reverend gentleman, it should be understood, although a regularly elected delegate, declined to be present and press his claims, lest an element of discord might be introduced into the Convention; and in this his action was far more manly and Christian than that of the men who excluded him. Their conduct savors too much of the bigotry of a book recently published in the South, written to prove the absurd doctrine that the negro is not a member of the human family, but only a superior species of brute without a soul.

Among the speakers was Governor COLQUITT, who, in delivering the address of welcome to the Canadian delegates, compared the proposed European Congress which is to decide "who shall hold the keys to two narrow channels of water, and who shall be made responsible for the government of a few desolated and blood-soaked patches of earth in the Balkan peninsula," to the Convention before him, the diplomacy of which "assumes that mankind is a great brotherhood; that the will of God, done on earth as it is in heaven, is peace and good-will between men; that justice and truth and mercy are the grand conservators of human happiness and greatness; and that the cheapest defense of nations is to live void of offense to God and man."

We can not afford space for a detailed report of the proceedings of the Convention, which consisted mainly of carefully prepared and interesting reports of past work, and debates upon the best method of directing the labors of the future. Certainly, from the showing of the statistics, it would appear that the delegates enjoy the best of all encouragements—success. At present there are 7,657,696 members in the Sunday-schools belonging to this Union in the United States and Canada alone. During the last year there were within this territory 7640 new schools established, and 790,943 new children added to the rolls.

FREDERICK DOUGLASS.

No man in America has had a more remarkable career than the new Marshal of the District of Columbia, whose portrait is given on this page. He was born at Tuckahoe, Talbot County, Maryland, about the year 1817. Reared as a slave, he taught himself secretly to read and write while employed in a ship-yard in Baltimore. While very young he formed a resolution to escape from slavery, but it was not until 1838 that he found the opportunity to run away. In September of that year he fled, made his way to New York, and thence to New Bedford, where he married, and supported himself for three years by working on the wharves and in various shops. He was known to be intelligent and trustworthy; but his genius as an orator was first displayed at an antislavery convention held at Nantucket in 1841, where he made a speech so eloquent and stirring that he was offered the agency of the Massachusetts Antislavery Society. For nearly four years thereafter Mr. DOUGLASS lectured constantly in Massachusetts and other New England States, rousing public sentiment against slavery, and gaining great distinction as an orator.

In 1845 Mr. DOUGLASS published an autobiography, and in the same year made a visit to England, and lectured to enthusiastic audiences in every part of the United Kingdom. His freedom was purchased by his English friends, in order to insure him against legal annoyance in his labors. After remaining two years abroad, Mr. DOUGLASS returned to this country, and estab-

lished at Rochester, New York, a weekly journal, under the title of The North Star, afterward changed to Frederick Douglass's Paper. During the height of the excitement produced by JOHN BROWN's celebrated raid, Governor WISE, of Virginia, endeavored to have Mr. DOUGLASS arrested for supposed complicity in that movement, and he deemed it prudent to go abroad again. After an absence of a few months, Mr. DOUGLASS returned to Rochester, and continued the publication of his paper.

When the civil war broke out in 1861, Mr. DOUGLASS strongly advocated the use of colored troops and the emancipation of the slaves in the South. When permission was given, in 1863, to employ such troops, he assisted in the work of enlisting colored men, and was especially active in organizing the Fifty-fourth and Fifty-fifth Massachusetts regiments. Slavery having been abolished, Mr. DOUGLASS discontinued the publication of his paper, and applied himself to lecturing, in which he was remarkably successful. His powers of oratory are unexcelled, and no man possesses greater influence over an audience. In 1870 he removed to Washington, D. C., and became the editor of the New National Era. The following year he was appointed secretary to the Santo Domingo Commission; and on his return the President appointed him one of the Territorial Council of the District of Columbia. In 1872 he was elected Presidential elector at large for the State of New York, and was appointed to carry the electoral vote of the State to Washington.

MEETING OF COLORED CITIZENS.

The colored citizens of Boston held a meeting on Tuesday evening, the 26th ult., in the vestry of the Twelfth Baptist Church, Southac street. Mr. John J. Smith called the meeting to order, and read the following list of officers, which was unanimously adopted :—

President—ROBERT JOHNSON.

Vice Presidents—Jonas W. Clark, William H. Logan, Coffin Pitts, John J. Sydney.

Secretary—John Stephenson.

The President, on taking the chair, made a brief speech, thanking the audience for the honor conferred upon him, and closed his remarks by urging upon the colored citizens the necessity of examining for themselves the present aspect of affairs ; and if there ever was a time when their rights, in common with all mankind, as men and citizens, should be asserted, defended and acted upon, that time has come.

Short speeches were made by Geo. L. Ruffin and Geo. W. Lowther. Mr. Julian B. McCrea then introduced the following resolutions :—

Resolved, That we, the colored citizens of Boston, will support with our voices and our votes, John C. Fremont, of California, as President of the United States, and Wm. L. Dayton, of New Jersey, as Vice President.

Resolved, That while we regard the Republican party as the people's party, the resolve in the Republican platform endorsing the Kansas free State Constitution, which prohibits colored men from going into that territory, and the determination of the Republican press to ignore the colored man's interest in the party, plainly shows us that it is not an anti-slavery party ; and while we are willing to unite with them to resist the aggressions of the Slave Power, we do not pledge ourselves to go further with the Republicans than the Republicans will go with us.

Mr. McCrea briefly supported the resolutions.

Dr. J. S. Rock was then introduced, and made an able, powerful and eloquent speech, which was received with the wildest demonstrations of favor. At one moment, it appeared as though every one's face was bathed in tears ; in the next, the whole audience was convulsed with laughter. The address was very brilliant, and one of Dr. Rock's best efforts. He is regarded here, in the 'Athens of America,' as one of our first-class lyceum lecturers, and if he was white, there would not be honors enough in the State to confer upon him. He is as brilliant on the stump as in the Lyceum, and he has now given up his whole time to the great questions of the day, and in the present campaign is devoting all his energies to secure the election of Fremont and Dayton.

Mr. John J. Smith next addressed the meeting, and urged upon them the necessity of seeing that their taxes were paid, and that their names were on the voting list.

A spirited discussion then arose in relation to the second resolution, in which Messrs Smith, Ruffin, Lowther, McCrea, Johnson and Sydney took part, after which, the resolutions were unanimously adopted.

Mr. George W. Lowther then referred to the petition which Dr. Rock had presented to the Board of Mayor and Aldermen to have the word 'colored' struck off of the voting lists and tax bills, and characterized the action of that body as illiberal and entirely behind the spirit of the age, and in the coming election, we should not forget those men at the polls.

The meeting, which was very large, adjourned at a late hour, with three rousing cheers for Fremont and Dayton, and three more for the Massachusetts delegation in Congress.

JOHN STEPHENSON, *Secretary*.

The Liberator, September 5, 1856

CALL FOR A STATE CONVENTION OF COLORED MEN.

OFFICE CIVIL AND POLITICAL RIGHTS ASSOCIATION, ATLANTA, GEORGIA, Sept. 7, 1868.

The colored Members of the House of Representatives of the General Assembly of Georgia, having been expelled therefrom, and having organized themselves into an Association, to be known as the "Civil and Political Rights Association," and having been unanimously elected President of said Association, I therefore issue this call

To the Colored Voters of Georgia.—The rights guaranteed to us by the Constitution of our State, and by the Constitution and laws of the United States, have been unlawfully and arbitrarily torn from us by one branch of the General Assembly, a body created and established very largely by our votes, and that at the risk, in many instances, of starvation and death. The Democratic party, having, by refusing the colored members the right to vote, unlawfully obtained a large majority in the House of Representatives, have decided, by a mere resolution, in defiance of the Constitution and laws of the United States, and of the State of Georgia, that colored men have no right to represent their race in the General Assembly, and have accordingly ejected them from their seats. By this act they have ignored our rights of citizenship and representation, rights established by the Constitution and laws, and recognized by every sound and impartial jurist in the country. (See Irwin's Code, Part 2, p. 332, sections 1,648 and 1,649.) By this act nearly 100,000 taxed voters of Georgia, are deprived of their right of representation, contrary to the cardinal principle

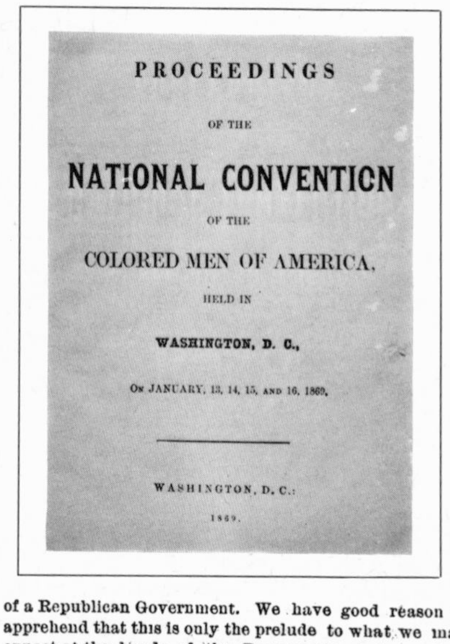
PROCEEDINGS

OF THE

NATIONAL CONVENTION

OF THE

COLORED MEN OF AMERICA,

HELD IN

WASHINGTON, D. C.,

ON JANUARY, 13, 14, 15, AND 16, 1869.

WASHINGTON, D. C.:

1869.

of a Republican Government. We have good reason to apprehend that this is only the prelude to what we may expect at the hands of the Democratic party, as they neither regard our established rights, as citizens and electors, or our condition and claims as freemen. In several counties we were advised by those we thought honest Democrats to elect colored representatives rather than loyal white men, while in several other counties not a white Republican could be found, or any white man who would accept the colored nomination; yet we are now censured and expelled for doing the best we could. And what is more astonishing, a number of white Representatives, who were professed Republicans at home, since their arrival here have become decided Democrats. In view of this state of things, we call upon the colored men of every county in the State to send delegates to a State Convention of colored citizens, to be held in the City of Macon, on the 1st Tuesday in October, 1868, for the purpose of taking into consideration our condition, and determining upon the best course for the future. There can be no doubt that our personal liberty is in as great danger as our civil and political rights. The same power which would override the Constitution in one thing will do it in another. It is, therefore, a solemn duty which every colored man owes to himself, his family, and his country, to maintain his manhood and his right of citizenship. It is our duty to meet and invoke Congressional aid in the security of our rights. Rally, then, rally colored voters, for your rights, your citizenship, and your personal liberty ! Send your delegates with sufficient funds to remain until the business of the Convention is completed. Guard against all disturbances, as this is a moral contest, a bloodless battle. Drunkards and fools fight in person, sober and wise men fight with thoughts and words.

As soon as this notice comes t hand, begin to get your delegates ready.

H. M. TURNER, President C. and P. R. Association.
JAMES PORTER, Secretary.

P. S.—The President may be addressed at Macon, and the Secretary at Savannah.

COLORED MEN EXCLUDED FROM THE JURY BOX—THE HOUSE RECONSIDER THEIR ACTION—THE NEWS FROM MAINE AND ITS EFFECT—ANOTHER COLORED MEMBER EXPELLED—WHAT WILL BE DONE NEXT—THE KU-KLUX BUSY—THE REMANDING OF GEORGIA TO MILITARY GOVERNMENT—THE STATUS OF HER SENATORS AND REPRESENTATIVES.

[FROM OUR SPECIAL CORRESPONDENT.]

ATLANTA, Sept. 15.—The House yesterday took another step toward the culmination of the counter-revolution which is in such rapid progress in this State. A bill was passed adopting the jury system of the old Slave Code, which forbids colored men sitting upon juries. This is practically denying to the colored citizen the right of trial by jury, for, while the prejudice of race remains so potent, he can have no justice in a suit with a white man; and the freedman is worse off, when accused of crime, than was the slave, for the latter was too valuable a piece of property to be wasted in hanging, while the freedman is the property of nobody but himself. The proceeding was in violation of the very Constitution from which this Legislature derives its existence and power to make laws, for that document prescribes but one criterion by which juries shall be selected, to wit: intelligence and uprightness, while the old system, perpetuated yesterday, establishes quite a different test, to wit: color. The Constitution says: "The General Assembly shall provide by law for the selection of upright and intelligent persons to serve as jurors," but the Code declares that such jurors shall be "*white* male citizens, above the age of twenty-one years." Ignoring the supreme law of the Constitution, the Legislature adopted the old slave law, rendered obselete by its inconsistency with the Constitution. A motion to amend, by providing that nothing in this act should disqualify any person from serving as a juror on account of race or color, was promptly voted down; so the Georgia Legislature, in the most solemn manner, declared that a colored man, no matter how upright or intelligent, shall be excluded from the jury box, and should be compelled to commit the custody of his life, liberty, and property to the white juries, no matter how ignorant or depraved they may be. Thus two vast strides have been made toward the disfranchisement of the colored man—he has been prohibited from holding office; he has been excluded from the jury box—it only remains to exclude them from the ballot-box. The bill was passed by a vote of 87 to 24, some dough faced Republicans dodging or voting with the majority.

THE RECONIDERATION AND ITS CAUSE.

But something occurred last night which naturally modified the views of the unterrified Democracy. Notwithstanding the large vote by which the bill was passed yesterday, a motion to reconsider prevailed this morning by some 14 majority. Whether the mysterious influence which thus urged the "unterrified" to repentance was the accounts of the Maine election which arrived last night, cannot positively be asserted, but it is difficult to ascribe any other cause for this sudden retrogression. The vastly increased Republican majority in Maine was an indication to some that, sooner or later, the conspirators against the National authority were to be called to account for their wrong doing. They cannot shut their eyes to the signs that the great heart of the loyal North still pulsates with patriotic vigor They cannot conceal from themselves that the vaticinations of their political prophets are turning out to be lies, yet it seems that the madness that precedes destruction still held its sway over them, and though the thunder from Maine may have for a moment startled them in their suicidal career, and caused them to review their action on the Jury bill, they quickly recovered their audacity, and proceeded with

THE EXPULSION OF THE REMAINING COLORED MEMBERS.

Fyall, who claims to be a Frenchman, was the first to be guillotined, and the Chairman of the Committee on Pedigrees (as it should be called) reported "that Fyall, having more than one-eighth negro blood in his veins, was ineligible to a seat, and that the clerk strike his name from the roll." Mr. Bryant asked for the testimony, which was read. It consisted of Fyall's own oath, who testified that his father and mother were both white, and French people. The other witness before the Committee was Mr. Alley, who swore that he knew Fyall's father and mother befor Fyall was born; his mother was a mulatto, &c.

Now, the above is a correct condensation of the journals of the House, as published in the Democratic papers here. It is the case as made by the Democracy itself. Fyall's oath is partly offset by Alley's, who swore that he knew Fyall's father and mother before he was born. Fyall is 47 years old, and Alley is apparently a much younger man. But, disregarding this flaw in the evidence, let it be noticed that the gist of the accusation is that Fyall *has more than one-eighth negro blood in his veins.* Nothing else is alleged against him.

New York Tribune, September 21, 1868

A BRIGHT RECORD—SHALL THE NEGRO OF OHIO VOTE?

WE learn from John M. Langston, Esq., of Ohio, that the Republican party of that State have accepted the issue of manhood suffrage for the negro of that State, and propose to give him the ballot by a majority of more than sixty thousand at their election, which occurs next October. In this struggle, Gen. Hayes, of Cincinnati, is the standard-bearer of the Republican party. The colored people of that State ought to be enfranchised at once, and without condition ; for, if Mr. Langston states the truth, there are sixty thousand colored inhabitants in that State, and they are the owners of taxable property to the amount of $15,000,000. The number of their children of legal school age, according to the numeration taken in September, 1865, is 21,706.

In the war of the late rebellion the colored men of Ohio supplied from their population to the 54th colored Massachusetts regiment four hundred men ; to the 50th regiment one thousand men ; and because this regiment was an Ohio one, Mr. Langston, on behalf of the colored men of Ohio, presented to it a stand of beautiful regimental colors at a cost of $225. To the 5th United States colored troops one thousand men, and to this Mr. Langston also presented a stand of colors worth $225. To the 27th United States colored troops, one thousand men ; to all other colored regiments during the war, three thousand six hundred men ; in all seven thousand men. In this estimate the colored regiment raised in Cincinnati, by Judge Dickson, during the Kirby Smith raid, for the defence of that city, is not included. This regiment numbered one thousand men. Mr. Langston speaks with full knowledge of these facts, because the colored troops of that State were recruited under his immediate direction and supervision ; and to him more than to any other single individual, belongs the honor of having made this record. In the charge at Fort Wagner, seventy-five of the men who fell there were from the State of Ohio, and were sons of several of the most wealthy and influential colored families of that State.

It cannot be the case that loyal men of Ohio, now so largely in the majority, can longer deny to their colored fellow-citizens the privilege of doing for their country, in the use of the ballot, what they did in the late rebellion in the use of the musket.—*N. O. Republican.*

During slavery many New York firms feared doing anything that might cause them to lose customers in the South. Among the firms that did not have this fear (or who at least had the courage to place advertisements in abolitionist newspapers) were Lord and Taylor, Arnold, Constable and Company, Brooks Brothers and Bowen and McNamee.

—see The Liberator, July 3, 1857.

In 1869 it was estimated that southern church members owned 600,000 slaves. Methodists, 219,000; Baptists, 125,000; Reformed Baptists, 101,000; Presbyterians, 77,000; Episcopalians, 85,000 and other denominations 55,000. As for Catholics, it was a bishop who suggested using Africans as slaves when a substitute was needed for the annihilated Indians.

—The Salem Observer, May 12, 1860.

The Philadelphia Inquirer, October 21, 1865

GOVERNOR SHARKEY ON NEGRO TESTIMONY.

He Orders it to be Received in the Civil Courts.

EXECUTIVE OFFICE, JACKSON, Sept. 25, 1865.— By an order, bearing date the 20th instant, Col. Samuel Thomas, Assistant Commissioner of the Freedmen's Bureau in this State, proposes to transfer to the civil authorities of the State the right to try all cases in which the rights of freedmen are involved, either for injuries done to their persons or property. This proposition is made, however, on condition that "the judicial officers and magistrates of the provisional government of the State will take for their mode of procedure the laws now in force in this State, except so far as those laws make a distinction on account of color, and allow negroes the same rights and privileges as are accorded to white men before their courts," by which I understand that negroes shall be allowed to testify in cases where their interest is involved. And believing that the late constitutional amendment which abolished slavery abolishes all laws which constituted a part of the policy of slavery, and in declaring that the negro shall be protected in his person and property establishes principles which of themselves entitle the negro to sue and be sued, and, as a necessary incident of such right, that he is made competent as a witness, according to the laws of evidence of the State.

Now, therefore, I, William L. Sharkey, Provisional Governor of Mississippi, with a view of securing to our citizens the rights of trial before their own officers and under their own laws, rather than by a military tribunal and by military law, do hereby proclaim and make known that in all cases, civil or criminal, in which the rights of negroes are involved, either for injuries done to their persons or property or in matters of contract, the testimony of negroes may be received, subject to the common law rules of evidence as regards competency and credibility which prevail in regard to white persons. And I do, therefore, accept the proposition of Colonel Samuel Thomas, Assistant Commissioner of the Freedmen's Bureau of this State, and request that no freedmen's Court shall hereafter be organized, and that those already in existence be closed and instructed to transfer the cases before them to the civil authorities; and I hereby instruct all judicial officers and magistrates to act accordingly, until the Legislature shall act upon this subject.

Given under my hand, and the great seal of the State affixed, this day and date above written.   W. L. SHARKEY, Provisional Governor of Mississippi.

A dispatch announces that a convention of whites in South Carolina have created a Commission to prepare a code of laws for the blacks. Now let us have a convention of blacks to make a code of laws for the whites—Congress to judge which convention does its work best, and admit representatives accordingly. If there are any who object to this, let them join us in advocating a convention of all to make laws for all. That is our idea of a "republican form of government."

New York Daily Tribune, September 30, 1865

In 1851, Mars Hill College at Mars Hill, North Carolina, fell behind on mortgage payments on its little building. Therefore, with the consent of college authorities, Joe Anderson, a slave who was owned by the school, was seized by the sheriff and held as guarantee for the debt.

It was not until after the 1954 Supreme Court decision that a black student entered Mars Hill College. She was the great-granddaughter of the mortgaged slave, Joe Anderson, who is buried on the college grounds.

NEGRO SUPREMACY IN THE SOUTHERN STATES.

THERE are but two States in the South where the negro population outnumbers the white—the States of South Carolina and Mississippi. In the other eight reconstructing States the whites are so largely in the majority that if they are outvoted it will be either because they refuse to register or because more are disfranchised than Congress intended. The following table gives estimates of population and voters for 1867, based on the census of 1860, without proper allowance for natural increase and for the losses during the war :

States.	Male Citizens.		Voters.	
	White.	Negro.	White.	Negro.
Alabama	243,180	164,265	81,033	54,755
Arkansas	154,712	42,185	51,571	14,062
Florida	37,016	28,852	12,339	7,961
Georgia	270,941	173,146	90,314	57,715
Louisiana	284,873	136,759	47,479	22,793
Mississippi	167,646	164,755	55,882	58,252
North Carolina	281,799	136,012	93,933	45,337
South Carolina	131,529	150,839	43,840	50,273
Texas	250,000	110,000	89,000	35,000
Virginia	316,761	108,128	105,583	66,043
Total	2,138,369	1,299,941	661,974	412,187

If all were registered, the white majorities would be as follows: In Alabama, 26,278 ; Arkansas, 37,519 ; Florida, 4,388 ; Georgia, 32,599 ; Louisiana, 24,686 ; North Carolina, 48,596 ; Texas, 45,000 ; Virginia, 39,540. The black majorities would be in Mississippi, 2,370 ; South Carolina, 6,439. If in the eight States where whites are dominant disfranchisement is limited by the conditions of the Reconstruction bills, the white majorities cannot be entirely wiped out, except possibly in Florida. The Southern obstructionists assert that the registers reject a great many white men who are not legally disfranchised, and as there is no appeal from their decisions, that it is impossible for white men to obtain their rights. This may be true in some localities, but it is not likely that it is the general fact. There is no evidence of any such general purpose of the military commanders to reduce the whites to a minority by unfair means, as the obstructionists allege. On the contrary, they show every disposition to administer the law strictly and fairly. The disfranchisement of whites, therefore, which gives the negroes a majority of voters in every State, except Arkansas, is voluntary. The whites refuse to register. If negro supremacy is established throughout the South, as now seems likely, it will be the fault of the whites themselves, who sullenly stand back and surrender their power because they dislike the conditions under which they are permitted to exercise it. If by registering and voting they endorsed these conditions, we might honor their pluck in standing out and bearing the consequences. But they do not endorse the Congressional scheme by voting under it. They merely go through with the process as an inevitable evil, and have full liberty to hate and denounce the scheme and its authors to their hearts' content, and keep doing so until they are satisfied. No, the abdication of power by the whites is cowardly and inexcusable, and they will themselves share the responsibility of the consequences, whatever they may be.

What the consequences of negro supremacy in the South are to be it is impossible to predict. George W. Kendall, of Texas, has written a letter, for the consolation of his white brethren, in which he predicts that the first colored vote will be the heaviest ever counted ; that the negroes will not continue to take an interest in politics after the novelty of voting has passed away. There may be something in this, but the negroes and their white friends will frame the new Constitutions for the Southern States, and do the first legislating, and if they hold their present purpose and leadership, they will adopt the Tennessee system, and there will be a much more sweeping disfranchisement of white men than under the confiscation acts, and the imposition of such other disabilities as even Brownlow has not attempted. The Southern white men must see that those who hold the power at the start will have every inducement so to fix things that they can retain it, and although Congress is to pass upon the new constitutions before they can stand, there is no probability that that body will require any greater leniency towards ex-rebels in the other States than in Tennessee. They will accept the constitutions made as true expressions of the popular will, and it will be a long time before the white men of the South can hope for any change. If they mean to have any voice in their State governments for the next dozen years they will do well to register and vote now.

New York Tribune, September 21, 1868

Letter written to W.E.B. Dubois by one Alvin Borgquest of Clark University in Massachusetts. The letter is dated April 3, 1905.

"We are pursuing an investigation here on the subject of crying as an expression of the emotions, and should like very much to learn about its peculiarities among the colored people. We have been referred to you as a person competent to give us information on the subject.

"We desire especially to know about the following salient aspects:

1. Whether the Negro sheds tears . . . . ."

Black women in the ante-bellum South were not permitted to dress with veils. Men were forbidden to carry canes or smoke cigars.

In Louisiana free colored women were forced to wear veils.

In 1854 the Know Nothing Party forced the discontinuance of Irish Stew being served in restaurants.

Ticket of admission to the impeachment trial of President Andrew Johnson. Johnson failed to be impeached by only one vote. His offense was acting contrary to the Congressional majority, which wanted to reconstruct the South.

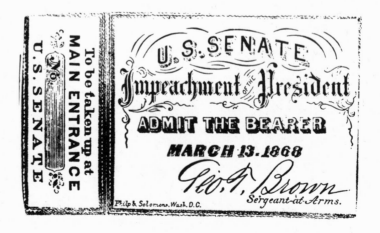

Executive Department.

IN THE NAME AND UNDER THE AUTHORITY OF THE

STATE OF FLORIDA.

Whereas, *Jonathan C. Gibbs* hath been duly appointed by the Governor Senate, according to the Constitution and Laws of said State to be *Secretary of State*,

Now, therefore, reposing especial trust and confidence in the loyalty, patriotism, fidelity and prudence of the said *Jonathan C. Gibbs*

I, HARRISON REED,

Governor of the State of Florida, under and by virtue of the authority vested in me by the Constitution and Laws of said State, Do hereby Commission the said *Jonathan C. Gibbs* to be such *Secretary of State* according to the Laws and Constitution of said State for the time aforesaid, and in the name of the People of the State of Florida, to have, hold, and exercise said office and all the powers appertaining thereto, and to perform the duties thereof, and to enjoy all the privileges and benefits of the same in accordance with the requirements of Law. In Testimony Whereof, I do hereunto set my hand and cause to be affixed the Great Seal of the State, at Tallahasse, the Capital, this *30th* day of *November* A. D. 186 and of the independence of the United States the *Ninety-third* year.

By the Governor. Attest.

Harrison Reed

Secretary of State.   Governor of Florida.

Document appointing black man Secretary of State in Florida during Reconstruction.

1862.

1866.

HOW AND IT WORKS. *Th. Nast.*

OTHELLO. DOST THOU MOCK ME?

IAGO. I MOCK YOU! NO, BY HEAVEN:

WOULD YOU WOULD BEAR YOUR FORTUNES LIKE A MAN.

—SHAKSPEARE.

"*Iago.* The Moor is of a free and open nature,
That thinks men honest that but seem to be so;
And will as tenderly be led by the nose,
As asses are.
Make the Moor thank me, love me, and reward me,
For making him egregiously an ass,
And practising upon his peace and quiet
Even to madness. 'Tis here, but yet confused:
Knavery's plain face is never seen, till us'd......
Though I do hate him as I do hell-pains,
Yet, for necessity of present life,
I must show out a flag and sign of love;
Which is indeed but sign......
Then devils will their blackest sins put on,
They do suggest at first with heavenly shows,
As I do now......
I humbly do beseech you of your pardon,
For too much loving you.....
I hope you will consider, what is spoke
Comes from my love;—But, I do see you are mov'd:—
I am to pray you, not to strain my speech
To grosser issues, nor to larger reach
Than to suspicion......

Are you a man? have you a soul, or sense?—O grace! O heaven defend me!
God be wi' you; take mine office.—O wretched fool,
That liv'st to make thine honesty a vice!—
O monstrous world! Take note, take note, O world!
To be direct and honest, is not safe.—
I thank you for this profit; and, from hence,
I'll love no friend, since love breeds such offense....
Work on,
My medicine, work! *Othello.*"

"I have been accused of being inimical to the true interests of the colored people: but this is not true. I am one of their best friends; and time, which tries all tests all, will demonstrate the fact.....I once said I would be the Moses of your people.....I have been blamed for vetoing the Freedmen's Bureau Bill, and have been also represented to the colored people as having done it because I was their enemy. This is not true.....The ordinary course of judicial proceedings is no longer interrupted. The courts, both State and Federal, are in full, complete, and successful operation, and through them every person, regardless of race and color, is entitled to and can be heard. The protection granted to the white citizen is already conferred by law upon the freedman. .....It can not be expected that men who have for four years been made familiar with the blood and carnage of war, who have suffered the loss of property, and in so many instances reduced from affluence to poverty, can at once assume the calm demeanor and action of those citizens of the country whose worldly possessions have not been destroyed, and whose political hopes have not been blasted, and the worst view of this subject affords no parallel in violence to similar outrages that have followed all civil commotions, always less in magnitude than ours. But I do not believe that this to-be-regretted state of things will last long."—ANDREW JOHNSON.

The first March on Washington took place in 1894, when a Midwestern social reformer named Jacob Coxey led about 500 men into the nation's capital following the depression of 1893. They had expected to press Congress to take action for relief of

Not Fair.

The question is often asked, why it is that the colored people claim an equality with the whites, and so few of them have manifested even a propensity for that equality; that we never have produced authors, writers, professors, nor geniuses of any kind, notwithstanding some of us have been free from the formation of this government, up till the present day.

To say nothing about the disadvantage that would naturally arise to the *few*, while the many continued in slavery and degradation; yet, when Mr. Jefferson, the 'apostle of democracy,' was asked by a British statesman, 'Why it was that America, with all her boasted greatness, had produced so few great men, and learned authors,' the American statesman quickly replied, that; when the United States had been an independent government as long as Greece was before she produced her Homer, Socrates, and Demosthenese, and Rome, before she produced her Virgil, Horace, and her Cicero; or when this country had been free as long as England was, before she produced her Pope and Dryden, then he would be ready to answer that question.

According to the above sensible position of the American statesman, so characteristic of himself, *we* answer, that more is asked of us, than ever was asked of any other people, and if it is expected that with all the disadvantages with which we are surrounded, that we should still equal the other citizens, it is giving us more than we claim; it is a tacit acknowledgement, that we are naturally superior to the rest of mankind, and, therefore, are much more susceptible than they.

With this cursory view of the subject, then, all that we have in conclusion to say is, that if we produce any equals at all, while we are in the present state, to say the least of it, we have done as much as Greece, Rome, England or America.

Article written by Martin Delaney in the Pittsburg Mystery, 1843

the unemployed, but instead many were arrested for trampling on the Capitol lawn.

As Coxey's army passed through Denver, the march was joined by a thirteen-year-old boy whose aunt snatched him out of the line as it passed by her house. Years later that youth had headquarters in Washington and for many years was known as "the little dictator" because of the tight reins he held as national head of colored Elks throughout the world. His name was J. Finley Wilson.

On June 6, 1900, leaders of black communities gathered from various parts of the nation. Among other matters, they discussed the possibility of forming a ticket to run for President and Vice-President of the United States. The suggested pairs were:

1. Judge W. Walker of Boston and P. B. S. Pinchback
2. Bishop W. B. Derrick and Dr. W. E. B. DuBois
3. Bishop Grant of Illinois and Reverend J. P. Simpson
4. Bishop Henry Turner and B. T. Washington
5. Bishop Alexander Walters and T. T. Alain of Florida

Bishop Levi Coffin presided over the meeting, which abandoned the idea of promoting an all-black ticket.

In 1929 the New York City Board of Education issued a directive that Negro should be spelled with a capital N. In 1930, the *New York Times* began to do likewise.

In 1919, after a bitter struggle, a black physician was placed on the staff of Harlem Hospital, situated in the heart of the black capital of the world and serving a predominately black clientele.

In the early 1930's, the wife of W.C. Handy (Father of the Blues), died on the doorstep of Sydenham Hospital, which refused to admit her on the ground that it was a private hospital and that she would have to be taken to a city hospital.

In 1910, 99.2% of all black Americans were native born and only 60% of all white Americans were native born.

—The Negro Population in the U.S., 1790–1910, U.S. Census Bureau.

John Chavis (1763–1838) was freeborn near the borderline between Virginia and North Carolina. He obtained an unusually fine formal education as a result of an experiment conducted half in jest by some white gentlemen of means. Out of curiosity, they sent him to Princeton in order to learn if a colored youth had the capacity to take higher education. At Princeton, Chavis acquitted himself well in private studies under President Witherspoon. Chavis also studied at Washington Academy, which was once called Liberty Hall Academy and later became Washington and Lee University. A certificate that he successfully passed his studies was once filed in the Manuscript Order Book of the Rockridge County Court in Virginia but has since been lost. It may have been placed there by the

gentlemen who had satisfied their curiosity.

In 1801, Chavis became a Presbyterian minister at Lexington and Hanover, Va., under the General Assembly. About 1805, he migrated to North Carolina where he preached to both white and black congregations. He has been described as "distinguished for dignity of manner" and as he knew Greek and Latin among other subjects he was asked to tutor sons of prominent white people. He established his school in Greensboro, N.C., and there under the black scholar sat youths who were to be among the future leaders in the state and nation. Governor Charles Manly and Senator Willie Mangum were among his more famous pupils.

In 1832, when Chavis was approaching 3 score and ten in age, a

law was passed which forbid blacks either to teach or to preach. This law was a consequence of fear among whites because of the late Nat Turner revolt in nearby Virginia. Thereupon, deprived of his means to earn a living, Chavis wrote a sermon entitled "The Extent of Atonement." Sales of the sermon and donations from friends and former pupils supported Chavis until his death in 1838. Today, the archives of the University of North Carolina contain many letters from former pupils to Chavis and more are in the files of the Library of Congress.

In many cases when the mother of a famous man was a black woman, biographers either skip details on parents or tell many different stories so as to confuse researchers. John

James Audubon's birthplace is variously given as Louisiana, France and Haiti. On rare occasions he is described as being of illegitimate birth or else of French parentage with no background on the mother. The fact appears to be that Audubon was born of a French father and a black woman on the island of Haiti at Jeremie, where Alexandre Dumas, another illustrious mulatto, was born. In those days the French had few reservations about color. Many of the mulatto children, like Audubon, Dumas and Norbert Rillieux, were sent to France for their schooling.

Another famous American born in the West Indies, and whose mother is a shadowy figure, was Alexander Hamilton. Not only is there a persistent rumor that his mother was a Negro, but in New York City there are black Hamiltons who claim direct descent from the illustrious first U.S. Treasurer.

Upon retiring from service in 1910, former Confederate soldier James Gordon had these remarks to say:

"I was born a multi-millionare, but was never happy untill I got rid of my millions. The largest portion of it went to feed a large number of slaves that I, unfortunately, inherited . . . I want to see you join me in taking away these bayonets that are on those guns you sent down there to a race of people who came out of a jungle and are only partially civilized. We cannot civilize them in half a century. We were not civilized in a thousand years as we are today . . . We do not want to hurt the nigger. We all love the nigger. I love the nigger. I want to read you here a little sentiment of mine . . . This is my poetry.
"The Old Black Mammy [Gordon's black nurse]
The dear old black mammy, so gentle and tender
So faithful and true to her trust;

I loved her so well I dared not offend her,
She is gone, yet I honor her dust . . ."

—The New York Evening Journal, February 25, 1910.

Archibald McMillan, resident of Cameron County, Texas, in a deed of manumission executed on December 13, 1859, freed six mulatto slaves: a twenty-three-year-old woman and her five children.

In the deed is written the reason for granting freedom to them:

"For the faithful service she has rendered for me until this time; the other four I free on account of believing them to be my own children . . ."

The fifth child was fathered by a black man who married the freed woman.

1932. Chapter 78. If any white person intermarry with a colored person, or any colored person intermarry with a white person, he shall be guilty of a felony and confined in the penitentiary for from one to five years.

1642. Act XXII. A punishment is provided for loitering runaways in the colony; for a second offense a runaway is to be branded in the cheek with the letter "R."

It is a felony for a runaway to carry powder and shot, punishable by death.

1705. Chapter XXIII. All Negro, mulatto, and Indian slaves within this dominion shall be held to be real estate and not chattels and shall descend unto heirs and widows according to the custom of land inheritance, and be held in fee simple.

1918. Chapter 301. In the penitentiary the races shall be kept separate.

1699. Act VI. The penalty for the first offense of hog stealing by a Negro or a slave is set at thirty lashes on the bare back, well laid on; for the second offense, two hours in the

pillory with boths ears nailed thereto, at the expiration of the two hours the ears are to be cut off close by the nails.

1705. Chapter XIV. It is enacted that if any person shall steal any hog or pig, for the first offense he shall receive on his bare back twenty-five lashes or pay ten pounds current money; and if a Negro or Indian, thirty-nine lashes well laid on, at the common whipping post, and moreover shall pay 400 pounds of tobacco for each hog. And if any person shall offend the second time, he shall stand in the pillory and have both ears nailed thereto, and at the end of two hours have the ears cut loose from the nails. And for the third offense he shall be adjudged a felon and shall suffer death.

1705. Chapter XIX. In Section 31 it is stated that Popish recusants, convicts, Negroes, mulattoes, and Indian servants, and others not being Christians, shall be incapable to be witnesses in any cases whatsoever.

1705. Chapter XLIV. In Section 34 it is declared that if any slave

resist his master, or owner, or other person, by his or her order correcting such slave, and shall happen to be killed in such correction, it shall not be accounted felony; but the master, owner, and every such other person so giving correction shall be free and acquit of all punishment and accusation for the same, as if such incident had never happened: And also if any Negro, mulatto, or Indian, bond or free, shall at any time lift his or her hand in opposition against any Christian, not being Negro, mulatto, or Indian, he or she so offending, shall for every such offense, proved by the oath of the party, receive on his or her bare back thirty lashes, well laid on.

1691. Act XVI. This act provides penalties because many times Negroes, mulattoes and other slaves unlawfully absent themselves from their masters' and mistresses' service and lie hid and lurk in obscure places, killing hogs and committing other injuries.

And for prevention of that abominable mixture and spurious issue which hereafter may increase as well by Negroes, mulattoes and Indians intermarrying with English, or other white women, it is enacted that for the time to come, that whatsoever English or other white man or woman, bond or free, shall intermarry with a Negro, mulatto, or Indian man or woman, bond or free, he shall within three months be banished from this dominion forever.

And it is further enacted, that if any English woman being free shall have a bastard child by a Negro she shall pay fifteen pounds to the church wardens, and in default of such payment, she shall be taken into possession by the church wardens and disposed of for five years and the amount she brings shall be paid one-third to their majesties for the support of the government, one-third to the of the parish where the offense is committed and the other third to the informer. The child shall be bound out by the church wardens until he is thirty years of age. In case the English woman that shall have a bastard is a servant, she shall be sold by the church wardens (after her time is expired) for five years, and the child serve as aforesaid.

1705. Act XLIX. This act, on servants and slaves, states that for a further Christian care of all Christian slaves it is enacted that no Negro, mulatto or Indian, although Christian, or Jew, Moor, Mohammedan or other infidel, shall purchase any Christian servant nor any other except of their own complexion, or such as are declared slaves, but if any Negro or other infidel or such as are declared slaves (i. e., those not Christians in their native country, except Turks and Moors in amity) shall notwithstanding purchase any Christian white servant the said servant shall become free, ipso facto, and if any person having such Christian white servant shall intermarry with any such Negro, mulatto or Indian, Jew, Moor, Mohammedan or other infidel, every Christian white servant of every such person so intermarrying shall, ipso facto, become free and acquit from any service due to such master or mistress so intermarrying. A woman servant having a bastard shall for every offense serve her

owner one whole year after her indenture has expired or pay 1,000 pounds of tobacco, and the reputed father, if free, shall give security to the church wardens to maintain the child, but if a servant, he shall make satisfaction to the parish after his indenture has expired. And if any woman servant shall be got with baby by her master, she shall be sold by the church wardens for one year after her indenture, or pay 1,000 pounds in tobacco. If a woman servant has a bastard by a Negro, or mulatto she shall pay for the use of the parish 15 pounds current money or be sold for five years at the expiration of her time. If a free Christian white woman should have a bastard child, she shall pay 15 pounds current money of Virginia or be sold for five years. In both cases the church wardens shall bind the child to be a servant until it shall be thirty-one years of age.

Whatsoever white man or woman being free shall intermarry with a Negro shall be committed to prison for six months without bail, and pay 10 pounds to the use of the parish. Ministers marrying such persons shall pay 10,000 pounds of tobacco.

1710. Chapter XII. If any white or other woman not being a slave be delivered of a bastard child and she endeavor to avoid shame and punishment by drowning or secret burying to conceal the death, the mother so offending shall suffer death, except such mother can make proof that the child was born dead; this act is to be read yearly in churches by the ministers under penalty of 500 pounds of tobacco for omission.

1753. Chapter VII. A woman servant having a bastard child shall serve one extra year or pay her master 1,000 pounds of tobacco and the reputed father, if free, shall give security to the church wardens for the child's maintenance and keep the parish indemnified; if a servant he shall make satisfaction after his time of indenture. If a woman servant be got with a child by her master when her time is expired, she shall be sold by the church wardens

for one year. If any woman servant has a bastard child by a Negro over the year due her master, she shall upon the expiration of her time be sold for five years or pay 15 pounds current money. If a free Christian white woman shall have a bastard child by a Negro, or mulatto, for every such offense she shall pay to the church wardens 15 pounds current money or be by them sold for five years and the church wardens shall bind the child to be a servant until it shall be thirty-one years of age. Whatsoever English, or white man or woman being free shall intermarry with a Negro or mulatto man or woman, bond or free, shall be committed to prison for six months without bail and pay 10 pounds to the use of the parish.

1765. Chapter XXIV. Bastard children of woman servants and Negroes or free Christian, white women by Negroes, shall hereafter be bound out, the males to serve until twenty-one years of age and the females to serve until eighteen years of age, only and no longer; the former law binding the child out until thirty-one years of age now declared an unreasonable severity to such children.

1785. Chapter LXXVIII. Every person of whose grandfathers or grandmothers anyone is or shall have been a Negro, although all his other progenitors, except that descending from the Negro shall have been white persons, shall be deemed a mulatto, and so every person who shall have one-fourth or more Negro blood shall in like manner be deemed a mulatto. This act is to be in force from January 1, 1787.

1792. Chapter 41. It is provided that every person other than a Negro, although all his other progenitors, except that descending from the Negro shall have been white persons shall be deemed a mulatto; so every such person who shall have one-fourth part or more of Negro blood, shall in like manner be deemed a mulatto.

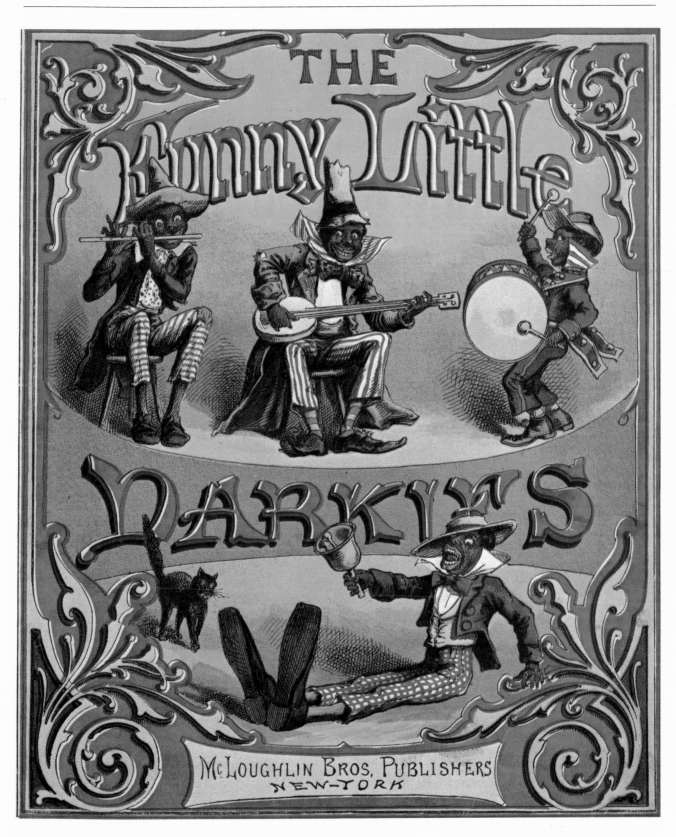

1792. Chapter 72. Every person not being a servant or slave committing adultery or fornication, and being convicted by the oaths of two or more credible witnesses or confession of the party, shall forfeit $20.00 for adultery and $10.00 for fornication.

1866. Chapter 17. Every person having one-fourth or more Negro blood shall be deemed a colored person, and every person not a colored person having one-fourth or more Indian blood shall be deemed an Indian.

1879. Chapter 252. All marriages between a white person and a Negro shall be absolutely void without any decree of divorce or other legal process.

1910. Chapter 357. Every person having one-sixteenth or more Negro blood shall be deemed a colored person, and every person not a colored person having one-fourth or more of Indian blood shall be deemed an Indian.

1924. Chapter 371. For the preservation of racial integrity, registration certificates shall be made out and filed for those persons born before June 14, 1912, showing the racial mixture for whom a birth certificate is not on file. It is a penitentiary offence to make a registration certificate false as to race or color. No marriage license shall be granted unless the clerk has reasonable assurance that the statements as to color are correct.

It shall be unlawful for any white person to marry any save a white person, or a person with no other admixture of blood than white and American Indian. The term "white person" shall apply only to the person who has no trace whatsoever of any blood other than Caucasian, but persons who have one-sixteenth or less of the blood of the American Indian, and no other non-Caucasic blood shall be deemed white persons. All laws heretofore passed and in effect regarding the intermarriage of white and colored persons shall apply to marriages prohibited by this act.

Oh these cold white hands manipulating they broke us like limbs from trees and carved Europe upon our African masks and made puppets

—Henry Dumas

One plays the drum, one sings a song,
One thumps the grand piano,
Another fiddles, on the top,
The tune of "Rosa Anna."

THE ALDEN FRUIT VINEGAR

USE CLEAR BAKING POWDER

GOLDEN COTTOLENE

J.&

40

DIXON'S
CARBURET of IRON
STOVE POLISH.

4,000,000
bottles sold annually
German
Syrup
and
August
Flower.

SAPOLIO

COATS' THREAD

ON'T FETCH YOU NOTHING WILL

J. A. BLUXOME,
SIXTH AVENUE,
cor. 21st St.

GREAT JERUSALEM

Under my hand the pyramids arose
I made the mortar
for the Woolworth Building

—Langston Hughes

Right: Dress made by slave, origin unknown; a remnant of a bedspread made on a plantation in Newcastle, Ky.; rice fanner.

Below: Coverlet, handwoven by a slave on a plantation in Virginia in 1800.

Left Bottom: Handbill advertising sale of 89 Negroes in Ryan's Mart, on Chalmers Street, S.C.

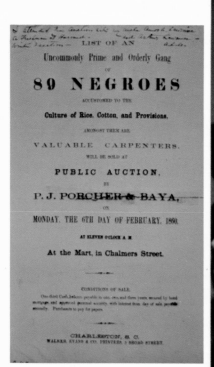

Center, Bottom Right: African rice fanner, slave made egg baskets and South Carolina coil baskets.

Center: Plaster cast taken from an iron balcony in Natchez, Mississippi.

Center, Bottom Left: Senegalese doll holding mat identical to contemporary mat at its feet. Mats from Liberia and other contemporary mats from South Carolina.

Right Bottom: Bronze portrait head from ancient Ife, 960-1160 A.D.

Bedspread woven by slaves on one of the Lovelace Plantations near LaGrange, Georgia. It appears to be an original design.

100

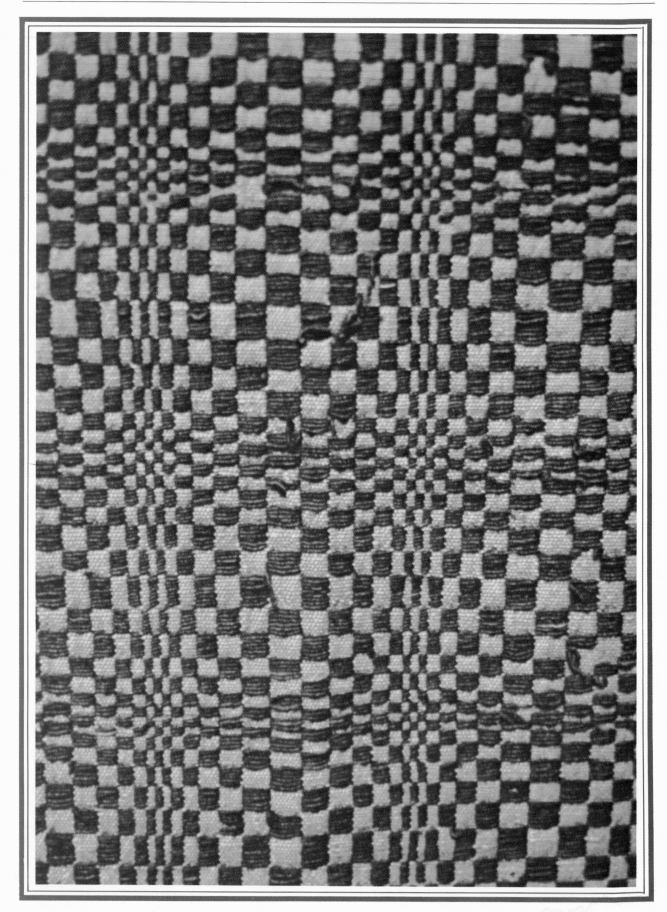

Hand tufted slave-made piecework quilt in eight pointed star.

101

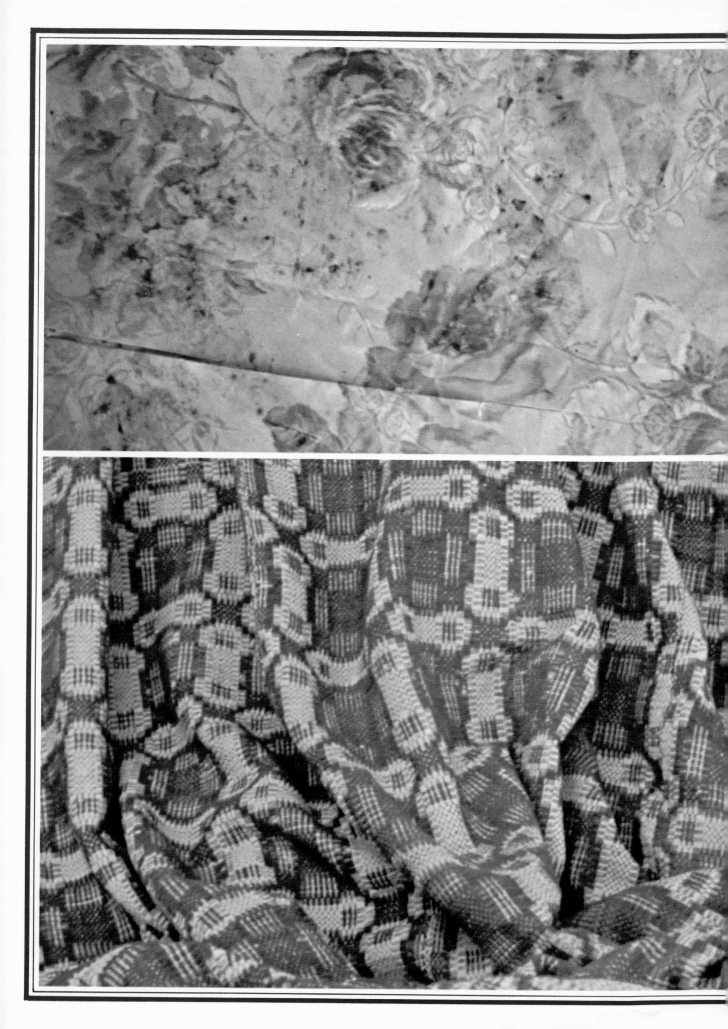

Left: Silk from a dress worn at a ball in Honor of President Washington on a visit to Charleston, S.C. Thought to have been woven by a slave.

Left Bottom: Bedspread woven by a slave near Macon Georgia, in Pattern called Catalpa Flower.

Right: Handwoven rug. Made in an original pattern by a totally blind Negro woman.

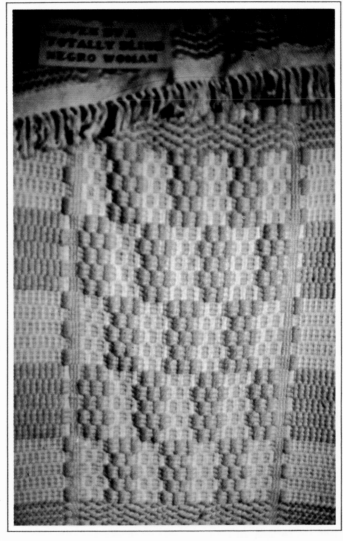

Gate at top of page was made by Peter Simmons, born a slave. Driveway gate at bottom of page is an original design by a Negro blacksmith.
Pair of wrought iron andirons from Mt. Hope Plantation.

Utensils and a pot trammel, made by slave blacksmiths.
Handforged nails, screws, bolts and hooks. Bottom: Locks and keys.
Waffle iron from a southern plantation.
Facing page; top left: Handturned mortar and pestle. Top right: Left handed
copper dipper made by a Negro blacksmith. Candle moulds made by a South
Carolina plantation tinsmith.

106

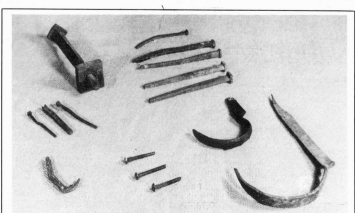

Center: Cast ironwork. Left: Gear pattern made at Riley Ironworks, Charleston, S.C. Right: Decorative cast ironwork, an acanthus leaf. Hedge clippers and a heavy garden tool that is a cross between a hoe and a pitchfork, made by a slave blacksmith.

Bottom: Wheel and gear wooden moulds for cast ironwork. Bottom left: Pee weight (block shape) used for weighing cotton; copper rice tester, mule snubber used to lock mule's jaw to prevent him from biting the farrier while being shod.

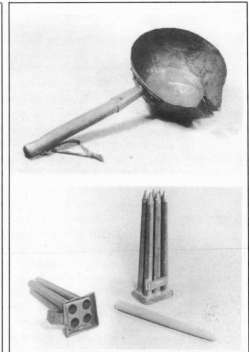

Corner china cabinet from Mt. Hope Plantation.

Slave made bureau; handturned wooden pilaster, used as a mould for cast ironwork; trunk made by a slave in 1870.

Top: Wedding shoes and dancing slippers, made by slaves.

Center: Mule shoe, worn to keep mule from sinking in muddy rice fields; child's egg basket made with curved sides so eggs would not roll out when carried on the head.

Bottom: Dolls made for white children by a slave named Emmaline.

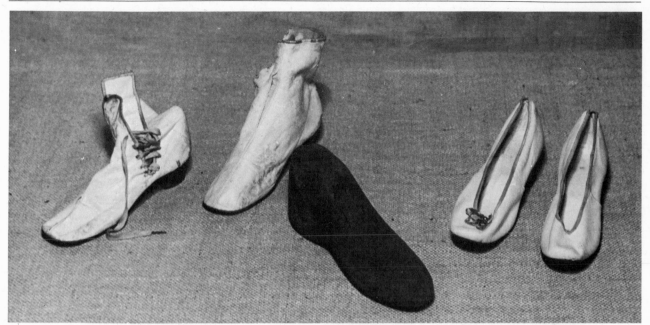

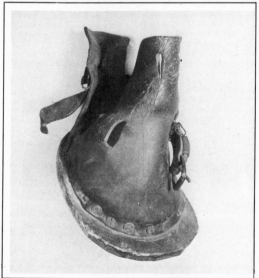

Black inventors created, developed and patented all of the following inventions
and improvements on the ideas of others.

110

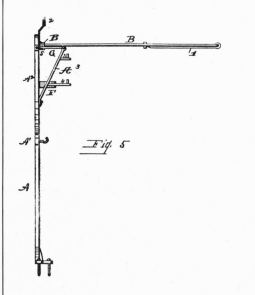

(No Model.)

W. B. PURVIS.
FOUNTAIN PEN.

No. 419,065.

Patented Jan. 7, 1890.

FIG. 2. FIG. 1. FIG. 3

Witnesses:

Inventor:
W. B. Purvis
by his Atty.

UNITED STATES PATENT OFFICE.

WILLIAM B. PURVIS, OF PHILADELPHIA, PENNSYLVANIA.

FOUNTAIN-PEN.

SPECIFICATION forming part of Letters Patent No. 419,065, dated January 7, 1890.

Application filed September 13, 1888. Serial No. 285,277. (No model.)

To all whom it may concern:

Be it known that I, WILLIAM B. PURVIS, of the city and county of Philadelphia, and State of Pennsylvania, have invented an Improvement in Fountain-Pens, of which the following is a specification.

My invention has reference to fountain-pens; and it consists of certain improvements, all of which are fully set forth in the following specification, and shown in the accompanying drawings, which form part thereof.

The object of my invention is to provide a simple, durable, and inexpensive construction of fountain-pen adapted to general use and which may be carried in the pocket. The construction is such that the ordinary action of writing causes, through the mediation of the ink-feeding devices, the ink to flow into the pen from the reservoir in volume commensurate with the duty required of the pen.

In carrying out my invention I form the holder into an ink well or reservoir in any of the well-known ways and support the pen flexibly over an outlet from said reservoir, and also provide an elastic ink-feeding tube between the reservoir and pen with a pressure-point carried by the holder to compress said elastic tube with each downward stroke of the pen, so as to expel a small quantity of ink from the reservoir-outlet in a positive manner.

My improvement will be better understood by an examination of the drawings, in which—

Figure 1 is a perspective view of my improved pen-holder. Fig. 2 is a longitudinal section of same on line $x\,x$ of Fig. 3; and Fig. 3 is a cross-section of same on line $y\,y$ of Fig. 2.

A is the holder proper and is made hollow, forming a reservoir C. The lower end of this holder terminates in two arms B and I, the former of which is the longer, preferably turned up, as at b, and made flexible at J, near the holder. Arranged between the parts B and I is an elastic tube H, connected at its upper end with the reservoir so as to receive ink, and having its other end curved upward toward the pen and terminating in a small orifice to supply ink to the pen. The elastic part or arm B has two lateral parts D, which support the pen-socket d, and which, with said socket, encircle the tube H and pressure-point I.

E is the pen and normally rests in contact with the orifice in the curved end h of the tube H.

G is a wire extending through the tube H and is preferably bent up or curved at its end as at g, corresponding to the curve in the end h of the rubber tube. This insures the orifice of the tube from becoming closed, in duces more ready flow of ink.

(No Model.)

2 Sheets—Sheet 2.

G. T. SAMPSON.
CLOTHES DRIER.

No. 476,416.

Patented June 7, 1892.

Fig. 5

Witnesses

Inventor
George T. Sampson
By His Attorney B. Pickering

UNITED STATES PATENT OFFICE.

GEORGE T. SAMPSON, OF DAYTON, OHIO.

CLOTHES-DRIER.

SPECIFICATION forming part of Letters Patent No. 476,416, dated June 7, 1892.

Application filed June 24, 1891. Serial No. 397,301. (No model.)

To all whom it may concern:

Be it known that I, GEORGE T. SAMPSON, a citizen of the United States, residing at Dayton, in the county of Montgomery and State of Ohio, have invented certain new and useful Improvements in Clothes-Driers; and I do hereby declare that the following is a full, clear, and exact description of the invention, which will enable others skilled in the art to which it appertains to make and use the same, reference being had to the accompanying drawings, and to the letters and figures of reference marked thereon, which form a part of this specification.

My invention relates to improvements in clothes-driers, the several features of which will be fully hereinafter described and claimed.

The object of my invention is to suspend clothing in close relation to a stove by means of frames so constructed that they can be readily placed in proper position and put aside when not required for use. This object I accomplish by the mechanism illustrated in the accompanying drawings, in which—

Figure I is a front elevation of the principal portion of the device with the drying-frame in a vertical position. Fig. II is a top view of the bracket. Fig. III is a front view of the

top drying-frame. Fig. IV is a side of the same. Fig. V is a side elevation at a right angle to Fig. I.

Like letters and numerals designate like parts throughout the several views.

A is a cast frame having a base, through which wood screws are driven to secure the same to the floor in the rear of a stove.

The dotted lines at H show the outline of a stove. The frame comprises the lateral arms A′, on which is a series of hooks to suspend cooking utensils, and the curved upwardly-extending arms A², to which is hinged the drying-frame B, and the left arm has an extension, to which the button 2 is pivoted. To the upper arms are bolted the arms A³, and in the upper ends of which is held the supporting wire G, on which the drying-frame B rests when the same is brought down for use to a horizontal position over the top of a stove. On these arms are lugs having pivots 3 and 4, on which are suspended brackets E., one only being shown. The rear ends of the supporting-wire G are held in orifices of the frame A. A straight rod could be substituted for this.

To the frame is attached the oblong pan F used as a receptacle.

The extension-bracket E comprises the frame with orifices for the pivots and the at

UNITED STATES PATENT OFFICE.

JOHN F. PICKERING, OF GONAIVES, HAITI.

AIR-SHIP.

SPECIFICATION forming part of Letters Patent No. 643,975, dated February 20, 1900.

Application filed July 19, 1899. Serial No. 724,406. (No model.)

To all whom it may concern:

Be it known that I, JOHN F. PICKERING, a subject of the Queen of Great Britain, residing at Gonaives, Haiti, West Indies, have invented a certain new and useful Air Ship or Launch, of which the following is a specification, reference being had therein to the accompanying drawings.

This invention relates to air ships or launches.

The object of the invention is to provide a ship or launch of great strength and durability and to combine with the float mechanism and appliances whereby the movements of the launch may be completely under the control of an operator—that is to say, that the propulsion horizontally or at any desired angle with relation to the horizon or the gradual raising or lowering of the float or the turning of the same to any desired point of the compass may be entirely and completely within the control of the operator.

The invention consists in certain constructions and combinations hereinafter described and claimed.

In the drawings, Figure 1 is a side elevation of my improved air ship or launch. Fig. 2 is a central vertical section through the same. Fig. 3 is a plan of that part of my ship below the gas dome or float, illustrating a suitable arrangement of the machinery and compartments. Fig. 4 is a rear elevation, the rudder being removed. Fig. 5 is a detail section through the gas dome or float, showing a fan and air-trunks leading upwardly and downwardly from the fan-casing. Fig. 6 is a detail section taken above one of the fan-casings.

1 is a gas dome, balloon, or float for sustaining or floating a structure 2, the latter being provided with a series of compartments and carrying a suitable motor or motors and mechanism for driving and controlling the motions of the ship. The gas dome or balloon part of my ship is preferably made in substantially the form shown in Figs. 1 and 2, and consists of a frame made of strong light tubing 3, of aluminium or like substance. The parts of the frame are securely braced or tied together. Extending through the dome and its cover are tubes 4 4 4 4, two at the forward or bow end and two near the stern. The braces or framework 5, leading from different parts of the dome, are perforated, as shown, and lead through the outer skin or cover of the balloon and are provided with safety-valves 6 6 to give relief to the dome or float in case the pressure from within becomes too great for any reason whatever. The space within the dome is entirely inclosed by silk or other suitable gas-holding fabric.

In order to charge or introduce gas to the dome, I provide an opening at one end, adapted to be closed by a cap 7 and a suitable gasket, and in order that the air within the dome may escape I provide at the other end a passage provided with a cap 8, similar to cap 7. As gas is introduced at one end of the dome air is forced out through the passage at the other end, and when it has been entirely expelled and the dome completely filled with gas the caps 7 and 8 are both closed and the balloon or float is ready for service. Suitably fastened to or connected with the dome or balloon is the structure 2, provided with compartment 9 for machinery and side compartments 10 10 for any desired purpose. The structure or hold 2 carries in compartment 9 a suitable motor 11, coupled with driving-shaft 12, the driving-shaft being operatively coupled through suitable multiplying-gearing with fans 13 near the bow of the ship and with fans 14 and driving-paddles 15 near the stern of the ship. The gearing between the driving-shaft and the driven parts consists, by preference, of sprocket wheels, pinions, and chains, as clearly indicated in the drawings.

The car or structure 2 is provided with a series of sight and ventilating ports 16 in the upper part thereof and with observation-ports 17 through the bottom of the car. An ordinary rudder 18 is connected with the ship for its general guidance and control. Leading upwardly from the fans 13 and 14 into the tubes 4 are air ducts or passages 19 19, and telescopically or loosely mounted on the ducts and within the tubes are other bent tubes or cowls 20. The crooked tubes 20 are each provided with a hole at the bend corresponding in size with that of the air-duct 19 and with a butterfly or flap valve 21, so that the air driven through the duct 19 may pass vertically through the opening or may be caused to follow the bend of the pipe. These bent tubes are conveniently operated by means of a rod or connection 22.

Leading downwardly from the cases of the fans 13 14 are air-ducts 23 23, and mounted in or on these air-ducts are other crooked or bent tubes 24, having openings at the bend or angle and adjusted to operate in a manner similar to the bent or crooked tubes 20. To control the blast from the fans, so as to cause the same to pass upwardly or downwardly, I provide gates or valves 25 for alternately opening and closing one or the other of said air-trunks. These valves are conveniently operated through connections 22ª.

In operation the balloon or gas-dome being charged and having a buoyancy sufficent to lift the car and its load the engine is started by the engineer or operator, and motion is imparted to the fans and propelling-wheels. In case it is desired to run both the fans and the propelling-wheels the crooked or bent tubes 20 and 24 are turned so that they project rearwardly, and the blast through them contributes to the propulsion or forward movement of the ship. In case the operator wishes to elevate the ship or carry it to a higher plane the cut-offs or gates to the upwardly-projecting air-trunks are closed and the valves in the downwardly-projecting crooked tubes are changed so as to direct the current downward, in which case the entire ship is driven upward. In case it is desired to lower the ship the downwardly-projecting air-ducts are closed by their valves or gates and the valve in the crooked tube 20 is turned so that the current is directed upward, in which case the ship is forced downward toward the earth. In case it becomes desirable to turn the ship around from end to end or through a considerable arc of a circle the crooked tubes projecting upwardly and downwardly are turned to the proper angle, in which case the ship may be turned promptly and readily to any desired direction much more rapidly and efficiently than could be

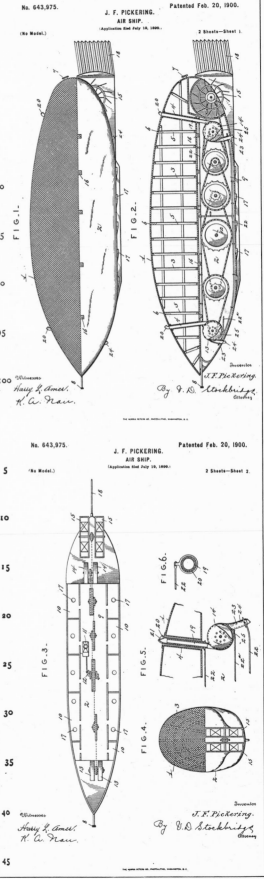

N. Rillieux.

Evaporating Pan.

Nº 4,879. *Patented Dec. 10, 1846.*

Sheet 2. 4 Sheets.

Sheet 1. 4 Sheets.

N. Rillieux.

Evaporating Pan.

Nº 4,879. *Patented Dec. 10, 1846.*

UNITED STATES PATENT OFFICE.

NORBERT RILLIEUX, OF NEW ORLEANS, LOUISIANA.

IMPROVEMENT IN SUGAR-MAKING.

Specification forming part of Letters Patent No. **4,879**, dated December 10, 1846.

To all whom it may concern:

Be it known that I, NORBERT RILLIEUX, of New Orleans, in the parish of Orleans and State of Louisiana, have invented new and useful Improvements in the Method of Heating, Evaporating, and Cooling Liquids, especially intended for the manufacture of sugar; and I do hereby declare that the following is a full, clear, and exact description of the principle or character which distinguishes them from all other things before known, and of the manner of making, constructing, and using the same, reference being had to the accompanying drawings, making part of this specification, in which—

Figure 1, Plate 1, is a longitudinal vertical section of the heater; Fig. 2, (same plate,) an end elevation of the upper part, A, thereof; Fig. 3, (same plate,) a plan; Figs. 4 and 5, (same plate,) a plan and vertical section of a modification of the mode of constructing the heater, and Figs. 6 and 7 (same plate) a plan and vertical section of another modification in the mode of construction. Fig. 8, Plate 2, is a plan of the cooler in connection with the entire apparatus, and Fig. 9 (same plate) an elevation of the same; Fig. 10, Plate 3, an elevation of a modification of the entire apparatus represented in Plate 2; and Fig. 11, Plate 3, a vertical section of the apparatus thus modified; Figs. 12 and 13, (same plate,) longitudinal and transverse vertical sections of one of the boilers or pans; Fig. 14, Plate 4, an elevation of a series of evaporating-pans; Fig. 15, (same plate,) a side elevation; Fig. 16, (same plate,) a plan thereof, and Fig. 17 (same plate) a horizontal section taken at the line X X of Fig. 14.

The same letters indicate like parts in all the figures.

My invention consists, first, of a heater for clarifying saccharine juices preparatory to the evaporating process, but which may be employed simply for heating the juice preparatory to clarifying; second, of a cooler employed in connection with the vacuum-pans or evaporators or boiling apparatus, by means of which the saccharine juices are cooled by a current of air that they may be employed as a means of condensation for the vacuum-pans, at the same time preparing them by partial evaporation for the evaporating-pans; and, third, of an arrangement of vacuum-pans or evaporators.

First, of the heater: This part of my invention is distinguished from all other things before known by so arranging it that the saccharine juice is conducted through a tube or pipe and delivered at the bottom of a vessel provided with tubes, through which the juice rises gradually to the top, receiving heat from the tubes which are heated by the circulation of hot water or steam around them, the upper part of the vessel being provided with a rim which has a pipe for the clarified juice to pass off, and a spout for the discharge of the scums which is placed a little above the connection of the pipe that carries off the clarified juice.

Of the cooler: The nature of this part of my invention consists of the employment of a current of air from a fan-blower, which passes up a vertical flume and meets the saccharine juice or other fluid falling in spray from a perforated pan or pipes above, and then in using the saccharine juice thus cooled and partly evapo-

rated for the condensing process by passing through the pipes of what is known as the "Hall Condenser" to make the vacuum in the pans. After this the juice is separated, a portion, in a partly-heated state, is fed into the first of the series evaporating-pans, and the rest returned to the cooler preparatory to another operation. By means of this arrangement I attain an economical result, for the cooling operation partly evaporates the saccharine juice, and at the same time avoids the necessity of using water for carrying on the process which saving is very important on account of the great scarcity of water in many parts of the sugar-growing country.

Of the evaporating-pans: A series of vacuum or partial vacuum pans have been so combined together as to make use of the vapor from the evaporation of the juice in the first to heat the juice in the second, and the vapor from this to heat the juice in the third, while the latter is in connection with a condenser, the degree of pressure in each successive one being less; but the defect in this plan is that when the last, called the "striking-pan," (so called from the fact that the sugar is there reduced to the condition in which it is to be transferred to the coolers or granulating-vats,) is stopped all the others in the series must be stopped also, and as this occurs every time the striking-pan is discharged and when it is used for reboiling the molasses it becomes a serious inconvenience. The object of my improvement is to avoid this inconvenience by connecting the striking-pan by a pipe governed with a cock with the first sirup-pan, so as to heat with the vapor from the said first sirup-pan, so that the connection can be closed at pleasure without interrupting the operation of the series of sirup-pans, the last of which is in connection with the condenser, instead of being in connection with the striking-pan. The number of sirup-pans may be increased or decreased at pleasure so long as the last of the series is in connection with the condenser, and it will be obvious that the striking-pan, instead of being heated with steam from the first sirup-pan, may be heated by vapor from either of the series except the last, although I prefer to take the vapor from the first; but this connection must be independent of the connection between the several sirup-pans with each other and that of the last of the series with the condenser.

In the accompanying drawings, Plate 1, A is the trough of the heater at the top of a vertical cylindrical vessel, B, containing a series of vertical tubes, b, the upper ends of which are attached to and open into the trough A and their lower ends attached to a perforated plate near the bottom of and opening into chamber, c, at the bottom of the vessel B, provided with a man-hole, c', for the purpose of cleaning out. One of the vertical tubes b extends up higher than the rest, and communicates with a pipe, D, through which the saccharine juice is introduced from the coarse strainers (in the usual manner) that separate the coarse impurities. The juice passes down this tube to the chamber c, and gradually rises in the tubes b into the trough A, and is, after being heated, discharged through the bent pipe a', the scum being discharged through spout, a, lower than the upper part of the discharge-pipe a', but above its connection with the trough, so that none but the clarified juice enter the discharge-pipe, and the scum rise sufficiently high to be discharged before the juice can escape through the discharge-pipe, to avoid the escape of any impurity with the juice. As the juice circulates through the tubes b it is heated by the waste water from the pans, which enters near the top of the vessel B, through a pipe, V, circulates around the tubes, and passes out through pipe, S, provided with a regulating-cock, s. For the purpose of starting the apparatus, and before the sugar-pans are heated, this part of the apparatus is heated by steam from a boiler, which is introduced through a branch pipe, which connects with the hot-water pipe.

The first modification of this part of the apparatus is represented in same plate, Figs. 4 and 5, and the second modification by Figs. 6 and 7, same plate. The first modification differs only from the above in having the vessel B divided into an upper and lower compartment by a horizontal diaphragm, and using two pipes, V V, for introducing the water to both of them, and two pipes, S, for discharging it, the hot water for the upper compartment being supplied from the pan working under the lowest pressure to commence heating the juice, and that for the lower compartment from the pan working under higher pressure to increase the heat of the juice as it approaches the top. And the second modification differs from the others in carrying the hot water for heating the juice through two coils of pipes or worms, b', the same being introduced into the vessel by the same means as above. This apparatus, under either of its forms, can be employed either as a simple heater to heat the saccharine juice to about 175° by the hot water from the pans or others, and then to be clarified in the usual way, or, as I prefer it, to clarify the juice by raising it to the boiling-point, but without ebullition, as the agitation would prevent the separation of the impurities, which, under the action of heat without ebullition, rise to the top in the form of scum and are discharged at the spout.

From the heater the saccharine juice is conducted to the filters in the usual manner, which is not require to be described or represented, and from these it is discharged in the vat of the cooler, (see Plate 2,) which is a large vessel, and from this it is forced through pipe N by a force-pump, I, into and through tubes of a Hall condenser, D'', through which it ascends, and a portion—about one-twentieth—is forced from the top of the condenser through a pipe, o, into the pan B'' of the boiling or evaporating apparatus, and the rest through the pipe z into a vessel, E, which delivers it to a series of horizontal perforated tubes, E'', which discharge it in spray at or near the top of a vertical chamber, G'', down which it falls into the receiving-vat F at the bottom. As the juice descends in the form of spray it is met by a current of air from a rotary fan-blower, G, which cools and partly evaporates it. When thus cooled, it is again forced, as before described, through the tubes of the condenser, and its passage through condenses the vapor from the vacuum-pan B, which escapes from the upper part of the bonnet through a pipe, F', (as represented in Fig. 1, Plate 3,) into the hollow support G', from whence through a valve in the back hollow bar, V', and thence along a horizontal pipe, to the condenser and outside the pipes thereof, (in the well-known manner of the Hall condenser, which needs no representation,) and then condensed the water and air are drawn by the air-pump H in the usual manner of exhausting a condenser. The vacuum-pan is heated by the vapor from the saccharine juice in the pan B'', and when condensed the hot waste water passes out through the pipe V to the heater, for the purpose before described. The air and feed pump is operated by eccentrics or cranks on the shaft P and the fan-

blower G by a belt from the belt-wheel Q on the shaft T, the shafts T and Q being geared together by cog-wheels R, receiving motion from some first mover. As the evaporating apparatus represented in this connection is similar to the one patented by me on the 26th of August, 1843, it is not deemed necessary to give a description of it in this connection, particularly as it must be obvious that my improved methods of heating and clarifying and cooling and condensing can be combined with any kind of evaporating apparatus, and I contemplate employing them in connection with the evaporating apparatus to be hereinafter specified. I have therefore simply described the manner of combining these improvements with an evaporating apparatus for making sugar.

From the foregoing it will be obvious that the effect of this arrangement is to condense the vapor from the vacuum-pans which communicate with the condenser, so that by the circuit the saccharine juice is partly evaporated and prepared for being introduced in the pans while it is used as a means of condensing the vapor from and keeping up a vacuum in the vacuum-pans, thus effecting a leading object of my invention—viz., carrying on the whole operation without the necessity of using water for condensation, as water is frequently very scarce in many of the best sugar-manufacturing regions of the country. The essential features of this part of my invention may, however, be used with water, but without waste, by arranging the apparatus as represented in Plate 3, Figs. 10 and 11. In this modification the quantity of water necessary for carrying on the condensing operation is placed in the vat F, and from this it passes through the pipe N to a common condenser, D'', to form the condensing-jet in the usual manner of working a condenser, and from the condenser it is drawn out and discharged into the hot well k'' by a common single-acting air-pump, H, and from the hot well the water of condensation is forced through the pipe Z by a force-pump, K, or by an air-vessel into the vessel E, which discharges it in spray through the perforated tubes, to be cooled in its descent to the vat F by the current of air from the fan-blower G, as above described. The water evaporated in the cooling-room during the descent of the spray is equal to the water produced in the condenser by the condensation of the vapor from the pans, so that the first charge of water with which the apparatus is started will continue to work it for any length of time.

Of the boiling or evaporating apparatus represented in Figs. 12 and 13 of Plate 3, and Figs. 14, 15, 16, and 17 of Plate 4: The pillars and frame-work that support the pans or boilers are made hollow to answer the purpose of the pipes for conducting liquids to be evaporated, the waste water, and the vapor by which the process is to be carried on.

The evaporating pans or boilers A' A'' A''' A'''' are all constructed alike. They are cylindrical, and the lower half at each end extends beyond the heads to form a chamber, B' and C', at each end, the heads being pierced in the lower half to receive the tubes D', that connect the two chambers. These tubes have a slight inclination downward from the front chamber, B', to the back one, C', sufficient to permit the flow of water produced by the condensation of the vapor that passes through them. The top is provided with a bonnet, E', and within there is a pipe, F', to take the vapor from the upper part of the bonnet to the front end, through which it passes into the hollow support G' in front, to be conducted to another pan or boiler. Each pan or boiler is provided with a discharge-pipe, H', at bottom, governed by a stop-cock, I', for the purpose of discharging the contents of each boiler when necessary. The series of pans having been properly charged, steam from a boiler or the escape-steam of the engine enters the first hollow pillar, K', through the pipe

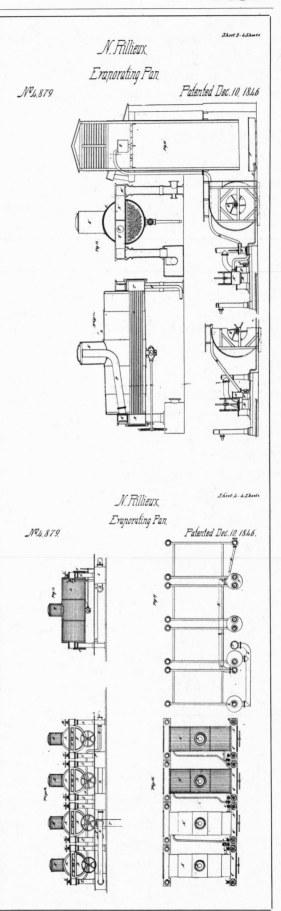

Sheet 3. 4 Sheets

N. Rillieux.
Evaporating Pan.
Nº 4,879
Patented Dec. 10, 1846.

Sheet 4. 4 Sheets.

N. Rillieux.
Evaporating Pan.
Nº 4,879
Patented Dec. 10, 1846.

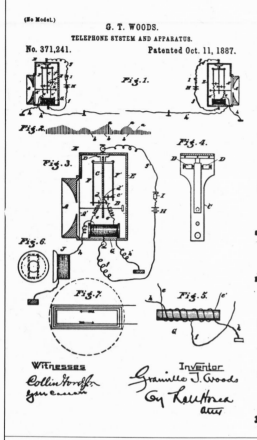

(No Model.)

G. T. WOODS.

TELEPHONE SYSTEM AND APPARATUS.

No. 371,241.   Patented Oct. 11, 1887.

Fig. 1.
Fig. 2.
Fig. 3.
Fig. 4.
Fig. 6.
Fig. 7.
Fig. 5.

Witnesses
Collin Hooffer
Inventor
Granville T. Woods
By Kall Horea
atty

UNITED STATES PATENT OFFICE.

GRANVILLE T. WOODS, OF CINCINNATI, OHIO, ASSIGNOR TO THE WOODS ELECTRIC COMPANY.

TELEPHONE SYSTEM AND APPARATUS.

SPECIFICATION forming part of Letters Patent No. 371,241, dated October 11, 1887.

Application filed June 1, 1885. Serial No. 167,140. (No model.)

To all whom it may concern:

Be it known that I, GRANVILLE T. WOODS, a citizen of the United States, residing at Cincinnati, Ohio, have invented new and useful Improvements in Telephone Systems and Apparatus, of which the following is a specification.

My invention relates to a method of and apparatus for the transmission of articulate speech and other sounds through the medium of electricity, its object being to obtain an increased force of transmission of the impulses controlling the action of the diaphragm at the receiving end; also, to obviate the disturbing effects now attributed to induction from neighboring lines.

The nature of my invention will be more clearly understood from the subjoined description, in connection with the accompanying drawings, forming part of this specification, in which the parts referred to are indicated by letters of reference.

In the drawings, Figure 1 is a diagram of the entire system arranged for use; Fig. 2, a graphical representation of the electrical current as modified and utilized in the transmission of speech or sound by my invention; Fig. 3, an enlarged vertical cross-section of the transmitting-instrument; Fig. 4, a detached side elevation of the "vibrator;" Fig. 5, a diagram explanatory of the construction of the

induction-coil and connections; Figs. 6 and 7, detail views of the receiving instrument.

My invention differs from the ordinary methods of electrical transmission of speech in two essential particulars: First, I employ in the primary or local circuit under control of the sending-diaphragm a non-continuous or intermittent current, which by the action of the sending-diaphragm is alternately shunted by media of varying conductivity in opposite directions through the primary of an induction-coil, producing, second, alternating currents of opposite polarity in the line-circuit.

By the first-mentioned feature I obtain a current of far greater inducing strength in the primary of the coil, and by the latter a reversal of the polarity of the diaphragm in the receiving-instrument, whereby the diaphragm is both attracted and repelled, thereby increasing the range and force of its vibrations and producing more vigorous air-vibrations and louder sounds. I also obtain a more forcible transmitting-current and the counteraction of static effects, whereby I am able to transmit through longer distances.

An explanation of the principles involved will be given in connection with the following description of the form of apparatus illustrated in the drawings. A designates the mouthpiece, and A' the ordinary diaphragm, of a transmitting apparatus. In rear of the dia-

---

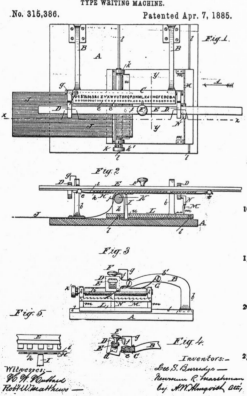

(No Model.)

L. S. BURRIDGE & N. R. MARSHMAN.

TYPE WRITING MACHINE.

No. 315,386.   Patented Apr. 7, 1885.

Fig. 1.
Fig. 2.
Fig. 3.
Fig. 5.
Fig. 4.

Witnesses:
96 W. Nuttall
Rob. W. Matthews

Inventors:
Lee S. Burridge
Newman R. Marshman
by A. W. Almquist atty

UNITED STATES PATENT OFFICE.

LEE S. BURRIDGE AND NEWMAN R. MARSHMAN, OF NEW YORK, N. Y.

TYPE-WRITING MACHINE.

SPECIFICATION forming part of Letters Patent No. 315,386, dated April 7, 1885.

Application filed March 22, 1824. (No model.)

To all whom it may concern:

Be it known that we, LEE S. BURRIDGE and NEWMAN R. MARSHMAN, citizens of the United States, and residents of New York, in the county and State of New York, have invented certain new and useful Improvements in Type-Writers, of which the following is a specification.

The object of our invention is to provide an inexpensive and yet complete type-writer of but very few parts, not liable to get out of order, requiring for its operation as few movements as in the case of expensive machines now in use, and which will admit of printing a sheet of paper of any length without the necessity of coiling or folding the same.

The invention consists in the combination, with a stationary letter-plate, of a type-plate fitted to slide parallel with the said letter-plate in hinged or only vertically-movable supports, a stylus rigid upon the said type-plate, an impression-surface, and means for feeding the paper the proper distance between the letters by the vertical movement of the type-plate.

It also consists in the combination of a laterally-movable type-plate carrying below its type-surface a plate perforated opposite to the

type-face of each letter, and an ink-ribbon interposed between the type-surface and the said perforated plate, with a stationary impression-stud, and means for moving the paper over the said stud.

It also consists in the combination, with the letter-plate and type-plate, of one or more supports, each consisting of a horizontal or overhanging arm or reach having at one end the aforesaid plates, and secured at its other end by a downward-projecting branch to the bed-plate or main support of the machine, as will be hereinafter described and claimed, with reference to the accompanying drawings, in which—

Figure 1 represents a top or plan view of our improved type-writer. Fig. 2 is a longitudinal vertical section of the same, taken on the line *x x* of Fig. 1, as seen from the front. Fig. 3 is an end elevation of the same, seen in the direction of arrow 1 in Fig. 1. Fig. 4 is a detail cross-section of the letter-plate and type-plate, as seen in the direction of arrow 1. Fig. 5 is a partial detail view, on a larger scale than the previous figures, to illustrate the operation and arrangement of the type-plate, ink-ribbon, perforated plate, and impression-stud.

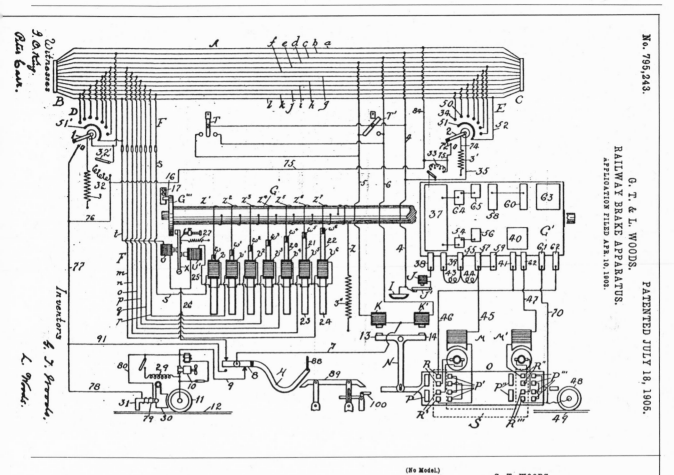

No. 795,243.

G. T. & L. WOODS.
RAILWAY BRAKE APPARATUS.
APPLICATION FILED APR. 10, 1903.

PATENTED JULY 18, 1905.

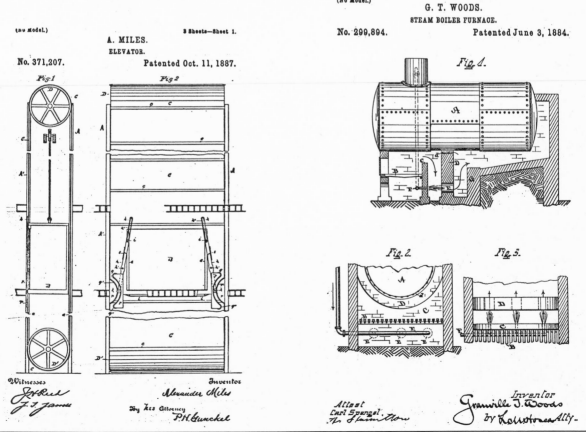

(No Model.)

A. MILES.
ELEVATOR.

No. 371,207.   Patented Oct. 11, 1887.

3 Sheets—Sheet 1.

G. T. WOODS.
STEAM BOILER FURNACE.

No. 299,894.   Patented June 3, 1884.

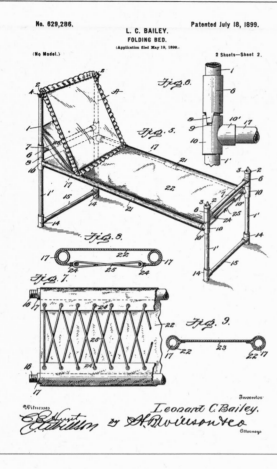

No. 629,286.

L. C. BAILEY.
FOLDING BED.

(No Model.)

Patented July 18, 1899.

(Application filed May 19, 1899.)

2 Sheets—Sheet 2.

Fig. 6.

Fig. 5.

Fig. 8.

Fig. 7.

Fig. 9.

Witnesses

Inventor
Leonard C. Bailey.
by A. H. Willson & Co.
Attorneys

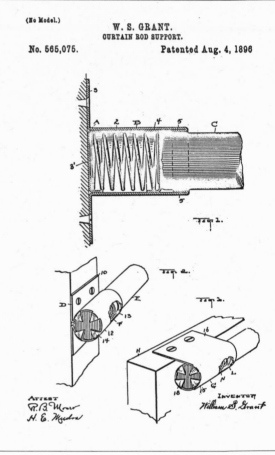

(No Model.)

W. S. GRANT.
CURTAIN ROD SUPPORT.

No. 565,075.

Patented Aug. 4, 1896.

Fig. 1.

Fig. 2.

Fig. 3.

Attest

Inventor
William S. Grant

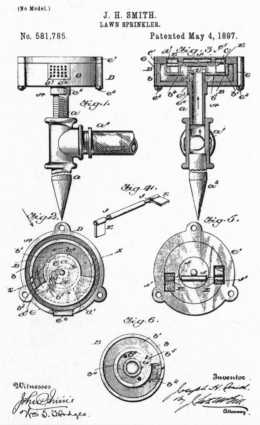

(No Model.)

J. H. SMITH.
LAWN SPRINKLER.

No. 581,785.

Patented May 4, 1897.

Fig. 3.

Fig. 1.

Fig. 4.

Fig. 2.

Fig. 5.

Fig. 6.

Witnesses

Inventor

Attorney

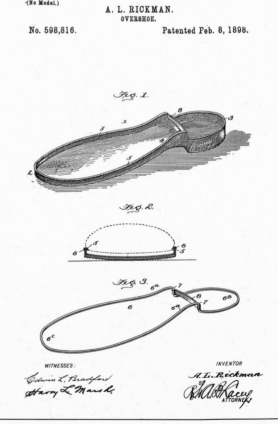

(No Model.)

A. L. RICKMAN.
OVERSHOE.

No. 598,816.

Patented Feb. 8, 1898.

Fig. 1.

Fig. 2.

Fig. 3.

WITNESSES:
Edwin L. Bradford
Harry L. Marsh

INVENTOR
A. L. Rickman
by
ATTORNEYS

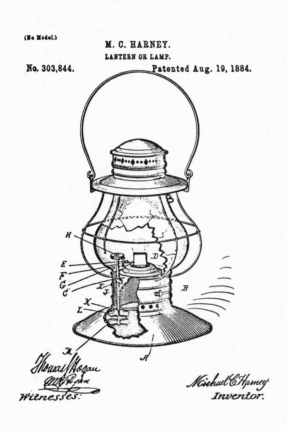

M. C. HARNEY.
LANTERN OR LAMP.

No. 303,844.   Patented Aug. 19, 1884.

Witnesses:
Thomas Hogan

Michael C. Harney
Inventor.

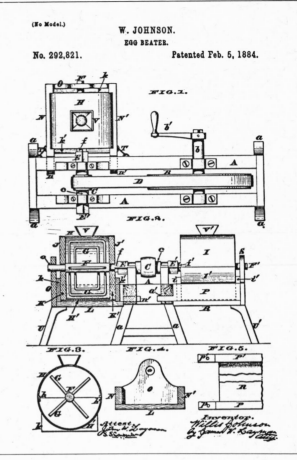

W. JOHNSON.
EGG BEATER.

No. 292,821.   Patented Feb. 5, 1884.

FIG. 1.

FIG. 2.

FIG. 3.   FIG. 4.   FIG. 5.

Attest:
John H. Leggman
S. Scornide

Inventor:
Willis Johnson
By James H. Layman
Atty.

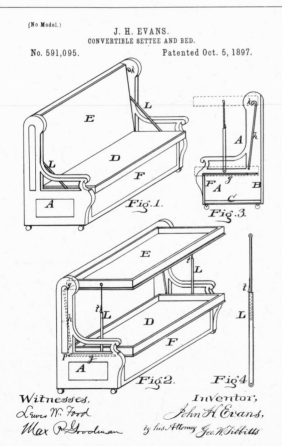

J. H. EVANS.
CONVERTIBLE SETTEE AND BED.

No. 591,095.   Patented Oct. 5, 1897.

Fig. 1.   Fig. 3.

Fig. 2.   Fig. 4.

Witnesses,
Lewis W. Food
Max R. Goodman

Inventor,
John H. Evans,
by his Attorney Geo. W. Tibbitts

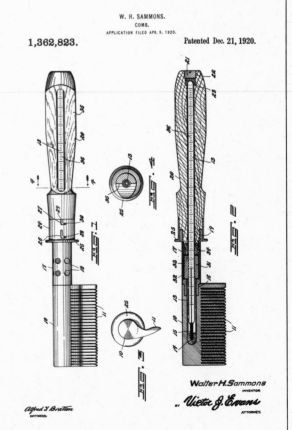

W. H. SAMMONS.
COMB.
APPLICATION FILED APR. 9, 1920.

1,362,823.   Patented Dec. 21, 1920.

FIG. 1.   FIG. 4.

FIG. 3.   FIG. 2.

Walter H. Sammons
INVENTOR

Alfred T. Bratton
WITNESS.

BY Victor J. Evans
ATTORNEY.

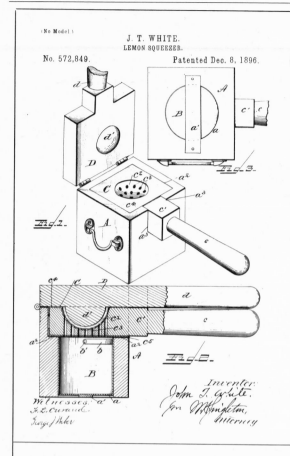

(No Model.)

J. T. WHITE.
LEMON SQUEEZER.

No. 572,849.   Patented Dec. 8, 1896.

Fig.3.

Fig.1.

Fig.2.

Witnesses: a' a
F. E. Orrand
George Aber

Inventor.
John T. White.
Jn. M. Singleton,
Attorney.

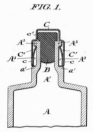
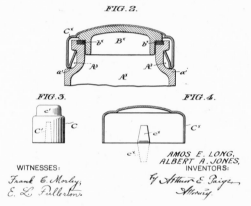

No. 610,715.   Patented Sept. 13, 1898.

A. E. LONG & A. A. JONES.
CAP FOR BOTTLES, JARS, &c.
(Application filed Mar. 10, 1898.)

(No Model.)

FIG. 1.

FIG. 2.

FIG. 3.   FIG. 4.

WITNESSES:
Frank C. Morley,
E. L. Fullerton.

AMOS E. LONG,
ALBERT A. JONES,
INVENTORS.
By Arthur E. Paige,
Attorney.

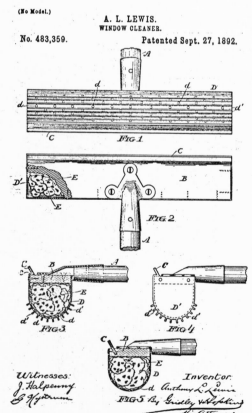

(No Model.)

A. L. LEWIS.
WINDOW CLEANER.

No. 483,359.   Patented Sept. 27, 1892.

FIG. 1.

FIG. 2.

FIG. 3.   FIG. 4.

FIG. 5.

Witnesses:
J. Halpenny
G. Wystrum

Inventor.
Anthony L. Lewis
By Gridley & Hopkins
His Attorneys.

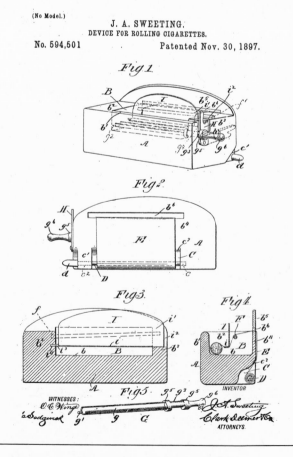

(No Model.)

J. A. SWEETING.
DEVICE FOR ROLLING CIGARETTES.

No. 594,501   Patented Nov. 30, 1897.

Fig 1.

Fig 2.

Fig 3.   Fig 4.

Fig 5.

WITNESSES:
O. C. Wing
A. Sedgwick

INVENTOR
J. A. Sweeting
Clark Deemer Co.
ATTORNEYS.

(No Model.)

R. P. SCOTT.
CORN SILKER.

No. 524,223.   Patented Aug. 7, 1894.

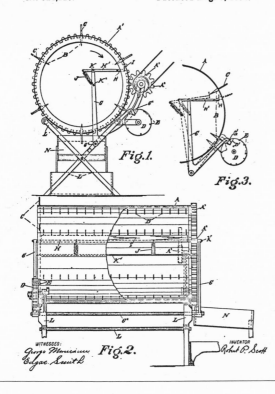

Fig.1.

Fig.3.

Fig.2.

WITNESSES:
George Monnion
Edgar Smith

INVENTOR
Robert P. Scott

(No Model.)   2 Sheets—Sheet 2.

G. T. WOODS.
APPARATUS FOR TRANSMISSION OF MESSAGES BY ELECTRICITY.

No. 315,368.   Patented Apr. 7, 1885.

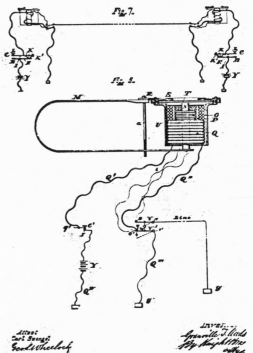

Fig.7.

Fig.8.

Attest:
Carl Younge
Geo. W. Wheelock

Inves.:
Granville T. Woods

(No Model.)

J. L. LOVE.
PENCIL SHARPENER.

No. 594,114.   Patented Nov. 23, 1897.

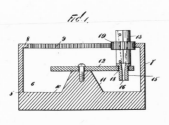

Fig.1.

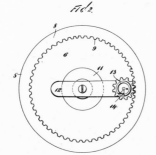

Fig.2.

WITNESSES:
John Buckler
C. Gerst

INVENTOR
John Lee Love.
BY
Edgar Tate
ATTORNEYS.

(No Model.)

G. W. KELLEY
STEAM TABLE.

No. 592,591.   Patented Oct. 26, 1897.

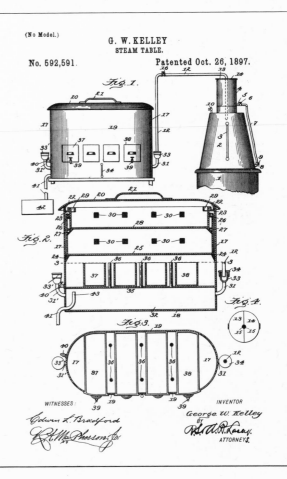

Fig.1.

Fig.2.

Fig.3.

Fig.4.

WITNESSES:
Edwin L. Bradford
J. H. McPherson Jr.

INVENTOR
George W. Kelley
BY
R. S. & A. P. Lacey
ATTORNEYS.

C. B. BROOKS.
STREET SWEEPER.

No. 556,711.   Patented Mar. 17, 1896.

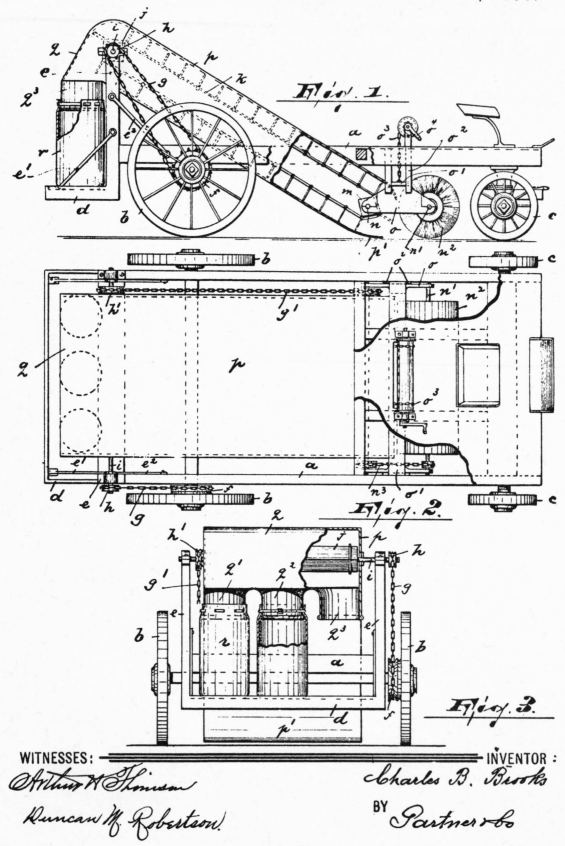

Fig. 1.

Fig. 2.

Fig. 3.

WITNESSES: INVENTOR:
Arthur H. Thomson   Charles B. Brooks
Duncan M. Robertson.   BY Partner & Co

                                              ATTORNEYS

H. L. JONES.
CORN HARVESTER.

No. 429,311. Patented June 3, 1890.

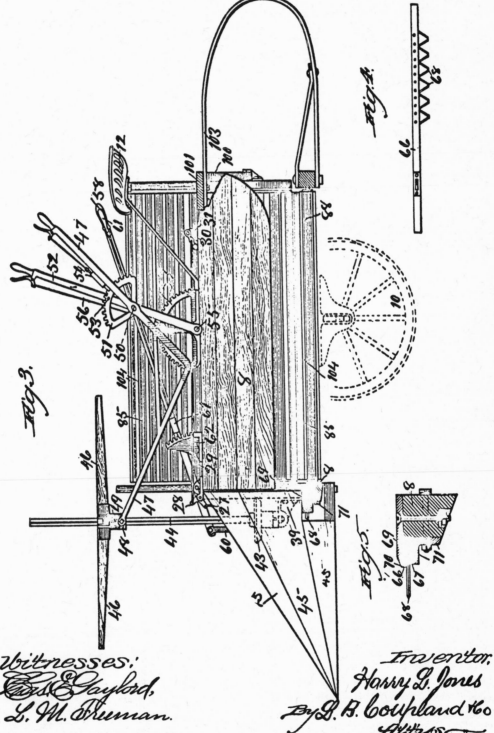

We hardly mourn his inevitable going so much as we rejoice in pleasant memory at having been associated with him in a great work for all peoples under a great man.

LEWIS HOWARD LATIMER

at his home, 64 Holly Avenue, Flushing, L. I.

December 11th, 1928

Mr. Latimer was born at Chelsea, Mass., September 4th, 1848. At ten years of age, after a few years of rudimentary education, Mr. Latimer seeming to sense the heavy load carried by his parents to support their family of four children, decided to subdue his thirst for knowledge as a school attendant and assist his father to the best of his ability, meanwhile devoting every spare opportunity, and utilizing every available source to acquire the education for which he yearned. At the age of 16 he enlisted in the Naval service of the Federal Government, serving as a "landsman" on the U. S. S. "Massasoit" from which he was honorably discharged in 1865, when he returned to Boston and secured employment as an office boy in the office of Messrs. Crosby and Gould, patent solicitors. In this office he became interested in draughting and gradually perfected himself to such a degree as to become their chief draughtsman, remaining with this firm for about eleven years. It was Mr. Latimer who executed the drawings and assisted in preparing the applications for the telephone patents of Alexander Graham Bell. In 1880 he entered the employ of Hiram S. Maxim, Electrician of the United States Electric Lighting Co., then located at Bridgeport, Connecticut. It was while in this employ that Mr. Latimer successfully produced a method of making carbon filaments for the Maxim electric incandescent lamp, which he patented. His keen perception of the possibilities of the electric light and kindred industries resulted in his being the author of several other inventions.

He was of the colored race, the only one in our organization, and was one of those to respond to the initial call that led to the formation of the Edison Pioneers, January 24th, 1918. Broadmindedness, versatility in the accomplishment of things intellectual and cultural, a linguist, a devoted husband and father, all were characteristic of him, and his genial presence will be missed from our gatherings.

Mr. Latimer was a full member, and an esteemed one, of the

EDISON PIONEERS.

40 West 40th Street New York City

First Black Commissioner
New York City – 1926

F. Q. MORTON, LL.B.
Secretary of the Commission

HOTEL CAFE OF NAIL BROS , NEW YORK.   ED NAIL
DINING ROOM.
JOHN B. NAIL   BILLIARD HALL

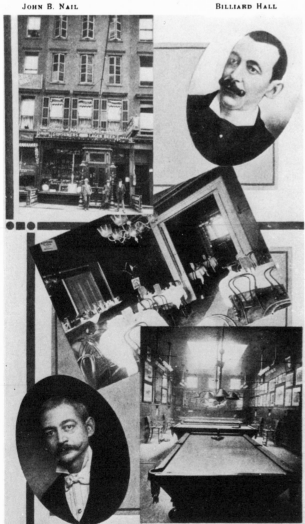

O. A. BROWNSON, AUTHOR OF *Chess Problems*, WAS BLACK.

Chess Problems

FOR SALE BY

O. A. BROWNSON, JR.,

DUBUQUE, IOWA.

LONDON: W. W. MORGAN, 67 BARBICAN, E. C.
PARIS: JEAN PRETI ET FILS, 72 RUE ST. SAUVEUR.

HARVESTER COMPANY
Centennial Medal
Honoring
JOE ANDERSON
Co-Inventor of the Reaper

OBVERSE   REVERSE

A Negro inventor: Robert Blair, inventor of anti-aircraft gun.

ADMISSION OF A COLORED LAWYER TO THE U. S. SUPREME COURT.

MANY of our readers will remember a series of engravings that were published in the Summer of 1878, illustrating a novel system of silk-culture that had been established in Huntsville, Ala. The founder of this enterprise was Samuel Lowery, a native of Nashville, Tenn., born December 9th, 1832. His father was Elder Peter Lowery, a slave, who purchased the freedom of himself, his mother, three brothers, two sisters and a nephew, and became the first colored pastor of a church in the South, preaching in Nashville from 1849 to 1866. His mother, Ruth Mitchell, was a free woman who added the pecuniary results of her energy to the funds Peter had accumulated for the purchase of his freedom. The amount, $1,000, was paid over forty-seven years ago. Samuel was the only issue of the marriage. At the age of twelve years he was placed at Franklin College, Tenn., where, in spite of his color, he commanded the respect of the faculty and pupils. At the close of the war he began reading law, and was the first colored man ever admitted to the Supreme Court of Tennessee and the Courts of Northern Alabama. In 1875 he removed to Huntsville, Ala., where he opened a school, his daughters, Ruth and Anna, introducing sewing, knitting and needlework among the poor girls, and in their leisure devoting their attention to the care of their silkworms. In the Summer of 1878 Mr. Lowery appeared before many of the agricultural and scientific societies of the North and South with specimens of the silk that had been produced at his school.

The next appearance of Mr. Lowery was in Washington on the afternoon of February 2d last, where he was one of a group of persons engaged in a scene of the most notable character. A motion had been made in the United States Supreme Court before Chief Justice Waite, that the Hon. Joel Parker, twice Governor of New Jersey, be admitted to the Bar of the Court. Mrs. Belva Lockwood, who was admitted to practice before that court by special Act of the last Congress, rose immediately and moved the admission of a lawyer from Alabama, who, she testified upon honor, possessed the necessary qualifications for practice before the Supreme Court of the United States. The lawyer whose admission she moved rose, and proved to be Samuel Lowery.

Mr. Parker and Mr. Lowery then stepped forward to the clerk's desk, placed their hands upon the same Bible and were sworn in together, standing very near to the niche where the bust of Chief Justice Taney, the author of the Dred Scott decision, is placed.

OLDEST WHALER LOST.

New Bedford Bark Canton Built at Baltimore in 1833.

[Special Dispatch to the Boston Herald.]

NEW BEDFORD, Dec. 6—For several years the oldest whaling craft in the world, the whaling bark Canton, built in Baltimore in 1833 for a merchantman, first a famous packet, and for 66 years a whaling vessel, is a wreck on the island of Maio, one of the Cape de Verde group. Word has been received here that the old craft is a total loss, although the crew was saved.

The Canton was bound on a whaling voyage from this port to the coast of Africa, and had put into the Cape de Verde Islands. There are no very good harbors in the islands excepting Fogo, where all the vessels go in the "hurricane months." In all probability a violent storm came up and the Canton dragged anchor.

Although the oldest vessel sailing from this port, the Canton was still considered the most com'ortable whaler afloat.

The Canton sailed Oct. 7 under command of Capt. Valentine Roza, fitted for about $15,500. The news of the wreck is the first from the vessel since she sailed.

Early in the 40s she was purchased by C. R. Tucker & Co. and fitted as a whaler. She also has been owned by J. F. Tucker & Son, E. D. Mandell & Co. and J. & W. R. Wing. Originally a

ship, her rig was changed to that of a bark in 1874.

She has been commanded by some of the best of New Bedford's deep sea sailors. At first she was named the Canton 2d to distinguish her from another ship of the same name. The first ship was lost. The Wings purchased the bark in 1895. She was partly rebuilt in 1883, and the repairs made on her 33 years ago, and later repairs, left her practically a new vessel.

She has chased the whale under the line where the rays of the sun started the pitch in her seams, and she has wintered in the far waters of Hudson bay, buried in snow and ice.

If the miles she has travelled could be reckoned up, the old whaler would undoubtedly be found to hold the record for long-distance sailing.

Her captain is hardly less interesting than the craft. A Brava Portuguese, he was picked up by a New Bedford whaler at the Cape de Verde islands and, starting before the mast, worked his way up to command. He began on the Josephine, that is about to sail from this port for Chili. On board the Josephine was Mrs. Marion Smith, wife of the master, Capt. Horace Smith. Mrs. Smith knew navigation, and finding young Roza willing to be taught, she gave him the instruction that made him capable of taking a vessel around the world.

After he became a navigator Roza was mate of several vessels, and finally was given command of the Canton. On the vessel with Capt. Roza was his wife, who was in the shipping articles as assistant navigator.

RUTH LOWERY, FOUNDRESS OF SILK-CULTURE IN ALABAMA.

Miss Ruth Lowery started a mid-nineteenth-century silk industry in Huntsville, Alabama. She started with a few silkworms given her by her father, Samuel Lowery, a law-yer-scientist who was admitted to U.S. Supreme Court practice in 1880. At a school in Huntsville, which was started by her father, Miss Lowery obtained silk from cocoons spun by her worms. Pupils of the school helped to spin the silk and make articles of it. The silk grown in Alabama by these blacks won prizes over Asiatic and European nations at international fairs.

Huntsville gave Miss Lowery a mulberry tree in the center of the city to provide nourishment for the silkworms. The early death of Miss Lowery ended the industry that had such a successful start.

The 15th Amendment, giving freedmen the right to vote, was passed on March 30, 1870. On March 31, 1870, in Perth Amboy, New Jersey, Thomas Mundy Peterson cast his vote. Fellow townsmen hailed him as the first black to vote after passage of the 15th Amendment, and prepared to honor him.

Princeton, New Jersey, had an election on April 4, 1870, and one Moses Schenck was the first of approximately one hundred blacks who voted, and his fellow townsmen gave him a medal for that distinction. However, when they learned that Peterson had voted on March 31, they had to identify Schenck as the first to vote *in Princeton*. Meanwhile, El Paso, Illinois, honored David A. Strother because he voted on April 4, 1870. To this day, people of that little Midwestern town claim the honor because news traveled slowly before the telephone and other electrical media of communication were invented.

Thomas Mundy Peterson got his medal from fellow citizens of Perth Amboy on May 30, 1884. Today that medal is in the collection of Xavier University in New Orleans. Following is the poem that honored Peterson when he got his medal:

And so we meet to decorate
By token on the Freedman's coat
The man who was in any State
The first to cast a Freedman's vote.

THE GREAT LAND SCHEME

In the late 1800's, Gerrit Smith, a wealthy white man, sold to city blacks, at twenty-five cents an acre, thousands of acres of land in Upstate New York. Much of it was rocky and hilly, thus unsuitable for farming. Most of the blacks abandoned the land and returned to the city. George Downing, a shrewd businessman, bought their unrecorded deeds to the land, but died before he could consummate his plan to establish a claim to the vast acreage.

Thomas Downing owned and operated a restaurant at the corner of Broad and Wall streets for forty-six years from 1820–1866, when he died. In the great fire of January, 1835, his quick wit saved the financial district from complete destruction. Water from the fire hoses froze and Downing suggested use of his large store of vinegar, which stayed the flames.

In 1842, when Charles Dickens visited the U.S., former Mayor Hone gave a reception and paid Downing $2,200 for being in charge of the service for the occasion.

THOMAS DOWNING

Thomas Downing, one of the pioneers of New York city. He at one time owned the property at No. 3 Broad street, now occupied by the Morgan-Drexler building, a structure valued at $3,000,000. Born in 1791, he knew intimately every New Yorker of prominence up to the days of the Civil war. It was he who saved James Gordon Bennett's New York Herald from going under by advancing a loan of $10,000 to Bennett.

NEGRO'S HEIRS CLAIM VAST GAME PRESERVES

Sue J. P. Morgan, Alfred G. Vanderbilt, T. L. Woodruff, and Others.

OLD DEEDS AS EVIDENCE

Assertion That Gerrit Smith, Abolitionist, Transferred Land to George T. Downing of Newport Years Ago.

Special to The New York Times.

NEWPORT, R. I., Nov. 17.—The heirs of the late George T. Downing, residing in Newport and Brooklyn, through Rufus L. Perry, a New York lawyer, have instituted proceedings to secure thousands of acres of land in St. Lawrence, Clinton, Jefferson, Lewis, Essex, and Hamilton Counties, in New York State, which are now held by ex-Lieut. Gov. Timothy L. Woodruff, Alfred G. Vanderbilt, J. Pierpont Morgan, and other wealthy men, and which it is alleged were purchased by the present holders under a misapprehension.

The territory in question takes in most of the Adirondack forests which have been turned into Summer camps.

MISS LEWIS—
THE COLORED ARTIST

From the same country as Miss Hosmer is Miss Edmonia Lewis, a colored lady, whose sex, extreme youth and color invite our warmest sympathies. Born of an Indian mother and a negro father, she passed the first twelve years of her life in the wilds, fishing, hunting, swimming, and making moccasins. Her love of sculpture was first shown on her seeing a statue of Franklin. "I will make something like that," she said to a benevolent gentleman who engaged an artistic friend in New York to permit her to visit his studio. Then she had some clay given her, and the model of an in-fant's foot, which she imitated so well as to merit praise and encouragement. "I often longed to return to the wilds," she said, "but my love of sculpture forbade it"; and here she is alone, a simple girl of twenty-three years of age, struggling against the prejudice entertained towards her race, and competing with the finished masters of the art. As she has been here only two months, she has not much to show. A bust of Col. Shaw, who commanded the first colored regiment ever formed, is a meritorious work, and has been ordered by the family of the brave Colonel who died fighting for his country. Another bust, of Mr. Dionysius Lewis of New York, is nearly completed as a commission. The first ideal work of our young artist is a freed woman falling on her knees, and with clasped hands and uplifted eyes thanking God for the blessings of liberty. She has not forgotten her people, and this early dedication of her genius to their cause is honorable to her feelings. Two other groups, the design of which are taken from Longfellow's Minnehaha, are nearly modelled. They represent first Hiawatha coming to the wigwam of his love, and laying down a deer at her feet, in token of an offer of marriage; and secondly, Hiawatha leading away his chosen bride: "So hand in hand they went."

Black and white whalers shipwrecked in the Arctic. They were rescued by the <u>Corwin</u>, U.S. revenue cutter, in 1898 after being stranded for several months.

Captain Absolom Boston, skipper of a Nantucket, Massachusetts, whaler in the 1800's, inherited his love for the sea from his father and grandfather, who were whalers before him. Edouard Stackpole, an authority on whaling, told how history was made by Prince Boston, who was the grandfather of Captain Boston.

Prince was a slave whose owner hired him out to be a crewman on a whaling ship. It was the custom for owners to collect the wages of slaves. After a year-long voyage in 1769, Prince Boston returned and the ship owner paid Prince instead of giving the money to William Swain, the slave owner. Swain brought a lawsuit, and after a jury trial, lost not only the wages but also lost a slave, as the judge ordered Prince Boston to be freed. This was believed to be the first instance of emancipation by act of a jury in Massachusetts and just about ended slavery in Nantucket.

For a time Captain Absolom Boston was skipper of the whaler industry that was owned by a group of black New Bedford residents. Included among them was Richard Johnson, who gave the name Douglass to Frederick Bailey to save him from capture as a fugitive slave.

LAND-RICH BLACKS OF COLONIAL DAYS

It is interesting to speculate on whether the attitude towards blacks in New York would be different had Dutch colonial blacks held on to their land bounties for several generations. The first eleven blacks brought to Manhattan to serve the Dutch West Indies Company were Paul D'Angola, Big Manuel, Little Manuel, Anthony Portuguese, Manuel de Gerrit de Gens, Simon Congo, Gracia, John Francisco, Peter Santomee, Little Anthony and John Fort Orange. In 1644, they presented a petition asking to be released from service. The petition was granted and each was given a large land grant by the Dutch.

Big Manuel and Angola were given a large chunk of what is now Greenwich Village. Not only did Peter Santomee get land for himself but his son Solomon also obtained thirty acres of land on part of which now stands the Flatiron building at 5th Avenue and 23rd Street. Solomon's holdings were further increased by his marriage to one of the land-rich D'Angola girls. Solomon's will in the New York Surrogates Court shows that he possessed land, houses, guns, silverware and other material things denoting wealth in those days. It must be remembered, however, that land in Manhattan increased in value only as the population was swelled by immigration. In Dutch colonial days land beyond Wall Street was considered the wilds and much of it was swampy.

A member of the Society of California Pioneers, Alvin Coffey came to the gold mines in California in 1849 as a slave. In the day he panned for gold and in the evening he cobbled shoes for the miners.

All the money he earned was confiscated by his master who then decided to take him back to Missouri. When they arrived in Missouri, Coffey was sold to a new master.

After describing his experiences in California to his new owner, he persuaded the man to permit him to return to California. The agreement

George Washington, founder of Centralia, Washington.

was that the slave would mail back an amount agreed upon by both master and servant.

Back in the California gold fields, Coffey made and saved a sum sufficient to pay his master and buy the freedom of his family. With the money he earned at the mines, Coffey bought a farm and became a wealthy man. He was able to educate his children well, one son becoming an engineer.

When he died in 1902 he was mourned by many friends. He is buried at the Oak Hill Cemetery in Red Bluff, California.

Biddy Mason, early Los Angeles landowner.

1781—Los Angeles was founded by "a strange mixture of Indians and Negroes."

With open heart surgery and heart transplants moving out of the experimental stage it is timely to go back and review the first successful operation on the human heart. It was performed by Dr. Daniel Hale Williams, a colored surgeon and some assistants at Provident Hospital in Chicago on July 10, 1893. James Cornish, a twenty-four-year-old black expressman had been stabbed and the only way his life might be saved was through an operation to close a wound in his heart.

Assisting Dr. Williams in the delicate operation were other surgeons attached to the hospital, which was founded by Dr. Williams so that black doctors and nurses could receive training and experience. The team consisted of Drs. Williams, George Hall, Howard Chislett, E. E. Barr, William Morgan and William Fuller. The patient survived and responded well. On August 2, 1893, another operation was performed to remove fluid from the pleural space. On August 30, 1893, Cornish walked out of the hospital and outlived Dr. Williams. Two years after the operation, Dr. Williams went to the Chicago stockyards just to see his former patient.

Writing for the *Medical Record* in 1851, Dr. Williams wrote that after a diligent search of medical records, he learned that the operation on Cornish was not only the first successful operation on the human heart but was also the first operation on that particular region of the human heart.

Onesimus, a slave owned by Cotton Mather, earned his freedom by suggesting a preventive against smallpox during an epidemic in 1721. It was a method of inoculation brought from Africa by the slave. Although there were many skeptics, Mather learned the method from Onesimus and persuaded people to try it, thus stopping the epidemic

But the sweetness of labour is share in the harvest...

—Damas

from spreading further. This inoculation against smallpox, introduced in America by an African slave, preceded Jenner's article on the subject by sixty-eight years.

Francisco Negro was an incorporator of the Village of Bushwick in Brooklyn. He owned land in Bushwick in 1633, three years earlier than any white man's acquisition of land there.

At Warren, Massachusetts, in 1802, died a colored man named James Marks, aged 115 years. He claimed that in his youth he sailed as a pirate with Captain Kidd and once saw Kidd cut off the head of a white boy who saw the pirate bury a treasure chest on Long Island.

According to *The Gazateer and Guide*, 1901, Vol. I, #1, free blacks in the U.S. from 1620 to 1830 owned real and personal property valued at $100,000,000.

Our Father which art in Heaven
White man owe me 'leven an pay
  me seven
Thy Kingdom come, Thy will be
  done
If I hadn't took that, I wouldn't get
  none.

LOUISIANA.   NEW-ORLEANS, SEPT. 17.
"HAUL OF PIRATES."

There are now lodged in jail in this city the following buccaneers, forming the crew of a picaroon lately captured by Capt. Loomis, in the revenue cutter, and confined on charges of piracy, &c. viz —*John Desfargues*, Captain; *Robert Johnson*, and *John Taichart*, Lieutenants; *Peter Morel, Charles Dickenson, Ephraim Tompkins, Isaac Tibbets, Thomas Thompson*, and *Wm. M'Clure*, and several others (18 in all) of French names, and negroes.— They have pretty good funds, and have engaged Counsellors to defend them. They say, their vessel is owned by *John Lafitte;* that she was commissioned at Galveztown, by the Independent Government of Texas; and that *Governor Long* approved of the equipment.—They deny having attacked the cutters; and that when they returned their fire, the cutters were under *Mexican* colours. They say, that none of their people were injured by the fire of the cutters; and that the latter had but one man wounded.

ENTERPRISE OF A COLORED MAN. James Forten of Philadelphia, is said by some to be worth $100,000, though not possessed of a dollar at twenty-one years of age. He served his time at the sailmaking business, in which he now employs over twenty hands, mostly colored persons, who cost him $10,000 a year. He is rather an old gentleman, and was in the state house yard, in Philadelphia, when the Declaration of Independence was first read. He fought also in the revolution, and is said to have been some months confined on board the infamous old Jersey prison-ship, where so many Americans died, and of which a curious account has recently been given (published by Wm Peirce) by the Rev Mr Andros of Berkley, who was also on board. The private character of Mr Forten is spoken of as highly respectable. [Journal.

On December 15, 1644, a Dutch land grant was issued to Lucas Santomee, "a physician" son of Pieter Santomee, free Negro.

The land on which Madison Square Garden in New York now rests once belonged to a black woman, Annie d'Angola.

The first land grant in the section of Brooklyn, New York, known as Gravesend was issued by Dutch governor Kieft on May 27, 1643, to a black man named Antonie Jansen Van Salee. Freely interpreted, his name was 'Anthony, sone of Jan from Salee' (Salee is in North Africa). Like most white colonists of that period, Jansen could not write and signed his land patent with his mark.

Potato Chips first introduced by Negro chef in 1865.

A black man of Indian descent has a town in Wisconsin named in his honor. He was Chief Oshkosh.

The Knights of Labor had 60,000 Negroes in a membership of 700,000 in 1886.

Hiram S. Thomas, introduced potato chips at his famous inn near Saratoga. They were first called "Saratoga Chips."

Pioneer Settlers.—Before the proper settlement of Gravesend by Lady Moody and her associates, there were two persons who took up farms within what afterwards became the town-boundaries, and for which they held individual patents.

The first patent, or ground-brief, was issued by Gov. Kieft, May 27, 1643, giving possession (retrospectively from August 1st, 1639) to one Antonie Jansen Van Salee, 100 morgen (200 acres) of land, one part to be called the *Old Bowery*, and the other the *12 morgen*.

Facsimile of Anthony Jansen's mark.

According to an old map, now on file in the town-clerk's office at Gravesend, the "Old Bowery" part of this farm was situated at the western part of the town, now covered wholly, or for the most part, by the village of Unionville; while the "12 morgen" (by which name the land is known to this day) lay a little distance from it in a south-easterly direction. Between these parcels of land lay a large strip of marsh or meadow-ground, worthy of special mention in connection with a certain "Neck" of land (or rather at that time of sand-hills) running south from the "Old Bowery," because of the legal efforts afterwards made for the possession of both.

The sternwheel steamer *Pocotempo* had a trial trip on Wednesday afternoon. She was built by Dawson Thomas (a colored man). Mr. Thomas has been long and favorably known as one of the best ship carpenters in San Francisco. The *Pocotempo* is the tenth vessel which he has either contracted or helped to build. The sloop *Angel Doll* was built almost alone by Mr. Thomas. We are proud to see our colored shipbuilder get so much encouragement. The *Pocotempo* is built for the produce trade.

From The Pacific Appeal (San Francisco), December 19, 1863.

John Chavis (1763–1838) was freeborn near the borderline between Virginia and North Carolina. He obtained an unusually fine formal education as a result of an experiment conducted half in jest by some

Dr. Alonzo McClennon, second Black appointed to the U.S. Naval Academy. When it was discovered that he was Black, he was forced to leave.

white gentlemen of means. Out of curiosity, they sent him to Princeton in order to learn if a colored youth had the capacity to take higher education. At Princeton, Chavis acquitted himself well in private studies under President Witherspoon. Chavis also studied at Washington Academy, which was once called Liberty Hall Academy and later became Washington and Lee University. A certificate that he successfully passed his studies was once filed in the Manuscript Order Book of the Rockridge County Court in Virginia but has since been lost. It may have been placed there by the gentlemen who had satisfied their curiosity.

Forten, the Sailmaker. James Forten (1766–1842) was a freeborn native of Philadelphia. During the Revolutionary War he served as a ship's cabin boy, was captured by the British, but finally exchanged so that he could return home. He followed his father's footsteps and became an apprentice sailmaker, but soon was shop foreman, and when an opportunity arose, he purchased the business from the owner, Robert Bridges.

A merchant and slave-ship owner, Thomas Willing, loaned Forten the money to make the purchase. Forten invented a new device for handling sails on a boat and his business prospered, so that he grew wealthy. He devoted much of his wealth to the abolitionist cause and for the aid of fugitive slaves. When he learned that it was the object of the American Colonization Society to colonize all free blacks outside the United States, he made the following comment:

From Some Recollections of Our Anti-Slavery Conflict, Samuel J. May. Boston, 1869.

The State Supreme Court handed down a decision in the suit by Lillie G. Taylor vs. State of Louisiana, Angelina Allen and George West, decreeing to the plaintiff a vast tract of land in the southwest section of Claiborne County, the land being rich in oil and gas deposits.

The case turned on Lillie Taylor's relation to her mother, who took the estate as daughter of Ison McGee . . .

The estate is estimated to be worth no less than twenty million dollars and it makes the litigant the richest colored woman in the world.

From Washington Colored American, May 5, 1921.

On January 14, 1895, blacks organized The National Steamboat Company and incorporated it under the laws of Washington, D.C. The corporation owned an excursion steamboat, *The George Leary*, which sailed between Washington and Norfolk, Virginia. The boat was a sidewheeler, 272 feet long, with three decks, 64 state rooms, 100 berths and a dining room—all lit by electricity. Capacity of the boat was 1,500 people.

Atlanta, Georgia, June 12—The Supreme Court of the State today sustained the will of the late David Dickson. This makes Amanda Eubanks the richest Negro in America, with a fortune of half a million. Dickson, who was related to the best families in the state, was before the war one of the heaviest slaveholders in the South, having on one plantation alone 300 Negroes. After the war he was the first prominent farmer to succeed under the new order of things and he made a fortune of $600,000. He died a bachelor, leaving many white relatives anxious for his property. They were disgusted, as well as disappointed, when they discovered that seven-eighths of his possessions were left to a colored woman and her daughter, Amanda. A fight was made on this will, the principal point made being that it was opposed to public policy to permit a white man to dispose of his property to his colored illegitimate child. The Supreme Court rules that the Negroes have the same civil rights as white people and that the will must stand.

From The New York Times, June 14, 1886.

Died May 25, 1919, at her fabulous country estate at Irvington-on-the-Hudson, Madam C. J. Walker, a colored millionairess. She was born in Louisiana, 1875, was married at age fourteen and at age twenty a destitute widow with a daughter to support. She was taking in washing in Denver, Colorado, when she got the inspiration to manufacture a line of cosmetics and develop a hair-straightening process for Afro-American women. In twelve years she was a millionaire and a philanthropist.

She spent $10,000 every year to educate colored youths in colleges, in addition to sending six youths to Tuskeegee Institute each year. Among other grants, she gave $5,000 to the National Conference on Lynching to assist their program to combat that blot on the nation. Heiress to the fortune was a daughter, Mrs. A'Leila Walker Robinson.

From The New York Times, May 26, 1919.

PAUL CUFFE, the first actual colonizer

In the early 1800's, what now is Radio City had a roadway called Cato's Lane which ran from Third Avenue near 52nd Street to the East River. It was named for Cato Alexander (1771–1858), who owned a famous roadhouse patronized by high society of the day.

William Dunlap, social arbiter of the period, wrote:

"Who has not heard of Cato Alexander's? Not to know 'Cato's' is not to know the world . . . Between four and five miles from the City Hall stands the celebrated tavern.

"Master Cato! Neither Rome nor Utica could boast such a bowl of iced punch as this! You are the Cato of Catos. Blush not, thou flower. of modesty. What do you laugh at? A flower may be dingy. Who calls you black? See how the red blood mantles your cheeks. The orange-tawny and crimson streaks, shine through the glossy ebony like northern lights through the darkness of a polar sky, cheering a six months night. Cato of Utica! Thou pride of Africa! Give me a bowl again."

From Memoirs of a Water Drinker, William Dunlap. 1837.

Some I love who are dead were watchers of the moon and knew its lore: planted seeds, trimmed their hair,

Pierced their ears for gold hoop earrings as the moon advised.

—Robert Hayden

Anti-voodoo bracelet to ward off evil. Amulets show one-eyed, legless, headless, and otherwise mutilated bodies.

VOODOO DOLLS

Voodoo dolls are most commonly used in hexing another individual. It must always be remembered that it is not the doll itself, for *it* is merely the medium which represents the intended victim. And the doll is the means by which thought transference is successfully transmitted. The doll is the means by which direct contact is established between the priest or priestess and the person to be made ill, wounded, or even sometimes killed. The actual act is the end result of powerful concentrated thoughts.

The best Voodoo dolls (most powerful and effective) *must* be made by the Voodooist who intends to cast a specific spell on someone. It must be created out of a number of items carrying the intended victim's vibrations—personal things which are used or worn by the individual, or a part of the victim's physical being. An item of clothing should be used for the doll's outer covering. Try to get something recently worn by the victim (a shirt, shorts, socks, etc.).

The doll is to be carefully stuffed with crushed straw or cotton in which a number of physical items have been blended. Such physical items would consist of some parts of the victim's body. These would include fingernail parings, skin shavings, toenail cuttings, and hair. All are known to be excellent vibratory materials for this use.

After all these materials are collected, and while the Voodoo doll is actually being constructed, an animal should be killed in a sacrificial ritual. Some of its fresh blood must be added to the doll's stuffing. Blood

is a very important ingredient, for it is said to form an extremely strong contact with life.

Better yet, if the intended victim is a woman, some of her menstrual blood is most effective. This type of blood is believed to be the most potent of all kinds and should certainly be used when obtainable.

Causing Disenchantment

Gun powder and red pepper, blended well and placed in a red flannel bag, is said to be a strong wanga.* It will create animosity between friends when tossed in their paths. This hexing agent will not really harm anyone, but it does cause many arguments and fights. Use with care.

If you would prefer to purchase similar dolls, simply locate one of the numerous stores which handle these materials. But, if you do buy dolls rather than make your own, it is advisable that you still add the same ingredients mentioned for maximum effectiveness. Open a small slit on one side and place the required materials as before. Blood, here again, is a necessity.

After the doll is properly prepared, the mental image of the victim is totally concentrated upon. His or her name is slowly repeated. Brand-new steel pins or needles are slowly stuck into the doll at various selected points. The victim will feel pain in the identical area, or may even die if the pin happens to strike a vital organ. Such practices have been commonly known to cause much physical pain and discomfort, and death. This type of wanga often gains more strength if two identical dolls are manufactured at the same time. One is to be placed between the mattress of the victim, while the other is utilized for pin sticking by the antagonist. It is said to bring about better results.

Another method of causing extreme discomfort is to tie a black cotton thread around the neck of the Voodoo doll. Use a slip knot. This can then be tightened and loosened

---

* Wanga—A terrible Voodoo hex, curse or spell. A work of black magic against an enemy.

at will. It causes the victim to choke, gag, and fight for air. This too is said to cause death if the houngan or mambo deems it necessary. Again, concentration is a major factor in proper thought transference of this type.

Voodoo dolls, jabbed full of pins, and accompanied by black wooden crosses, burning black candles, tiny black coffins, and black crepe wreaths, are often placed on the doorstep of an enemy to bring evil down upon him. This has been popularly practiced in New Orleans for over two centuries.

When the cloth for making the doll has been carefully cut out, sew the pieces together but leave an opening in one side for stuffing. After everything has been carefully added, hand stitch the final section. Use only white cotton thread for this purpose. Size is of no consequence.

CASTING A HEX

To Bring a Quick Death

Write the person's name on a small piece of plain white paper. Repeat seven times. Split a fresh fish down the middle with a brand-new steel razor blade and insert the paper inside. Pour a whole can of black pepper over the paper. Sew the fish back up with black cotton thread. Bury in your enemy's backyard without his or her knowledge.

Death with a Cow's Heart

Purchase a fresh cow's heart from your local market. Split it open. Write the person's full name on a scrap of plain white paper and insert it in the heart. Cover with a very strong tobacco (cigar or pipe) and carefully wrap in a clean cotton cloth. Tightly tie with black cotton thread. Bury near the market where the heart was purchased. Its Voodoo power will take effect within two short weeks.

To Hex a Person's Mind

Mix a pot of your favorite vegetables and make into a tasty soup. Catch and skin a live rat. Drop it into the boiling soup blend. This is

considered to be a very easy wanga to prepare, and also one of the most effective. It is said to work almost instantly after you induce a person to eat some of the soup.

Butter Imagery

Voodoo images are often made from molding butter into a human male or female shape, according to the sex of your victim. The completed butter figure is then baptized with holy water and given the complete name of the person to be conjured. Then proceed to stick with numerous new pins, or better yet, a honey-locust thorn. The butter image is carefully placed where the bright sun will readily strike it. As it begins to melt and eventually disfigures, the human counterpart is said to dwindle away. He or she eventually dies unless the hex can be broken.

Clay Dolls

Voodoo-hexing dolls can be shaped out of raw mud, but such material must come from a crayfish hole. If none is available, use clay taken from a river's mouth. Either one will work. This completed doll is also to be given a name and thoroughly stuck with many pins, then placed in the oven to bake until it is completely dried out. It is believed to cause great discomfort to an enemy, and causes him to lose weight. Rheumatism is said to harshly strike the hexed person. Death could easily be an end result of this hexing method, especially if vinegar is poured over the baked image while it is still hot.

Paper Dolls

Take a newspaper and cut human images out of it on the change of the moon. Cut seven in all. Place one on top of the other and give it the name of anyone you desire to place a hex upon. A brass pin is then to be stuck in the image, starting at the head and slowly working downward to the feet. Then place the perforated newspaper figure in a small box and bury it when the sun goes down. This wanga is generally believed to bring death to an enemy in a very short period of time, usually within seven days or seven weeks.

SORCERY WITH A VOODOO DOLL

To Attract Great Wealth

Take plain parchment paper and carefully write down the amount of money you desire. Use only Dove's Blood Ink for best results. Be sensible and request only the amount you really need (the cost of a new suit, a dress, automobile, etc.). Ask for enough to cover the price of any *one* item. If more is requested, the energy force will be scattered and nothing will be accomplished.

After having written the amount you desire on the piece of parchment paper, tape, pin, or glue it to the bottom of the Voodoo doll's feet. Stand the doll on a piece of clean white cotton cloth and carefully anoint it with Money Oil beThen sprinkle liberally with Money Drawing Powder. Tie a green ribbon or string around the doll's waist while repeating the following words:

Money is really needed,
Money is really desired,
Money rightfully mine,
Come at the present time.

Light some Money-Drawing Incense and read Psalm 4. Carefully wrap the doll in a white cotton towel and hide in the corner of a dark closet. Repeat this entire procedure every evening after the sun sets. You should receive the cash you need by the seventh day. When you do obtain the necessary money, burn the doll and scatter the ashes in the wind. If the doll cannot be burned, simply bury it some place other than your own yard.

To Attract a Lover

Write the name of a particular person on a piece of parchment paper with Dove's Blood Ink. If no one special is on your mind, and you seek a lover, simply write "My true love." Tape, pin, or glue this paper to the bottom of the Voodoo doll's feet. Stand the doll on a clean red cloth and anoint with Luv, Luv, Luv Oil, and sprinkle with French Love Powder. Mix equal parts of Compelling Incense and Love Incense and light. While burning, re-

cite Psalms 45 and 46. Wrap the doll in red cloth and carefully hide it in a dark place. Repeat this entire procedure daily until you have gained your objective. When a lover appears, burn or bury the doll in an isolated area.

To Stop Infidelity

Write the name of the unfaithful person (husband, wife, or lover) on a piece of clean parchment paper and attach to the back of the Voodoo doll. Anoint the entire doll with Compelling Oil and lay it on a piece of scarlet satin. Sprinkle the doll thoroughly, on both sides, with Come To Me Powder and say the following:

With powerful love powders all over thee,
Hurry, hurry—Come right back to me!

Repeat this entire procedure for three consecutive days. On the third day, after completing the entire ritual, wrap the doll in the scarlet satin and carefully hide it in a dark closet or any other secluded place. The mate or loved one will be forced to return and will stop playing around.

To Cross a Person

The "Doll in a Jug" is one of the oldest methods of Voodoo conjuration known today. And it is one of the easiest to perform satisfactorily. Take a cloth doll and stuff into a brown porcelain jug. Tightly cork and then bury it in any cemetery on the breast of a grave. Your enemy is said to die in nine days or less, or nine months or less. Death may be made to come even sooner if you also take a quart of ashes and bury them in the victim's backyard.

To Torment Someone

Take a vase-shaped Voodoo doll (Paquet Congo) and anoint the feathers with some Black Art Oil, and the body with Obeah Perfume Oil. Write the full name of the person you desire to curse on a clean piece of parchment paper. Use only Dove's Blood Ink.

To Help Lonely People Find Lovers

Take a piece of parchment paper and using Dove's Blood Ink, write the following poem:

Loved one to be, possible mate,
Come forth now, it is fate.

Anoint the Voodoo doll with Attraction Oil and then pin, glue, or tape the parchment on the back. Lay the doll on a clean piece of white cotton cloth, and sprinkle both the back and the front with Love Powder (Red). Recite the following seven times:

This is a person I sincerely woo,
It is my love, my lover so true.

When finished, wrap the doll tightly in the white cotton cloth and hide it in a secluded place. No one must be able to see it. This ritual must be accomplished each night until you meet the person you desire. When he or she finally comes to you, burn the doll and toss the ashes in the wind.

To Hinder Someone's Success

Write the person's full name on a clean piece of plain white paper. Use only black ink in this instance. Take a Voodoo doll and cut open the back. Stuff the paper inside. Add some bitters, red pepper, and black pepper. Sew the back tightly with black cotton thread. Then proceed to tie the doll's arms behind it, and place a black veil over the face. Anoint with Black Art Oil and sprinkle with Crossing Powder. Place the doll in a dark corner of the room, in a kneeling position. This procedure is said to create great frustration in the person you have hexed. He or she will not be able to get ahead in life. Obstacles will be encountered at every turn so long as the doll is not disturbed. Anoint with fresh Black Art Oil once every seven days.

WARDING OFF EVIL

To Protect Yourself

If you known of someone who is trying to cross or hex you, it is a relatively easy matter to avert evil.

Blend the following ingredients in bathwater:

Garlic	7 small pieces
Thyme	A pinch
Dry basil leaves	7
Parsley flakes	7 can shakes
Sage	7 can shakes
Geranium Oil	7 drops
Salt peter	A pinch

Carefully mix the above items well, and use for a special protective bath on Tuesday, Thursday, and Saturday. After bathing for fourteen minutes, dry completely off and thoroughly rub down with bay rum. Follow this with a second rub down using Verbena Perfume Oil. This procedure is said to uncross any hexed person, and also prevents them from being hexed for a period of seven weeks.

Miscellaneous Hex Breakers

Get a friend to read a Bible verse backwards to you. Then fold the page, place a silver fork on it, and close the book. Put the Bible under your pillow before going to sleep. Even further precautions may be taken in this regard. Recite the "Lord's Prayer" backwards before actually lying down.

Burning an old pair of shoes sprinkled with sulfur is said to force all evil spirits out of a home.

Pasting newspapers on your walls is said to be a good protection from evil spirits. The spirits will have to stop and read every word before causing any harm to the occupants.

Fingers tightly crossed while passing a cemetery is said to protect an individual from evil spirits of the dead.

Salt sprinkled all over a house stops evil spirits from doing harm. Black pepper carried in the pockets of any piece of clothing accomplishes the same thing. A brand-new knife carried in a left pant's pocket protects men, and matches carried in the hair of a woman will stop all evil from doing her harm.

A Blood Hex Breaker

Fresh drops of human blood must be placed in a pan of sugar or cane syrup. This is said to help overcome many evil influences. It also removes obstacles in your path.

Protection from Evil

Brick dust has always been popular in New Orleans as a strong protector from evil spirits. People merely scrub their front door stoop with some of this dust.

Another extremely common protective device is attained by nailing a dung-coated horseshoe above the door, or one which has been sprinkled with Four Thieves Vinegar.

Catholics often nail a saint's picture over their doors in an effort to offset an evil curse or hex. The saints represent various Voodoo loas.

To Avoid Harm

Find a live turtle and cut its heart out. Eat the heart raw while it is still warm. This is a very old Voodoo secret which is said to protect one from all harm.

Goat's milk is also a good hex breaker. Boil a pint of this liquid and blend with a small can of parsley flakes. Let cool but drink down while still warm. It is said this recipe will protect you from coming under the power of anyone who might attempt to hex you.

VOODOO CHARMS

Human Hair Charms

Many Voodoo believers claim that the hair of a person, or the dust from a footprint, make the most powerful wangas known today. Care is taken to never leave loose hair lying around in a home, for someone may pick it up and use this material against its owner. Human hair is commonly used in creating death potions or harmful medicines, for use against the individual from whom the hair was obtained.

When anyone walking through a house happens to leave footprints, these prints must be carefully swept up prior to leaving. An enemy can collect the dust from such a print and utilize it in a wanga against the person who made it.

Garlic Charms

Garlic is believed to turn away spirits of the dead and protect an individual from all evil. Pieces of garlic are placed in a small cloth sack and tied around the neck as a powerful Voodoo charm. Use red flannel when possible.

Cat Charms

Voodoo practitioners place a great deal of faith in charms made from cat's teeth, claws, or whiskers. This is especially true when such items are taken from a lion or a tiger, but a domestic cat will usually suffice. Wrap any of the above in a cloth sack and carry with you at all times.

Hanging a black cat's tail over your front door is said to keep all evil away from your home.

The hair of a black cat should always be saved and tossed over the left shoulder when under any kind of duress. It is believed to change bad luck to good.

Simple but Unusual Charms

A broom hung over a door is said to keep sickness and disease away from a home. An old, well-used broom is best to use for this purpose.

Snake vertebrae are to be placed in a sealed container and buried in the backyard at midnight. This charm is said to cure backaches and prevent back disorders.

Champagne poured on all four corners of your property, on a moonless night, is said to guarantee the assistance of good spirits in time of need.

Mustard seed planted by your front and back door will bring success and luck in everything attempted. This charm has always been extremely popular with Voodooists.

To Make Dreams Come True

Take a large seashell and fill it completely with tar. Cover the mouth of the shell with an ember of charcoal and allow to smolder for one minute. Sprinkle powdered Ambergris on the coal and proceed to meditate and pray for what is desired. Then, on the first Friday following, at 3 A.M., go outside and pick three Violet Leaves. Repeat the names of any three helpful loas, one loa for each leaf picked.

Place these three leaves and the now cooled seashell under your pillow. Do this just prior to retiring for the night. Upon awakening, write down your dream of the evening before. Tell no one about it or the spell will be broken.

A Good Luck Charm

All of the following materials are to be carefully collected and blended in a large cast iron pot. After thoroughly mixing, place the feet in the pot and soak. Then scrub.

Beer	1 bottle or can
Cider	1 pint
Raspberry soda	1 bottle
Dried Orris Root	1 pinch
Dried Basil Leaves	1 pinch
Cornmeal	¼ cup
Gingersnap	1
Birdseed	1 pinch
Cinnamon	1 pinch
Cloves	1 pinch
Congris	1 tablespoon
Olive oil	1 tablespoon
Sugar	1 tablespoon
Gin	1 shot

After completing the above instructions, allow the feet to dry. Before putting any shoes on, dust their insides with dried Basil Leaves, cinnamon, cornmeal, and steel dust. Good luck will always be with anyone who follows these directions. The gods are said to remain ever close at hand to guide the feet to eventual success. This is an extremely potent recipe and it is commonly utilized in Voodoo groups.

LEGAL AIDS

Triumph in a Lawsuit

When you are served with legal papers, fold in four parts and place in a piece of red flannel. Then add some Five Finger Grass and sprinkle with Geranium Oil. Hide all these items under your bed for seven days and nights. It is said to soothe the anger of the law until the time you are to come before the judge.

During this same period, sprinkle every corner of your house with Peace Water, and carry a piece of John the Conqueror Root with you at all times. Allow no one to see or touch this root until the trial is over.

On the night before you are to

appear before the judge, you must burn three Peace Candles and an equal mixture of John the Conqueror Incense and Helping Hand Incense. This is said to make the testimony of an enemy unbelievable to the judge and to confuse him while speaking against you in court. Follow the above procedures, and you can triumph over all enemies.

To Control a Court

Take a plain piece of white paper and write the name of the accused three times. Follow this by writing the name of the judge and the prosecuting attorney three times each. Give this paper to the accused and have him wear it in his left shoe. Then mix the following ingredients:

Rose Geranium Perfume Oil	3 drops
Verbena Perfume Oil	3 drops
Lavender Oil	3 drops
Jockey Club Perfume Oil	½ ounce

Shake the above items thoroughly and give to the accused to use as needed. Instruct him to rub seven drops on his body every day before each court appearance and to rub a little all over his right hand.

While all the above is being accomplished, a trustworthy friend must be induced to go into the courtroom while it is empty, and sprinkle all four corners, the judge's seat, jury box, and the prosecutor's chair. Victory is certain if each step of this ritual is properly carried out.

To Silence a Witness

Go to your local market and purchase a fresh beef tongue. Take it home and split it open with a brand-new razor blade. Write the name of each court witness on a plain piece of white scrap paper. Cut each name carefully from the paper and mix them all up. Stuff into the split tongue and add plenty of red pepper.

Pin the tongue together with nine brand-new needles and tie a wire around it. Hang in your oven to dry for thirty-six hours. A fireplace works even more suitably, for you can smoke the tongue for a higher

degree of magic potency. Then take the dried tongue out of the oven or down from the fireplace, and carefully place it on a fresh cake of ice or on a large pile of ice cubes. Stick seven Black Candles in the ice and light. Have the accused read Psalm 22 for general legal problems and Psalm 35 if the charge involves murder.

LOVE SORCERY

Voodoo Aphrodisiacs

Sucking the juice from codfish bones is believed to be one of the best restorers of sexual potency. Voodooists use this with great regularity.

Bamboo shoots are also said to be an excellent aphrodisiac, as are almonds when properly prepared. Almonds are believed to produce fertility, as well as act on both sexes as a love charm.

Special types of grass are utilized in Voodoo as potent love charms or aphrodisiacs.

When a male becomes impotent, a special love gris-gris should be made from a black cat's testicles. Completely dry the testicles and place them in a chamois sack. Sew the top tightly together. This charm is to be worn by the impotent male's genitals for a period of at least thirty days. His sexual vigor will renew itself after this period of time.

To Force a Proposal

Take a pumpkin and carefully hollow it out. Stuff with boiled potatoes and fresh bread. Wrap a new bar of castile soap with the pumpkin vine itself. Place both items near a lover's front door. This must be done by a girl's mother or a boy's father in order to make it work effectively. It is said to force the one you love to propose within a short period of time.

A Simple Contraceptive

Both prospective lovers must drink a glass of fresh rainwater and turn the glasses over on a table before going to bed. This act is said to make conception impossible.

When You Are Spurned

If a girl is spurned and finds a lover

will not seriously consider marrying her, she can easily get even with him. A bright red candle is nailed over his front door. This act is said to bring the wrath of evil loas down upon his head until he finally repents.

A Simple Love Charm

Two garlic bulbs are punctured with a steel nail which is left in to hold both bulbs together. The top bulb represents the individual making the charm, and the bottom bulb represents the desired lover. Hide in the corner of a dark closet until the one you care for begins to respond. This garlic charm is said to make a lover overflow with passion.

To Make a Man Impotent

If a man has sexual relations with a woman and then treats her rather badly or breaks his word, she can very easily get even with him. According to ancient Voodoo practices, all she must do is keep the cloth used for cleansing both parties after their relations. This towel, washcloth, or rag is first tied in seven knots. It is then weighted down and dropped into a river. The man is said to lose his sexual virility until amends are made or until the girl forgives him and retrieves the cloth. Only she can break the spell by untying the seven knots. If the knotted wiping rag is lost, he will never again regain his ability to perform sexually.

Keeping a Woman Faithful

The ground spine of a fish (any kind) mixed with the yolk of one hard-boiled egg and placed in a woman's navel will keep her true. If any other man makes love to her, he is liable to die within seven days. And this mixture is said to make her desire only the man who placed it in her navel. She is unable to respond to another lover's advances.

The Handkerchief Trick

A handkerchief wiped under the armpits and then wiped across the face of someone of the opposite sex is believed to secure a new lover. This is a very ancient Voodoo trick which gained widespread popularity in New Orleans.

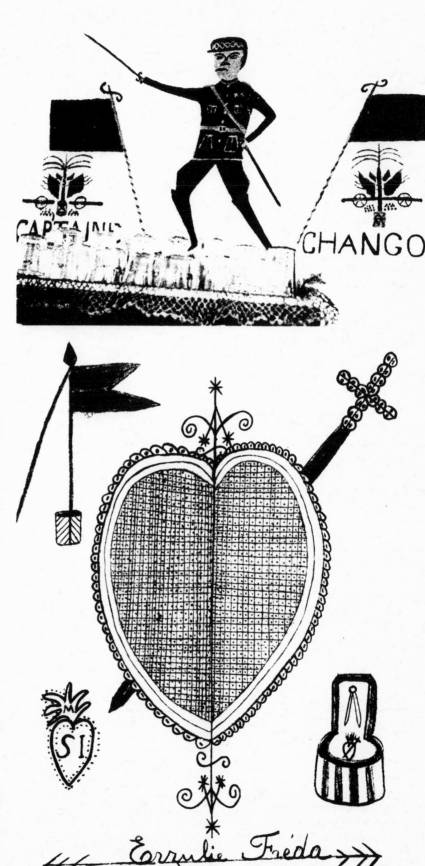

No power can stay the mojo
when the obi is purple
and the vodu is green
and Shango is whispering,
Bathe me in blood.
I am not clean.

—Henry Dumas

In 1822, when the verdict was handed down to execute Denmark Vesey and his fellow conspirators for their plot against the whites of Charleston, S.C., the first to be executed was Gullah Jack. He had caused many slaves to join the conspiracy because they were convinced that he was invincible. At one meeting of the plotters he placed a chicken on a table. Gullah Jack performed a witchcraft ceremony over it and the men scrambled to get pieces of it. Then Jack said, "Just like that we pull the Buckra to pieces."

For people in love, who wanted the beloved to return their love, "High John, the conquerer" has had a long and successful pull on the market.

A remedy for poison brews made from the Jamestown weed or from the deadly nightshade was finely ground green glass sifted through muslin, which the patient had to swallow in food or drink. When not finely powdered, flinty particles of glass sometimes worked their way through the walls of the intestines and caused inflammation and lingering death.

SANITÉ DÉDÉ was succeeded by the celebrated Marie Laveau, who was at once the most powerful of all the Voodoo queens and the most feared of the hobgoblins with which the mothers and nurses of early New Orleans frightened their unruly children; so awe-inspiring was the bare mention of her name that a decade

after she died it still had a salutary effect upon mischievous youngsters. In Negro folk-lore Marie Laveau was ranked even higher than Bras Coupe or Annie Christmas; her magical gifts were infinitely superior to those of the one-armed outlaw, and it was recognized among the blacks that with her powers of sorcery she could easily have performed, had she wished, any of the feats attributed to the legendary heroine of the river. She dominated Voodooism in New Orleans for at least forty years, and only once was her supremacy even threatened. That was about 1850, when a quadroon woman named Rosalie, who for several years had aspired to the Voodoo throne, imported from Africa a large —almost life-size—doll which had been carved from a single tree-trunk. Painted in brilliant colors and bedecked in beads and gaudy ribbons, this doll formed such an impressive spectacle, and was so obviously a source of magic, that Rosalie began to make considerable headway in her schemes of rebellion. But Marie Laveau met the situation in a characteristically masterful manner. She simply walked into Rosalie's house on a day when the quadroon was absent, and walked out with the doll. Rosalie immediately had her arrested, but the Voodoo queen presented such an imposing and carefully prepared array of proof that the court decided she was the rightful owner of the doll and awarded it to her. Possession of this potent fetish, together with a magic shawl which she said had been sent to her by the Em-

peror of China in 1830, made her authority secure.

Marie Laveau was a free mulatto, and was born in New Orleans about 1796. On August 4, 1819, when she was in her early twenties, she was married to Jacques Paris, also a mulatto, the ceremony being performed by Pere Antoine. Paris died in 1826, and a year or so afterwards Marie Laveau went to live with a mulatto named Christophe Glapion —there is no record of their marriage. She had a daughter in February 1827—whether by Paris or by Glapion is unknown—who was named Marie and who subsequently married a man named Legendre. In her youth Marie Laveau was renowned among the free people of color for her beauty, and especially for the symmetry of her figure. By profession she was a hairdresser, and as such gained admittance to the homes of fashionable white ladies, where she learned many secrets which she never hesitated to use to her own advantage. As a lucrative side-line she acted as procuress for white gentlemen, furnishing quadroon and octoroon girls for their pleasure, and also served as go-between and letter-carrier in clandestine love-affairs among her white clients. She became a member of the Voodoo cult about the time her husband died, and usurped Sanité Dédé's place as Queen half a dozen years later. Sanité Dédé was then an old woman.

For several years after she became queen of the Voodoos, Marie Laveau spent much of her time in a flimsy shanty on Lake Pontchartrain, which was sometimes used for meetings of the cult. One day while she was there a hurricane passed over New Orleans and the lake, and the shanty was torn from its foundations and hurled into the water. Marie Laveau sought safety on the roof, but when several of her followers tried to rescue her, she discouraged their efforts, crying out that the Voodoo god wanted her to die in the lake. She was finally induced to accept assistance, however, and according to the tale which was freely spread among the Negroes, the moment Marie Laveau reached the shore the fury of the storm abated and the lake became as smooth as the surface of a mirror.

A few years after this extraordinary manifestation Marie Laveau performed the feat which made her a woman of property and enormously enhanced her prestige among both whites and blacks. The son of a wealthy New Orleans merchant, having fallen in with bad companions, was arrested in connection with a crime, and although he was certainly innocent, the police had gathered a great deal of evidence which appeared to prove his guilt.

In desperation the young man's father implored the aid of Marie Laveau. On the day of the trial the Voodoo queen placed three Guinea peppers in her mouth and went to the Cathedral, where she knelt before the altar rail for more than an hour. Then she hurried to the Cabildo, gained admittance to the courtroom, and deposited the three peppers under the judge's bench. The trial was duly held, and although the evidence was overwhelmingly against the young man, he was found not guilty. His happy father was so impressed by this display of Marie Laveau's power that he not only fed her handsomely in cash, but also gave her a cottage on St. Ann Street between Rampart and Burgundy, not far from Congo Square. This house was the home of her descendants until 1903, when it was torn down.

Marie Laveau was born a Roman Catholic, and appears to have returned to the Church—if, indeed, she ever left it—a decade or so after she became the head of Voodooism in New Orleans. Throughout the remainder of her life she was extraordinarily devout and attended mass almost daily at the Cathedral. At the same time she retained her office as queen of the Voodoos, and in this guise sold vast quantities of "gris-gris" and other charms and conducted an extensive practice in sorcery so successfully that even among otherwise intelligent whites the belief was widespread that she possessed supernatural powers. So great was the fear in which she was held by the Negroes that her open allegiance to two faiths was never questioned. Nor did the Voodoos protest when she revised the ritual of the cult to include worship of the Virgin Mary and the Catholic saints, so that Voodooism became a curious mixture of West Indian fetish-worship and perverted Catholicism. Before Marie Laveau's time Voodooism in New Orleans was not only frowned upon by the authorities, but every effort was made to suppress it. But Marie Laveau surmounted this obstacle by popularizing the worship of the Voodoo god, and obviated the likelihood of police interference by inviting politicians, police officials, sporting men and newspaper reporters to attend the annual festivals on St. John's Eve.

Dancing was one of the slaves' favorite pastimes, enjoyed on special holidays and Saturday nights. One observer described the jogs and shuffles as "dancing all over," every part of the body moving at the same time.

During her reign these celebrations became almost as popular among sightseers as the weekly dances of the slaves in Congo Square; frequently the white spectators outnumbered the Voodoos. Under cover of these public ceremonies, however, Marie Laveau presided over many secret meetings, either in the chapel on Lake Pontchartrain or before one of the dozen altars which the cult maintained in New Orleans, at which the real magic of Voodoo was invoked, and the dancing carried to orgiastic extremes not possible before the easily shocked whites.

Most of these gatherings were for definite purposes and were paid for by the persons on whose behalf they were held. And secret and mysterious though they were supposed to be, Marie Laveau never lost her sense of the value of publicity and occasionally admitted a reporter. The New Orleans *Times* of March 21, 1869, described a meeting of the Voodoos at the lake chapel, in which the central figure was a young white

girl who had chosen this method of regaining the affections of her lover. Most of the celebrants were women, with a few quadroon men, and each carried a burning brand. Said the *Times:*

"These women were all dressed elaborately, some of them in bridal costumes, and with an extraordinary regard for the fineness and purity of their linen. At one end of the chapel a corpse was exposed. The rites having been commenced, an elderly turbaned female dressed in yellow and red [Marie Laveau], ascended a sort of dais and chanted a wild sort of fetish song, to which the others kept up an accompaniment with their voices and with a drum-like beat of their hands and feet. At the same time they commenced to move in a circle, while gradually increasing the time. As the motion gained in intensity the flowers and other ornaments disappeared from their hair, and their dresses were torn open, and each conducted herself like a bacchante. Everyone was becoming

drunk and intoxicated with the prevailing madness and excitement. As they danced in a circle, in the center of which stood a basket with a dozen hissing snakes whose heads were projecting from the cover, each corybante touched a serpent's head with her brand. In the midst of this saturnalia of witches, the pythoness of this extraordinary dance and revel was a young girl, with bare feet, and costumed *en chemise.* In one hand she held a torch, and with wild, maniacal gestures headed the band. In this awful state of nudity she continued her ever-increasing frantic movements until reason itself abandoned its earthly tenement. In a convulsive fit she finally fell, foaming at the mouth like one possessed, and it was only then that the mad carnival found a pause. The girl was torn half-dead from the scene, and she has never yet been restored to her faculties."

This was the last Voodoo ceremony over which Marie Laveau presided, for some two months later, on June 7, 1869, the Voodoos held a meeting in the chapel at Lake Pontchartrain, dethroned her on the ground that since she was well over seventy she was too old to perform the onerous duties of her high post, and crowned Malvina Latour as queen. Thereafter, until her death about ten years later, Marie Laveau devoted herself entirely to her self-imposed duties as unofficial spiritual adviser to the criminals in the condemned cells at the Parish Prison, an office which she had assumed during the early 1850's. This phase of her activity was wholly Catholic, into which she permitted no trace of Voodooism to creep. As soon as a man had been sentenced to hang, Marie Laveau made daily visits to his cell, taking him bowls of hot gumbo and platters of fried fish and otherwise consoling him in every way possible. If he consented, she prepared an altar in his cell before which she prayed with him—a box about three feet square, surmounted by three smaller boxes rising pyramidically to an apex, on which the Voodoo queen always placed a small figure of the Virgin Mary.

General de Buys was well known in New Orleans as a remarkably kind and indulgent master; he petted, coddled, and spoiled the Negro Squier, taught him to shoot, and permitted him to go alone on hunting expeditions in the forests adjacent to the city. And Squier practiced assiduously with the General's rifle; premonition, he said afterwards, warned him that he would eventually lose an arm, and so he became an expert marksman with either hand alone. The taste of freedom which Squier experienced on his journeys into the woods after game was too much for him. He began running away, and received only slight punsihment when he was captured and returned to General de Buys. Early in 1834 Squier was shot by a patrol of planters searching the swamps for runaway slaves, and his right arm was amputated, whence the sobriquet Bras Coupe, by which he was thereafter known. As soon as his injury had healed, Bras Coupe fled into the swamps and organized a gang of escaped blacks and a few renegade white men, whom he led on frequent robbing and murdering forays on the outskirts of the city, with an occasional venture into the thickly settled residential districts. He was New Orleans' most feared outlaw for nearly three years, and the successor of the *Kaintock* as the hobgoblin with which nurses and mothers frightened the Creole children. Reviewing his career, the *Picayune* after his death described him as "a semi-devil and a fiend in human shape," and said that his life had been "one of crime and depravity."

He was, of course, fireproof and invulnerable to wounds, for he was familiar with the miraculous herbs described by the French travelers Bossu, Perrin du Lac, and Baudry des Lozieres, and with many others which these avid searchers after botanical wonders had not discovered. Hunters returned to New Orleans from the swamps and told how, having encountered Bras Coupe, they fired at him, only to see their bullets flatten against his chest; some even said that the missiles had bounced off the iron like body of the outlaw and whizzed dangerously close to their own heads, while Bras Coupe laughed derisively and strode grandly into the farthest reaches of the swamps. And according to the slave tradition, detachments of soldiers sent after him vanished in a cloud of mist. Moreover, his very glance paralyzed, if he so wished, and he fed on human flesh.

The popular belief in Bras Coupe's invulnerability received a rude shock when, on April 6, 1837, he was wounded by two hunters who braved his magical powers and shot him near the Bayou St. John. And it was dissipated entirely on July 19 of the same year. On that day a Spanish fisherman named Francisco Garcia, who was known to the slaves as a friend of Bras Coupe's, drove slowly through the streets of New Orleans a cart drawn by a decrepit mule, and watched with tender solicitude an ungainly bundle, wrapped in old sacks, which jounced in the bed of the vehicle. Garcia stopped in front of the Cabildo and carried his bundle into the office of Mayor Dennis Prieur, where he unwrapped it and disclosed the body of Bras Coupe. The fisherman told the authorities that on the day before, the 18th, he was fishing in the Bayou St. John when Bras Coupe fired at him and missed, whereupon the indignant fisherman went ashore and beat out the brigand's brains with a club. The truth, however, appears to have been that Bras Coupe was slain as he slept in the fisherman's hut. Garcia demanded the immediate payment of the two-thousand-dollar reward which he had heard had been offered for Bras Coupe dead or alive, but he received only two hundred and fifty dollars. The body of the outlaw was exposed in the Place d'Armes for two days, and several thousand slaves were compelled to march past and look at it, as a warning.

"Cunjuh is magic some folks is bawn wid," she explained. "It gibs um powuh obuh tings udduh folks dohn unnuhstan. Dey kin wuk dat powuh fuh good aw bad. Dey kin put spells on yuh an lif duh spell some udduh root wukuh hab put on yuh. Ef a root wukuh break yuh spirit, he kin hanl yuh lak he want tuh. A witch is a cunjuh man dat somebody paid tuh tawment yuh. I know folks dat wuz rid so much by witches dat dey jis pine way an die."

The case of a man who had been conjured was described to us by James Moore. "He jis mope roun—couldn git spirit nuff tuh wuk. Den all ub a sudden he swell up an duh doctuhs couldn tell wut ail im. We tink he gonuh die. Den long come a man we call Professuh. He say ef we kin git any money he kin lif duh spell. We git some money tuhgedduh and he go out in duh stable an wen he come back he hab a lill black sack. He say dis hab duh cunjuh in it. Den he bile up some mullen leaves and bathe muh frien in um. He tell us tuh keep on doin dis. In two weeks duh swellin go down an he all right. Deah's root men wukin gense yuh all duh time. Dey kin lay tings down fuh yuh an ef yuh walk obuh dis, yuh fall unduh duh spell. Less yuh kin fine somebody else wut kin wuk roots an kin lif duh spell, yuh is doomed.

"Deah wuz a man wid duh powuh. He draw a ring roun anudduh man an dat man couldn git out dat ring till duh root man come an wave tuh um. Den deah wuz a uhmun done up so bad by somebody dat ants wuz crawlin out tru uh skin. Wenebuh a pusson go crazy, wut is dat but conjuh?

"I dohn lak tuh talk bout muhsef, but I caahn nebuh fuhgit duh time I hab a dose put on me by a uhmun uh didn lak. I wuz a good frien ub uh huzbun an she didn lak fuh us tuh go out tuhgedduh; so she tole me not tuh come tuh uh house no mo. I ain pay no tention. Well, suh, duh nex night soon as uh laid down, uh feel muhsef swoon. Ebry night it happen. Dis ting keep up till uh git sick. I couldn eat an jis git tuh pinin way. Duh doctuh he caahn hep me none. Finally I went tuh a root man. He say right off somebody done gib me a dose. He say 'I'll be roun tuhnight. Git some money tuhgedduh cuz I caahn do yuh no good less yuh staht off wid some silbuh.'

"Wen he come dat night an git

duh silbuh, he look all roun duh house an den dig a hole unduh duh doe step. Deah he fine a bottle. He tro it in duh fyuh an holluh, 'Git gone, yuh debil.' Attuh dat I git bettuh, but I ain nebuh bin tuh dat uhmun's house since. An I dohn lak tuh talk about it."

"Cunjuh? That's what is wrong with this ahm of mine. As I sit heah, I know that my enemy brought about this affliction. One night two, three yeahs ago, I put out my hand to open my gate. Pain went into my palm jus like stabbin with a shahp needle. This ahm has been no use since then."

"Perhaps it is rheumatism?" we suggested.

"No, sir. It isn't. I know. An cunjuh must be fought with cunjuh. If I know my enemy's name I could get somethin frum a cunjuh doctuh to help me seek revenge. But I am helpless."

"What would the doctor do about it?" we asked.

"The toe nails, the finguh nails, even the scrapins frum the bottom of the foot are all very powuhful. If the doctuh could get any of these frum my enemy, he would mix them in whiskey an make my enemy drink. That is all."

"Cunjuh," he said again. "You ask me if I know about these dahk things. I know too well. My wife Hattie had a spell put on uh fuh three long yeahs with a nest of rattlesnakes inside uh. She just lay theah an swelled an suffuhed. How she suffuhed! Jus like the foam that comes on a snake's mouth when he is hungry, she would foam, But she couldn't eat."

"Did she die of snakes?" we wanted to know.

"No. It was predicted that she would have a spell put on uh to die by fyuh and sho enough one night she was burned to death with the snakes still inside uh."

"But how were the snakes given to her?"

"That I can't tell. She maybe drank them in a little whiskey. But I can't tell."

"You like my gahden?" Lewis said mournfully. "That's all I can think of, my gahden. Theah's a bush

out theah that's goin to protect me frum any othuh enemies. Nobody can cunjuh me now because of that bush. If only I'd had a little piece of that plant befo, Hattie would be alive an me well an strong. But I kept puttin off goin to get a piece. You have to go to the woods in the dahk of night an find it faw yuhself. If you get caught at sunrise in those woods, you can't get out till night again. You plant a piece of the bush in somebody's yahd. They can't go out till you let them. You plant it in yuh own yahd. Nobody can get in to do you hahm. That's why I'm safe now. But," he concluded, with a melancholy look around his meagerly furnished domain, "I should've had it befo. My enemy has even prevented me from gettin on relief."

"Me an [my husband] couldn git long so I lef im. He went tuh a root doctuh fuh him tuh make me come back home. Den duh root doctuh put me down sick so duh wite people I wuz wukin fuh would dischahge me. I had pains runnin up an down muh whole body, an I knowed I wuz cunjuhed but uh wouldn gib in. I call me in a man who use tuh try tuh sell me a han tuh wawd off cunjuh. He rub muh legs down twice a day, an one mawnin a big black snake run outuh muh big toe. 'Deah goes duh devil,' say duh root man, an frum den on I git bettuh. A cousin uh mine git a dose once an wen duh root doctuh rub uh all ovuh wid a cleah liquid, bugs begin crawlin out of uh skin. Duh doctuh say if she had wait one mo day it would uh bin too late."

"Did your husband ever try any more conjure on you?"

She laughed with great amusement. "He sho did. He went tuh duh same man dat cuo me an give him thutty dolluhs tuh make me go back tuh him. One Sunday attuh chuch wen I ain had thought of evuh livin wid muh huzbun agen, I walked out duh chuch straight tuh muh huzbun's house. An dis happen," concluded Ellen, "widout duh root man evuh seein me. I didn know nuthin bout it till long attuh we wuz reconcile."

"Dey kin fix yuh wid mos anyting," Kelsey said. "Duh chinch bug

is use a lot an Ise sked ub em. I wouldn put muh han on dem ting fuh ten dolluhs. I hab a sistuh name Ida Walker wut wuz fix wid candy. She ate duh candy an den uh ahm swell up an tun blue. Yuh could see lill animals runnin up and down uh ahm. She got a root doctuh name Sherman. Soons he look at it, he know wut it wuz. He come Toosday an he gie uh a rub tuh use, and he say tuh rub down an he would come back Friday. Wen he come, duh tings all done come intuh duh finguhs. He tuk a basin wid some wome watuh, an he put muh sistuh han in it. Den he ketch hol uh duh han an duh tings run out in duh watuh. Dey wuz puppy dogs.

"He ax uh did she want em tuh go back weah dey come frum, an she say yes. So he say he know duh man wut sen em, an he went tuh duh winduh an tro duh watuh wid duh puppy dogs in it in duh direction uh duh man house an say, 'Go.' One week latuh duh man wuz in he fiel ploughin an he drop duh plough an fall down. Wen duh people git tuh im, all he could say wuz, 'Dis is my wuk. Dis is my wuk.' He went plumb crazy an died, but muh sistuh got well an fine.

"One ting I do blieb in is signs. Ef yuh watch signs, dey alluz mean good aw bad luck tuh yuh. Ef muh lef eye jump, I kin look fuh bad nooz, and ef muh right eye jump, I kin look fuh good nooz. Same ting wen yuh han itch. Yuh lef han mean yuh gwine tuh git a piece uh money; yuh right han say yuh gwine shake hans wid a strainjuh. Wen yuh foot itch, yuh gwine tuh walk on strange lan aw go tuh duh grabe-yahd. Dogs an chickens an buds all make signs dat mean sumpm. Ef somebody is comin, a roostuh come right up tuh duh doe an crow. Ef a dog sets up a howlin, somebody in duh neighbuhhood gwine die. A screech owl screechin roun tells yuh somebody neah by gwine die."

"'Tis bad luck fuh girls tuh wistle. It will suttnly lead tuh misfawchun. Yuh should nevuh put noo bodes on a ole house but yuh should git a ole bode das good tuh men duh place dat yuh hab tuh fix. An nevuh put anudduh ruhm on a house das already buil. It sho mean bad luck, eeduh sickness aw det tuh some uh yuh fambly aw close friens, wen yuh heah duh owl holluh by yuh house. Now yuh kin watch it. I ain see it fail yet."

"Deah's many tings wut's bad luck. Ef we come in duh house wid our hat on we hab tuh go back an den pull it off an den come in. Wen yuh clean duh house in duh day an duh flo git duhty agen by duh night time an yuh sweep duh flo, yuh musn sweep duh dut out duh house, but yuh hab tuh sweep it behine duh doe till mawnin.

CHARLES THE GRINDER

There was a Negro in West Baton Rouge parish called Charles the Grinder who went about the plantations and villages offering to sharpen scissors, knives, plows, tools or anything that needed sharpening. He never worked more than half a day, for he said "a man who works half time lives twice time, and in relaxation there is double expectation, scientifically speaking." Translated this meant that a lazy man lives twice as long as a hard-working and ambitious man. He never worked for wages, his reason being that the hours were too long, and pay-days too far apart. But he made ten times as much money as any laborer ever made in those days (about 1905), for he was a Voodoo priest (so he said) quietly practicing his profession, and bleeding the Negroes white. His sharpening business was merely a blind, but he made money from that, too, for he was an expert at it; he could sharpen a common pocket-knife to split a hair.

He had been a seaman, and remained for some years in Haiti, where he became acquainted with Voodooism, and said that he taught the Voodoos in New Orleans (including Marie Laveau II—which, of course, was not true), and was "run out of the city because of my superior knowledge." He lived in a houseboat on the Mississippi, and it was there he conducted his Voodoo rites, secretly and for his own purpose. He kept a snake in a box; and

a rooster with golden feathers, tame as a cat and fat as a pig, strolled about his boat, sometimes flapping its wings and spreading gold dust on the floor. Charles said the dust was pure gold, and the rooster was a "golden legend." What he meant by that nobody ever knew. He loved to use big words, and whether they were in the right place of a sentence to make sense was of no importance to him. He kept a large stock of shells, fish bones, and skulls of small animals, some gilded and some stained black or purple. These he sold as good-luck charms. For expensive gris gris he had dried bladders of hogs, which he gathered up among the plantations at hog-killing time; for these he charged two dollars and fifty cents. They were used almost exclusively for putting terrible curses upon an individual or his whole family.

There was a Negro, Sol Jefferson, who had been unjustly cursed and struck by the overseer of the plantation where he worked, and being a follower of Charles' cult went to him for means of revenge.

Charles said, "Leave it to me, and do what I say. The moon in the sky is a scientific object, which percolates and stimulates according to certain mineral matter exposed to it. Take this bladder, which has been vitalized by the golden rooster and the snake, Zombie, who is in touch with the great spirits of Haiti, fill it with sand from the shores of the great Mississippi, and fling it under the overseer's house on the dot of twelve, midnight. He will wish that he had never struck you, and you will hear from him to that effect."

Sol, half believing, took the bladder, and filled it with sand, as instructed. That night at midnight he threw it under the overseer's house. The next morning he went to work as usual, but did not see his boss. There was another man in his place. Wondering what had happened, and being alarmed, he inquired why the overseer did not come out. A Negro working next to him said, "Ain't you heard? He fell down at fo' o'clock dis monin' and broke his leg."

"That's a lie," cried Sol, forgetting himself," "—it couldn't 'av

been that quick."

"What you mean by that?" asked the other Negro, "is you mixed up in it?"

"What makes you ask that?"

"Just what you just said."

"I ain't said nothin'."

"Yes, you is, you just said 'it couldn't be this quick,' and I put two and two together and figured you'd put some gris gris on that man, fo' I knows that you's a friend of Charles the Grinder."

"I sho know 'im," said Sol, "and if you is actin' lak you is, I'm sho' gwine have him put some gris gris on you."

"Lawd, have mercy," cried the Negro, "I don't fool in none o' dat stuff, and you lay off me."

"I sho' will," said Sol, "onless you say something to bring trouble."

The Negro said that was something "I sho' won't do," and Sol was satisfied. But the outcome of the gris gris was very unexpected: Sol did not think it would work at all; and now he had unlimited faith in Charles the Grinder.

Sol did not know, however, that this surprise was nothing compared to what he was later to encounter. The overseer was sent to a hospital in New Orleans, and after several weeks recovered, but he had no sooner reached home when his wife was nearly burnt to death owing to the explosion of a can of kerosene which she used to light a fire in a wood stove, and before she was fully recovered her daughter eloped with a simpleton who had a police record, and as a result of this she nearly lost her mind. Sol, being a good man at heart, and thinking that these calamities which befell the overseer's family were results of the hog's bladder filled with sand which he had placed under the house, decided that he had better retrieve it. He waited until the moon was low and the night was dark, and then crept under the house to find the bladder, but could not locate it; he searched for a full hour without success. Meanwhile the overseer, having heard a noise under his house (for Sol had bumped his head on a rafter several times) decided to take his lantern and gun and go to investigate. As he shined the light on the intruder he thought he recognized Sol, whom he knew very well. "Is that Sol?" he asked.

"No, sir, dis ain't Sol," came the reply.

"Thank goodness," said the overseer, "for I'd hate to shoot Sol."

"Look out, Boss, dis IS Sol—don't shoot dat gun."

Sol came out from under the house and confessed everything. The overseer was not impressed, however, with the gris gris. "Leave it there," he said, "it can't do any more harm than it's already done."

Sol was relieved and went home happy. But the next day a storm blew the roof off of the overseer's house. Whereupon he sent for Sol and told him to find that bladder or he'd kill him.

Sol found the bladder, and took it home—to his sorrow. He was a middle-aged man, and was married to a very attractive mulatto girl. They had no children. She was very angry with her husband because of his association with Charles the Grinder, and said that she intended to go to see him and give him a "piece of her mind," and get him to move down the river.

Since the bladder was removed from under the overseer's house there was a change in his luck. His wife recovered, and his daughter left the simpleton whom she had married, and returned home, and the owner of the plantation gave him a better house to live in. He had become fond of Sol, and often laughed with him over the "crazy idea" of the gris gris.

Meantime the gris gris was working, not against the overseer, but against Sol himself, now that he had taken it to his own home. His wife had several times gone to see Charles the Grinder, and had become fascinated by his golden rooster, his bones, skulls, and his snake. He told her of his years in Haiti, and of the wonderful life in that country; he told her also of the many countries he had visited while a seaman, and his "big words" interested her; she did not know what they meant—neither did he—but they sounded

wonderful; they were not like the "Nigger talk" she heard from her husband, and Voodooism, which she once detested, had now become very interesting. She had been asleep; now she was awake, and saw before her a life of excitement and romance. What had she been doing all these years? Nothing—only getting meals for an ignorant Negro, and that was what she would continue to do; that was all she had to look forward to—living in a cabin, and perhaps never in her lifetime going farther than Baton Rouge—perhaps never as far as New Orleans even. These were the thoughts that Charles the Grinder had put into her innocent head. Her name was Rose-Marie, a pretty name, Charles thought, well suited to a very pretty girl.

The appointed morning came; the house-boat's ropes were pulled in, and it drifted down the current of the Mississippi, never to return, and Rose-Marie was on it with Charles the Grinder. When Sol found his house dark and empty as he returned from work, he suspected, and went to the landing where the boat had been tied up for years. No spot had ever seemed so desolate to him. The boat was gone, and it had carried Rose-Marie away. He knew that. He went home and got the fateful bladder, returned and threw it to the current, hoping that it would curse the river and all that floated on it. But Charles and Rose-Marie were far ahead of it, and they were safe; it would never overtake them. Sol went home, and as he told his story Voodism became very unpopular in his community.

GRIS GRIS ON HIS DOOR-STEP DROVE HIM MAD

Many of the old houses of New Orleans were built close to the sidewalk, and entered by steps, usually of three or four flights. It is today a wonder to strangers why these steps are kept so clean, but that is a time-honored custom; they are scrubbed daily, and sometimes when they are not perfectly clean pulverized brick is spread over them. There has

never been any satisfactory explanation for the pulverized brick being spread on perfectly clean steps. The inside of the house can be dusty and grimy, but the steps must be clean, for this gives the public the impression that the whole house is likewise clean. (This is the best explanation I can give of the clean steps of New Orleans; there may be a better one, but I have not heard it.)

There was a man of doubtful morals who had two names, J. D. Rudd and J. B. Langrast. Around 1850 he owned a house on Dumaine Street with a large yard, and there he made his living selling junk, which he stored on the premises, inside the house as well as in the yard. But his steps were always immaculate, and any person entering his quarters was stunned to see the filth —the old clothes, the bed that had not been changed for weeks, and the various items, such as demijohns, broken furniture, cart wheels, and bird cages. But he made considerable money, for half the junk he sold was stolen, and a good portion was given to him. He bought very little. Yet there was not a day he did not makes sales amounting to a sum close to a hundred dollars, which in that day was considerable.

The reason he had two names was that he had two wives, one in the uptown section, and one in the downtown section; neither knew of the existence of the other, and as one spoke only French and the other only Spanish they were not likely to meet and compare notes. In the uptown area he was known as Langrast, downtown as Rudd, and when uptown he wore a beautifully tailored suit, and a clean shirt, in fact, dressed like a gentleman, while downtown he wore work clothes, for his wife there, having been bred in a shack, was not very particular. Why he wanted two wives is to this day unexplained, for he spent most of his time at his headquarters-for-junk on Dumaine Street, and slept in a bed hardly fit for animals, much less a man who sometimes dressed like a gentleman and assumed urbane manners. He lived happily in this arrangement for several years, and felt that he was a genius at deception.

Marie Laveau was at the height of her fame and glory about this time, and was dazzling the people with her incredible achievements, but Langrast hated her and her cult, and all individuals who professed Voodooism. He said they were "the scum of the earth and thieves who would just as soon murder as steal." Whenever there was a mysterious murder in the city he attributed the crime to "some Voodoo." But one morning when he opened his front door he saw on his polished steps a cross and a small bag containing the head of a rooster. This infuriated him, and he started immediately to report the matter to the police, but he had only gone a few blocks when it occurred to him that he was not in a position to invite publicity concerning himself, for he was using two names, and was married to two women. It also occurred to him when his temper had cooled that the police could do little, if anything, about it. The more inconspicuously he lived the better. He turned back, and wondered what he could do with the rooster's head, which he carried with him to show the police, and, being unable to decide, he sauntered into a bar-room and ordered a drink of whiskey. Standing beside him at the bar was a wretched-looking man who seemed to be purposely getting drunk, for he ordered one drink after another.

As Langrast turned to go, this man faced him and said: "You see me? Look at me, I was once a prosperous gentleman. But look at me now. I'm a bum. Why? Would you like to know? It's an interesting story, and I'll tell you. The Voodoos put a curse on me. I was in love with a girl; but that I'll not mention—for reasons better known to myself, sacred reasons, very sacred. The gris gris appeared on my doorstep every morning—every morning—and then my luck began to change. A mocking bird that came and sang at my window every morning vanished; my gold fish died, my dog, Rex, the finest animal that ever lived, was shot, and died in my

arms, bidding me farewell, like a human would." Here tears came to his eyes. "I was in the tobacco business, handling perique tobacco grown up here in St. James parish, and I made money; I was on the way to becoming a millionaire, even though I spent money like water."

Langrast did not wish to hear this story, and started out but the man grabbed him by the arm. "Don't be in a hurry; this might happen to you, and I advise you to hear so you can be on guard. My name is John Spiker, and I'm from Kentucky."

Langrast was frightened. It seemed that the gris gris was already working on him. "I'll buy a drink," he said, "and that's all."

As John Spiker waved to the bartender to "bring us two drinks," Langrast slipped the rooster's head into his pocket.

The drinks were served, and Spiker began to talk again. "Yes, as I was saying, I kept a carriage, and the best men in the city shook hands with me on the street; but now they don't know me, don't even know my name anymore, don't know my face—as if they'd never seen me. But let me show you my cancelled check for ten thousand, made to cash—pin money—" He reached in his pocket, and as his hand felt the rooster's head his face turned white, and he seemed unable to move a muscle. He turned to see if there was anybody behind him, his hand still in his pocket clutching the rooster's head. Presently he took it out, examined it, and flung it with all his might at the mirror of the bar, breaking two bottles of whiskey.

The bartender went to the rear room of the saloon, and returned with a double-barrelled shot gun, which he pointed toward Langrast and Spiker as he said, "Now, git out o' here, the both of you."

"Why me?" asked Langrast.

"Because I saw you put that rooster's head in Spiker's pocket."

When Spiker heard this he remembered all the curse-words he had ever heard in old Kentucky, and let Langrast have them, swearing that he would kill him if he had a gun, and declaring that if he ever

met him when he did have a gun he would lay him low without notice, for this incident simply renewed the curse which had been placed upon him, prolonging it—"no telling how long."

The bartender, having cooled down, put his gun away, and having enjoyed Spiker's magnificent cursing, said that the boys could have a drink on the house, and to show them that gris gris meant nothing to him he would preserve the rooster's head in a glass of his best whiskey and keep it on the liquor stand.

Spiker stood still for a moment; then, with fresh tears running down his cheeks, shook hands with Langrast. Having enjoyed the drink on the house, they decided that they would get drunk together, and they swore that they would "clean up Voodooism in New Orleans," and expose it "as the dirtiest racket that ever existed or go back to a civilized country, either Tennessee or Kentucky, where a man would shoot you face to face, but wouldn't stoop to putting gris gris on your door-step and causing your death by slow humiliation and starvation."

They nearly drank the bar-room dry, at Langrast's expense, for he was prosperous. Sometime in the early morning they staggered homeward, and when Langrast reached his house he saw a fresh cross and another rooster's head on his steps. This drove him mad. He went into his house, took his shotgun, and began shooting the steps away, at the same time cursing the Voodoos and swearing that he would kill the last one "infesting this city." The neighbors called the police, and Langrast was lodged in jail.

When he was released, after paying a heavy fine, he sold his business for a song, deserted both of his wives and left the city.

Thirty years later an old man arrived in New Orleans from Peru, and registered at the St. Louis Hotel as J. B. Langrast. He spoke Spanish fluently, and was very wealthy, for he caused a sensation in banking circles by depositing half a million in a New Orleans bank. After a while he began to search for Mrs.

J. D. Rudd and Mrs. J. B. Langrast. He found that Mrs. Rudd was dead, and Mrs. Langrast, now fifty, was working as a waitress in the St. Louis Hotel. He went into the restaurant and recognized her. But she did not recognize him; he had grown very old, and since he had nearly forgotten the English language she could not recall his voice—his intonation had changed. But he finally convinced her that he was her husband, and took her with him to Tennessee, which to him was a civilized country wherein he wished to spend the rest of his life—where a man never shot you in the back, nor tortured you with gris gris and put a curse on you.

One fine mornin I'm gonna reach up and grab me a handfulla stars Swing out my long lean leg And whip three hot strikes burnin down the heavens And look over at God and say How about that!

—Paul Vesey

The Unwritten Law of Baseball that Barred Blacks Until 1946:

"It is not presumed by your committee that any club who have applied are composed of persons of color, or any portion of them; and the recommendation of your committee in this report are based upon this view, and they unanimously report against the admission of any club which may be composed of one or more colored persons."

The reason given—an ingenious bit of casuistry and evasion:

"If colored clubs were admitted, there would be in all probability some division of feeling—whereas by excluding them, no injury could result to anybody."

From the 1867 Official Records of the National Association of Baseball Players.

The original Cuban Giants and the Gorhams were baseball clubs composed of colored players who worked at such summer resorts as the Argyle Hotel in Babylon, Long Island, and played ball in their leisure time against professional white teams who played baseball for a living.

In the summer of 1887, the Cuban Giants played and lost 11–5 to Cincinnati, a major-league team. The same season the Gorhams beat the Metropolitans, a New York major-league team, by the score of 2–1. George Stovey, later a pitcher for Newark in the International League, pitched for the Gorhams, which also had a second baseman named Grant whom McGraw tried to sneak into the lineup of major-league Baltimore as an Indian.

The following open letter was sent to President McDermit of the Tri-State (formerly Ohio) League, by Weldy Walker, a member of the Akron, Ohio team of 1887. The letter was dated March 5, 1888. The law prohibiting the employment of colored players in the league was rescinded a few weeks later.

Steubenville, Ohio, March 5, 1888
Mr. McDirmit,

Sir:

I take the liberty of addressing you because noticing in "The Sporting Life" that the "law," permitting colored men to sign was repealed, etc. at the special meeting held at Columbus, February 22, of the above named league of which you are the president. I ascertaining the reason of such an action. I have grievances. It is a question with me whether individual loss subserves the public good in this case. This is the only question to be considered—both morally and financially—in this as it is, or ought to be, in all cases that convinced beyond doubt that you all, as a body of men, have been impartial and unprejudiced in your consideration of the great and important question—the success of the national game.

The reason I say this is because you have shown a partiality by making an exception with a member of the Zonesville Club, and from this one, would infer that he is only one of the three colored players—Dick Johnson, alias Dick Neals, alias Dick Noyle as the Sporting Life correspondent from Columbus has it; Sol White of the Wheelings,

John Henry "Pop" Lloyd—considered by many sports writers and reporters to be the greatest baseball player in the history of the national sport.

An integrated professional baseball team from Bismarck, North Dakota which won the National Semi-Pro Championship in 1935. Among its members were three outstanding black athletes—Satchel Paige, Chet Brewer and Quincy Troup.

National Semi-Pro Champions – 1935

Charlie Grant, an outstanding second baseman who was registered in 1901 by the manager of the Baltimore Americans as Charlie Tokahama of Indian extraction.

whom I must compliment by saying he was one, if not the surest hitter in the Ohio League last year, and your humble servant who was unfortunate enough to join the Akron club, just ten days before they busted.

It is not because I was reserved and have been denied making my bread and butter with some clubs that I speak, but it is in hopes that the action taken at your last meeting will be called up for reconsideration at your next.

The law is a disgrace to the present age, and reflects very much upon the intelligence of your last meeting and casts derision at the laws of Ohio—the voice of the people that says all men are equal. I would suggest that your honorable body, in case that black law is not repealed, pass one making it criminal for a colored man or woman to be found in a ball ground.

There is now the same accommodation made for the colored patron of the game as the white, and the same provision and dispensation is made for the money of them both, that finds its way to the coffers of the various clubs.

There should be some broader cause—such as lack of ability, behavior and intelligence—for barring a player rather than his color. It is for these reasons and because I think ability and intelligence should be recognized first and last—at all times and by everyone—I ask the question again, why was the law permitting colored men to sign repealed, etc.?

Yours truly,
Weldy W. Walker

Had Henry "Hank" McDonald of Canandaiqua, New York, lived in a big city, his name would be a household word among sports fans. Certainly he ranks with some of the old-timers who are better known. His exact age is a well-guarded secret but it is known that he is well over eighty years old, and is still an active referee and umpire at sporting events and, in addition, is active in local political circles.

Hank was a four-letter man at East High School and Canandaiqua Academy. He played pro-football seven years with the Rochester Jeffersons against such well-known stars as Jim Thorpe, Lou Little, Fats Henry, Greasy Neale, Milton Ghee, Lud Wray and many others better known than he. For six seasons he played baseball for the Cuban Stars and Pittsburgh Colored Stars, which puts him in major league class as a ballplayer.

Black Jockeys Who Won the Kentucky Derby

1875 Oliver Lewis on *Aristides*
1877 Billy Wakers on *Baden Baden*
1882 Babe Hurd on *Apollo*
1884 Isaac Murphy on *Buchanan*
1885 Enoch Henderson on *Joe Cotton*
1887 Isaac Lewis on *Montrose*
1890 Isaac Murphy on *Riley*
1891 Isaac Murphy on *Kingman*
1892 Alfie Clayton on *Azra*
1895 J. (Soup) Perkins on *Haima*
1896 Willie Sims on *Ben Brush*
1898 Willie Sims on *Plaudit*
1901 Jimmy Winkfield on *His Eminence*
1902 Jimmy Winkfield on *Alan-a-Dale*

On July 10, 1891, at Washington Park race track in Chicago, a black jockey named "Monk" Overton won six straight races. Sixteen years later, in 1907, the feat was repeated by another jockey named Jimmy

Isaac Murphy, the first jockey to win three Kentucky Derbys.

Lee. According to *The New York Times:*

The riding of Jimmy Lee, a colored jockey, was the feature of Churchill Downs this afternoon. He won all six races on the card and some of the mounts were at long prices. One dollar parlayed on Lee's mounts would have netted $15,000. This record has been equalled but twice by Fred Archer and George Fordham in England. Monk Overton, another Negro, one day at Washington Park in Chicago, 16 years ago won the first six races. When Lee rode back to the stand after winning the last race, he was cheered by the crowd. In the race on Foreigner, he lowered the track record for a mile and three furlongs by nearly two seconds.

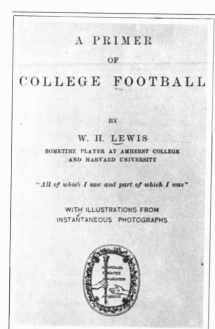

A PRIMER

OF

COLLEGE FOOTBALL

BY

W. H. LEWIS

SOMETIME PLAYER AT AMHERST COLLEGE
AND HARVARD UNIVERSITY

"All of which I saw and part of which I was"

WITH ILLUSTRATIONS FROM
INSTANTANEOUS PHOTOGRAPHS

The Renaissance Team, the greatest collection of black basketball players, first organized by Mr. Bob Douglas in 1923.

The author, William H. Lewis, was a black man who played center for Harvard. He was picked for the all-American football team in 1892 and 1893. When Walter Camp selected his all-time all-American football team, William H. Lewis was chosen for center. Mr. Lewis became a lawyer and Assistant U.S. Attorney in Boston.

American sprint champion from 1898–1900, Taylor toured Europe and Australia to meet and beat the best riders in what was then the most popular international sport. More than once his life was jeopardized during a race when other riders ganged up on him. It helped greatly that he was considered the best-conditioned athlete of his day.

Marshal "Major" Taylor (1878–1932), the Fastest Bicycle Rider in the World

In 1928, after his career had ended, he published his autobiography, *The Fastest Bicyle Rider in the World* It was out of print until 1972, when it was re-issued by the Stephen Greene Press of Vermont.

In 1910, the Philadelphia North American newspaper assigned Mike Murphy, George Murphy's father, to report on the Jeffries Johnson fight in Reno, Nevada. He was the only reporter who telegraphed back to his newspaper that it was impossible for the champion who had neglected himself for three years, to win. In connection with that message he coined the phrase "They never come back."

TOP: Joe Louis winning the Heavyweight Championship in boxing from James J. Braddock.
BOTTOM: Jesse Owens making his record breaking broad jump leap that won for him a gold medal
in the 1936 Olympics.

We looks like men a marchin' on, We looks like men of war.

1

2 The name of one of my poor fellows who was killed ought to be registered in the book of fame, and remembered with reverence as long as bravery is considered a virtue; he was a black man by the name of *John Johnson*; a 24 lb. shot struck him in the hip and took away all the lower part of his body. in this state the poor brave fellow lay on the deck, and several times exclaimed to his shipmates, "*fire away my boy, no haul a color down.*" The other was also a black man, by the name of *John Davis*, and was struck in much the same way: he fell near me, and several times requested to be thrown overboard, saying, he was only in the way of others.

AMERICANS!
DEAR IN REMEMBRANCE
The HORRID MASSACRE
Perpetrated in King-street, Boston.
New-England.
On the Evening of March the Fifth, 1770
When FIVE of your fellow countrymen,
GRAY, MAVERICK, CALDWELL, ATTUCKS,
and CARR,
Lay wallowing in their Gore!
Being *basely*, and most *inhumanly*
MURDERED!
And SIX others badly WOUNDED!
By a Party of the XXIXth Regiment,
Under the command of Capt. Tho. Preston.
REMEMBER!
That Two of the MURDERERS
Were convicted of MANSLAUGHTER
By a Jury, of whom I shall say
NOTHING,
Branded in the hand!
And *dismissed,*
The others were ACQUITTED,
And their Captain PRESENT...

1. **Negro seamen in Revolutionary War**
2. **Extract from a letter by Captain Shaler, dated at sea January 1, 1865.**
3. **The <u>Boston Gazette and Country Journal</u> (March 12, 1770) noted "A mulatto man, named Crispus Attucks" among those killed in the first battle of the American Revolution**
4. **Army pay check issued to William Kitchen, a slave who served as a "substitute" for his master**

4

3

Revolutionary War certificate for one hundred acres of bounty land issued to Agrippa Haull, black Revolutionary War veteran. Most veterans, both black and white, sold their rights to the land to speculators for a few ready dollars. Generals received as much as 20,000 acres of bounty land for their war services.

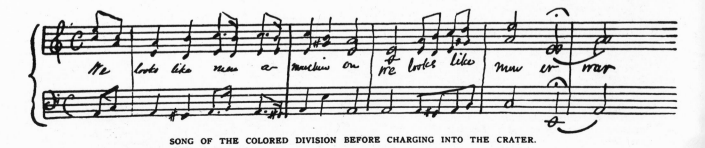

LAWS OF NORTH CAROLINA—1784.   639

CHAPTER LXX.

An Act for Enfranchising Ned Griffin, Late the Property of William Kitchen.

I. Whereas, Ned Griffin, late the property of William Kitchen, of Edgecomb county, was promised the full enjoyments of his liberty, on condition that he, the said Ned Griffin, should faithfully serve as a soldier in the continental line of this State for and during the term of twelve months; and whereas the said Ned Griffin did faithfully on his part perform the condition, and whereas it is just and reasonable that the said Ned Griffin should receive the reward promised for the services which he performed;

II. Be it therefore Enacted by the General Assembly of the State of North Carolina, and it is hereby Enacted by the authority of the same, That the said Ned Griffin, late the property of William Kitchen, shall forever hereafter be in every respect declared to be a freeman; and he shall be, and he is hereby enfranchised and forever delivered and discharged from the yoke of slavery; any law, usage or custom to the contrary thereof in anywise notwithstanding.

CHAP. XVIII.

An ACT to authorise the raising of two regiments of men of Color.

Passed October 24, 1814.

I. *Be it enacted by the people of the state of New-York, represented in Senate and Assembly,* That the governor of the state of New-York be, and he is hereby authorised to raise, by voluntary enlistment, two regiments of free men of color, for the defence of the state, for three years, unless sooner discharged.

Two regiments to be raised.

II. *And be it further enacted,* That each of the said regiments shall consist of one thousand and eighty able-bodied men; and the said regiments shall be formed into a brigade, or be organised in such manner, and shall be employed in such service, as the governor of the state of New-York shall deem best adapted to defend the said

Their number.

We looks like men a marchin on we looks like men er war

SONG OF THE COLORED DIVISION BEFORE CHARGING INTO THE CRATER.

THE UNITED STATES OF AMERICA,

TO ALL TO WHOM THESE PRESENTS SHALL COME, GREETING:

Indian Lands

CERTIFICATE No. 2575

Whereas *George W. Smothers of Cowley County Kansas* has deposited in the GENERAL LAND OFFICE of the United States a CERTIFICATE OF THE REGISTER OF THE LAND OFFICE at *Wichita Kansas* whereby it appears that FULL PAYMENT has been made by the said *George W. Smothers* according to the provisions of the Act of Congress of the 24th of April, 1820, entitled "An Act making further provision for the sale of the Public Lands," for *and The Act of the 15th of July 1870 for the North West quarter of Section Twenty-seven, in Township Thirty four South, of Range Three East, in the District of Lands subject to sale at Wichita Kansas, containing One hundred and sixty acres*

according to the OFFICIAL PLAT of the Survey of the said lands, returned to the GENERAL LAND OFFICE by the SURVEYOR GENERAL, which said Tract has been purchased by the said *George W. Smothers*.

Now, know ye, That the UNITED STATES OF AMERICA, in consideration of the premises, and in conformity with the several Acts of Congress in such case made and provided, HAVE GIVEN AND GRANTED, and by these presents DO GIVE AND GRANT, unto the said *George W. Smothers* and to *his* heirs, the said Tract above described; To Have and to Hold the same, together with all the rights, privileges, immunities, and appurtenances, of whatsoever nature, thereunto belonging, unto the said *George W. Smothers* and to *his* heirs and assigns forever.

In testimony whereof, I, *Ulysses S Grant*, PRESIDENT OF THE UNITED STATES OF AMERICA, have caused these letters to be made Patent, and the Seal of the GENERAL LAND OFFICE to be hereunto affixed.

Given under my hand, at the City of Washington, the *Tenth* day of *June*, in the year of our Lord one thousand eight hundred and *Seventy three*, and of the Independence of the United States the *Ninety seventh*.

BY THE PRESIDENT: *US Grant*

By *S D Williamson*

R A Ficke, Recorder of the General Land Office

RECORDED, Vol. 4, Page 349.

Land grant issued to George Smothers. Smothers was one of the black Civil War veterans who chose to homestead in Kansas. His descendants kept the land and continue to be progressive farmers.

A THIEF'S PUNISHMENT

A correspondent of *The New York Times*, writing from Morris Island, S.C., says:

It has been conceded that the efficiency of an army may be judged by its discipline. That being the case, the Army of the South stands all right according to the popular standard, for discipline surrounds it on all sides. A square piece of board, large enough to cover a man's back and bearing the striking inscription:

THIEF—
This man, JOHN TOMPKINS,
Company C,
55th Regiment Massachusetts,
stole money from a wounded friend

is being carried about today by an individual, John Tompkins. His head is closely shaved, and he is divested of his coat. His beat extends up and down the island as far as our lines admit so that he may be viewed by all the regiments. In order to accelerate his movements, when occasion requires, a guard of two soldiers with fixed bayonets follow at his heels, and that the camp may receive due information of his approach, a drummer and a fifer who accompany the party, play their instruments to the tune of "The Rogues' March" with a will. The ingrate receives not the slightest token of pity from anyone, and looks to all appearances as if he considered the whistle dearly bought.

The spectacle forcibly reminds one that "the way of the transgressor is hard."

—From Anti-Slavery Standard, September 19, 1863.
   Photo: Chicago Historical Society Collection.

George Washington and Martin Van Buren served in Company E, 55th Massachusetts Regiment during the Civil War. They were both colored men named after Presidents of the U.S. Washington died in service at the General Hospital in Beaufort, South Carolina, in 1865, shortly before the mustering-out of his comrades. Van Buren lived a long life after the war and died in Moline, Illinois, in 1920.

Private James Stone was a fugitive slave from Kentucky who settled in Ohio after his flight to freedom. He was white in appearance, married a white woman and raised a family. When the war began Stone enlisted in a white regiment; Company E of the 1st Light Artillery of Ohio on August 23, 1861. This was a full two years before blacks were allowed to enlist in the Union Army. He fought in Kentucky, where he had been enslaved, then died in the General Hospital in Nashville, Tennessee, on October 30, 1862, while still in service. Not until after his death did blacks who knew him as a slave reveal his true identity.

Negro Teamsters, Virginia, 1864

Band of the 107th U.S. Colored Infantry, Fort Lincoln, 1865

Company E, 4th U.S. Colored Infantry, District of Columbia, 1865

In 1880, Cadet Johnson Whittaker, a young native of Washington, D.C., was found under his bed—tied, gagged and mutilated. He claimed some unknown men entered his room and assaulted him. After an investigation by authorities Whittaker was charged with having injured himself and trying to cast blame on others. He was convicted and ordered dismissed from the army academy at West Point. However, influential persons, in the interest of justice, caused authorities to reverse the decision and permit Whittaker to continue at West Point. He was dropped soon after on the grounds that he failed to pass a course in Philosophy.

The first Afro-American youth who received an appointment to be a West Point cadet was Michael Howard of Mississippi. Upon receiving the appointment he presented himself at the Academy on May 27, 1870. His appearance was the signal for great excitement both at the Academy and in the nearby towns. There was no lodging available to him at the local hotel, so he had to secure a room with a colored family

nearby to await the entrance exam which had to be passed before final admission to the Academy.

The West Point staff considered his appointment premature and more of a social experiment than the elevation of Hiram Revels to the Senate of the U.S.

The whole matter ended when results of the entrance examination revealed that Howard did not obtain a passing mark. Thus passed his opportunity to become the first Afro-American to enter West Point Military Academy.

From The New York Times, May 28, 1870.

The U.S. Military Academy at West Point was founded in 1802 to prepare young men to become Army officers. Blacks became eligible for appointment to the Academy in 1866, with passage of the 14th Amendment, which provides citizenship for all Afro-Americans.

The first test as to whether a black citizen could enter West Point came about in 1867, when James M. Gregory of Virginia was recommended to President Andrew Johnson for appointment to the Academy on recommendation of General Benjamin F. Butler. The President refused to appoint him because of the prejudice against blacks immediately following the Civil War. When Gregory filed his application at the U.S. War Department, he met General O. O. Howard, founder of Howard University. As a consequence of the good impression obtained at that meeting, Gregory attended Howard University, and after graduating with honors, became an instructor in Latin and mathematics.

When the 15th Amendment of 1870 made it possible to elect blacks to Congress during the Reconstruction

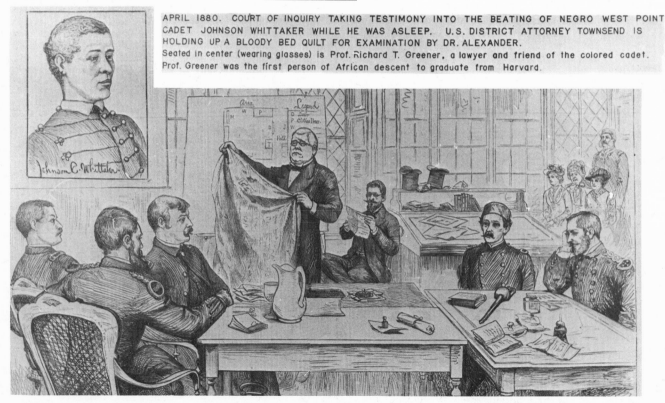

APRIL 1880. COURT OF INQUIRY TAKING TESTIMONY INTO THE BEATING OF NEGRO WEST POINT CADET JOHNSON WHITTAKER WHILE HE WAS ASLEEP. U.S. DISTRICT ATTORNEY TOWNSEND IS HOLDING UP A BLOODY BED QUILT FOR EXAMINATION BY DR. ALEXANDER.
Seated in center (wearing glasses) is Prof. Richard T. Greener, a lawyer and friend of the colored cadet. Prof. Greener was the first person of African descent to graduate from Harvard.

Period, it also made possible selection and appointment of black cadets. Between 1870 and 1886, thirteen black youths were nominated for appointment, pending their ability to pass an entrance examination. Some of the youths were appointed by white Congressmen.

1870	Michael Howard—Mississippi
1870	James W. Smith—South Carolina
1871	Henry A. Naxier—Tennessee
1872	Thomas Van R. Gibbs—Florida
1874	John W. Williams—Virginia
1876	Johnson C. Whittaker—South Carolina
1877	Charles A. Minnie—New York
1877	Henry O. Flipper—New York
1883	John H. Alexander—Ohio
1884	Charles Young—Ohio
1885	William A. Hare—Ohio
1885	William T. Andrews—South Carolina
1886	Henry W. Holloway—South Carolina

Only Flipper, Alexander and Young passed the entrance exam and successfully completed the course, later receiving commissions in the U.S. Army. No other blacks were admitted until the twentieth century.

When Mr. Flipper, the colored cadet, stepped forward and received the reward of four years of as hard work and unflinching courage as any young man can be called upon to go through, the crowd of spectators gave him a round of applause. He deserved it. Anyone who knows how quietly and bravely this young man —the first of his despised race to graduate at West Point—has borne the difficulty of his position.

For four years he has had to stand apart from his classmates as one with them but not of them—and to all the severe work of the academic offices, he has had added the yet

Cadet Smith's Defence.

The trial of Cadet Smith, colored, was concluded January 12th.

MAY IT PLEASE THE COURT:—I stand here to-day charged with a most disgraceful act, one which not only affects my character, but will, if I am found guilty, affect it during my whole life. And I shall attempt, in as few words as possible, to show that I am as innocent of this charge as any person in this room. I was reported on the 18th of December, 1870, for a very trivial offence. For this offence I submitted an explanation to the Commandant of Cadets. In this explanation I submitted the real cause of my committing the offence for which I was reported. But this cause, as stated, involved another cadet, who finding himself charged with an act for which he was liable to punishment, denies all knowledge of it. He tries to establish his denial by giving evidence which I shall attempt to prove absurd. On the morning of the 13th of December, 1870, at guard mounting, after the new guard had marched past the old guard, and the command of "Two's left—halt!" had been given, the new guard was about two p three yards to the front and right of the old guard Then the command, "Left backward dress," was given to the new guard. "Order arms, place rest." I then turned around toward Cadet Anderson and said to him, "I wish you would not tread on my toes." This was said to him in a moderate tone, quite loud enough for him to hear. He replied, as I understood, "Keep your d—d toes out of the way." I said nothing more, and he said nothing more. I then heard Cadet Birney say to another cadet (I don't know who it was) standing by his side, "It (or the thing) is speaking to Mr. Anderson. If he were to speak to me, I would knock him down." I heard him distinctly; but as I knew that he was interfering in an affair which did not concern him, I took no further notice of him, but turned around again to my original position in the ranks. What was said subsequently I do not know, for I paid no further attention to either party. I heard nothing said at any time about taking my eyes away, or of Cadet Anderson compromising his dignity.

Having thus reviewed the circumstances which gave rise to the charge, may it please the court, I will say a word as to the witnesses. Each of these cadets testifies to the fact that they have discussed the case in every particular, both with each other and with the other cadets. That is, they have found out each other's views and feelings in respect to it, compared the evidences which each should give, the probable result of the trial, and one has even expressed a desire as to the result. Think you that Cadet Birney, with such a desire lurking in his breast, influencing his every thought and word, with such an end in view, could give evidence unbiased, unprejudiced and free from that desire that "Cadet Smith might be sent away and proved a liar?" Think you that he could give evidence which should be the truth, the whole truth, and nothing but the truth, so help me God?" It seems impossible for me to have justice done me by the evidence of such witnesses, but I will leave that for the court to decide. There is another question here which must be answered by the finding of this court. It is this: "Shall Cadet Smith be allowed to complain to the commandant of cadets when he considers himself unjustly dealt with?" When the court takes notice of the fact that this charge and these specifications are the result of a complaint made by me, it will agree with me as to the importance its findings will have in answering that question. As to what that finding will be I can say nothing; but if the court is convinced that I have lied, then I shall expect a finding and sentence in accordance with such conviction. A lie is as disgraceful to one man as another, be he white or black, and I say here as I said to the commandant of cadets, "If I were guilty of telling a falsehood, I should merit and expect the same punishment as any other cadet," but as I said before, I am as innocent of this charge as any person in this room. The verdict of an infallible judge—conscience—is "not guilty," and that is the finding I ask of this court.

Daily Alta California,
February 5, 1871

The Colored Cadet—His Hardships at West Point.

The following letter from J. W. Smith, the colored cadet at West Point, to his home folks at Hartford, Connecticut, certainly makes out pretty hard times for that young pioneer:

West Point, N. Y., June 29, 1870.—Your kind letter should have been answered long ere this, but really I have been so harrassed with examination and the insults and ill-treatment of these cadets that I could not write or do anything else scarcely. I passed the examination all right and got in, but my companion, Howard, failed and was rejected. Since he went away I have been lonely indeed, and now these fellows appear to be trying their utmost to run me off, and I fear they will succeed if they continue as they have begun. We went into camp yesterday, and not a moment has passed since then but some one of them has been cursing and abusing me. All night they were around my tent, cursing and swearing at me so that I did not sleep two hours all night.

It is just the same at the table, and what I get to eat I must snatch for like a dog. I don't wish to resign if I can get along at all; but I dont think it will be best for me to stay and take all the abuses and insults that are heaped upon me. The examination was very hard this year—harder than ever before—and since I have been successful in getting in I will stay as long as I possibly can. One of the cadets refused to drill the squad because I was in it, and they reduced him from corporal to a private for disobedience of orders, and they are all mad about that. The one who drills the squad now is the meanest specimen of humanity I ever saw. After marching us out to the drill ground this morning he said to me, "Stand off one side from the line, you d—d black son of a b—h. You are too near that white man.— I want you to remember that you are not on an equal footing with the white men in your class, and what you learn here you will have to pick up for I won't teach you a d—d thing." And thus he kept me standing until the captain came around inspecting, when he pretended that he put me there to teach me a movement which I had never practiced before. And I could say nothing at all, or I would have been locked up for disobedience of orders or disrespect to "superior officers." If it ever happens again I shall deny it too his face and then resign.

If I complain of their conduct to the commandant I must prove the charges or nothing can be done; and where am I to find one from so many to testify in my behalf? If this afternoon's drill is conducted as this morning's was, you need not be astonished at hearing that I have resigned. I have borne insult upon insult until I am completely worn out. I have written a plenty of bad news, and I wish I had some good news for you, but alas! it seems to be getting worse and worse. I forgot to tell you that out of ninety-one appointees, five failed physically, forty-seven failed mentally, leaving thirty-nine admitted. They had prepared it to fix the colored candidates, but it proved most disastrous to the whites.
                                    J. W. SMITH.

Lancaster Intelligence,
July 9, 1870

more severe mental strains which bearing up against a cruel social ostracism puts on any young man— and knowing that he had done this without getting soured and losing courage for a day.

Anyone, I say, who knows all this would be inclined to say that the young man deserved to be well taken care of by the government he is bound to serve.

Everybody here who has watched his course speaks in terms of admiration for the unflinching courage he has shown. No cadet will go away with heartier wishes for his future.

—From The New York Times, June 15, 1877.

— Richmond papers say that the negroes employed there on fortifications are literally starved. The rations given them are: For dinner, three-quarters of an ounce of meat and three and three-quarters ounces of bread; the same of bread without meat for breakfast and supper—and the bread is heavy and indigestible; altogether, 12 ounces of food per day. The owners of the negroes are raising a row about the matter.

Insignia of the 9th and 10th Cavalry takes note that they were Indian fighters who also were called "Buffalo Fighters" by the Indians because their hair resembled the coat of a buffalo.

The Colored Troops.

ADJUTANT-GENERAL THOMAS'S REPORT.

The report of Adjutant-General Lorenzo Thomas to the Secretary of War in regard to the operations under his direction in organizing colored troops in the Southwest between the spring of 1863 and the termination of hostilities, eight months ago, has just been published. Of course only the more important facts in the document are now of general interest.

General Thomas states that the policy of recruiting negroes was enthusiastically received by the white troops in the Southwest, with the exception of one Chicago regiment. He says that Lieutenant-General Grant very heartily supported and seconded his efforts. Good officers for the troops offered themselves very slowly at first, but as the prejudice against the scheme of negro enlistments wore away, they came more rapidly than they could be appointed. The account of operations in 1863 is thus concluded:—

"Major George L. Stearns, Assistant Adjutant-General, having been ordered to Nashville, Tenn., to superintend the organization of colored troops, reported to me, and I found that he entered into

BANNER OF THE THIRD UNITED STATES COLORED TROOPS.

BELOW: Troopers of the 10th Cavalry near Chloride during the Apache Campaign. RIGHT: Colored Troops liberating slaves

the duty with great zeal and rendered good service. In the month of December I was compelled to leave the Mississippi River in consequence of sickness. The year's operations may be summed up as follows:—

Organizations.	Officers.	Enlisted men.	Aggregate.
One Regiment Cavalry	22	390	412
Four Regiments Heavy Artillery	151	3,956	4,107
Four Battalions Light Artillery	11	385	396
Twenty-four Regiments Infantry	745	15,767	16,512
One Independent Company	3	93	96
Total	932	20,591	21,523

"Other regiments were authorized, but as they were incomplete at this date, no returns were rendered. The above numbers are taken from returns in the Adjutant-General's office, and are below the numbers actually enlisted, as the loss in battle, by death and by desertion, could not have been less than 5000. This may seem a large estimate, but it is known that raw troops early contract diseases, especially the measles, and it is further known that when the blacks become sick, not having the vitality of the white race, they sink under disease, and the percentage of mortality is very great. The able-bodied men were largely employed in the several staff departments, especially at the principal dépôts, and by the troops themselves, as cooks and servants, and some commanders organized them into pioneer parties, without being mustered into the service of the United States. Many were induced by high wages to take employment on the transports; others again readily found employment as wood-choppers, also as laborers, in towns on the

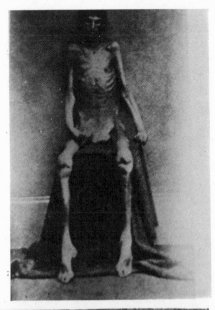

White Union soldier after being freed from the Confederate prison at Andersonville, Georgia, where many black and white Union prisoners died from neglect and harsh treatment. The camp commander, Wirz, was tried and convicted for violating the rules of war. When black soldiers first entered the war, the Confederates refused to recognize them as soldiers and threatened to sell them as slaves if captured or to kill them. Only a promise that the Union would retaliate in kind forced the rebels to cease the slaughter of black soldiers at their mercy.

river. Admiral Porter stated to me that in the naval fleet under his command he had over 1000 negroes. I state these facts to show why a larger amount of colored men were not enlisted."

Early in 1864 General Thomas was dissuaded from attempting to recruit negroes in Kentucky, by the representations of Governor Bramlette:—

"I represented that slavery was forever at an end, to which the Governor assented; and that as the negroes, were constantly passing the borders of the State, and it could not be prevented, I urged that I might take the able-bodied men and organize them into troops, whereby the owners of the negroes would receive certificates of their muster, and the State receive credit on the quota for the draft. The Governor, while generally assenting, urged that I would not establish recruiting stations in the State, but desist from my purpose, stating that the subject was one of peculiar delicacy to the people of Kentucky, that they did not desire the general government to interfere, and that they desired to manage the institution in their own way. He especially deprecated any agitation at that time, stating also that Kentucky would come up to the measure of her duty in this respect, and by a legal enactment provide for the extermination of slavery. He remarked that, under their present laws, some four or five years would be necessary to fully accomplish this measure. I conversed with most, and perhaps with nearly all, the members of the Legislature, which was then in session, all of whom took the ground advocated by the Governor, and some of them even requested that I should remove my recruiting stations in Tennessee, on the borders of Kentucky. Finding this feeling so prevalent in the State, I withdrew from it without their doing any thing."

"The whole of my operations in the West and Southwest, in the organization of colored troops may be given as 2804 officers and 76,040 enlisted men; aggregate, 78,844.

Two regiments were organized in Kansas from negroes, I understand, obtained from Arkansas, though not under my superintendence. A regiment of 1000 men was recruited at Evansville, Ind., from Kentucky negroes, and the latter State received credit for them on her quota of the draft. This regiment is not enumerated in the tabular statement.

RECAPITULATION.

Organizations.	Officers.	Enlisted Men.	Aggregate.
Four regiments cavalry	163	..	..
Eight battalions light artillery	40	..	...
Nine regiments heavy artillery	612	..	..
Fifty-seven regiments infantry	2052	..	..

I have the honor to be, very respectfully, your obedient servant,
L. Thomas, Adjt.-Gen. U. S. A.

The report of Adjutant-General Foster, of the bureau for colored troops, makes the following statements:—

On the 15th of July, 1865, the date on which the last organization of colored troops was mustered in, there were in the service of the United States 120 regiments of infantry,

Numbering in the aggregate	98,938
Twelve regiments of heavy artillery	15,662
Ten batteries light artillery	1,311
Seven regiments cavalry	7,245
Grand aggregate	123,156

The foregoing is the largest number of colored troops in service at any one time during the war.

The entire number of troops commissioned and enlisted in this branch of the service, during the war, is 186,057.

The loss during the war, from all causes except mustering out of organizations in consequence of expiration of term of service, or because service was no longer required, is 68,178.

The number of colored troops already mustered out, or under orders for muster out, is 33,234.

The aggregate of colored troops remaining in service, after the execution of all orders to this date for the muster out of organizations, is 85,024.

The whole number of claims for compensation on account of the enlistment of slaves in the service of the United States, filed with the boards in Delaware and Maryland, is 3971; compensation, varying in amount, was awarded upon 733. Of these claims, 294 have been rejected by the commission as not being well founded, and the remainder are still before the board. The total amount of compensation awarded loyal men is $213,883. Twenty-five claims have been paid, amounting in the aggregate to $6900, leaving 708 claims unpaid, amounting to $206,983.

Boston Semi-Weekly Advertiser,
December 27, 1865

The morning we landed at Daiquiri, Cuba, June 23, 1898, we first contacted the colored troops of the 9th Cavalry when a boat load of them was capsized by the violent surf beating against a partly wrecked dock. Most of them could not swim, and at least two of them were rescued from drowning by one of our men named Knoblouch, a swimming champion and graduate of Yale University. He also dived in time after time, retrieving most of the rifles lost in water.

Col. Wood and then Lt. Col. Roosevelt, assembled our boys after dark and marched us up the coast to Siboney, where we climbed the steep bluff bordering the ocean, reaching the apex of a ridge running inland along a deep valley laying to our right. This valley came to a blind end about three or four miles inland where a Spanish block house was located atop a steep ridge, forming the head of the short valley so that any of our troops marching up the valley would be exposed to gunfire from the block house.

Unfortunately, the officers of the 9th Cavalry who followed us from Daiquiri on the morning of June 24, chose to march up this "dead end" valley where they suffered numerous casualties just after we had attacked the block house from the right flank. No doubt the diversion set up by the 9th saved us many casualties and the diversion set up by our flank attack, like-wise saved many lives of the 9th Cavalry troops who were at a great disadvantage being exposed to direct gunfire from the block house, while we were only exposed to gunfire from the right flank of the Spanish troops in the block house and trenches.

By making a direct attack against the left flank of the Spanish troops, we were able to dislodge them from the block house and inflict heavy casualties, forcing all the Spanish troops to retreat. Meanwhile, the 9th and other U.S. regulars found their way around the right side of the block house and Spanish trenches. So we met members of the 9th as well as the U.S. 6th and 3rd Cavalry that same evening.

Wood and Roosevelt saw to it

Negro Troops of the U.S. Tenth (Colored) Cavalry, San Juan Hill, Cuba, July, 1898

that we made our marches toward Santiago at night and early mornings, so we got the jump on the rest of the U.S. troops. This kept us in the first line of combat all the time.

We reached the San Juan hills ahead of all other troops, closely followed by the 9th and 10th colored troops, a part of whom along with other regiments infiltrated with our regiment because they knew we came to Cuba to see action—most of our outfit being "to the manner born," a gun in hand.

As we crossed the cane brakes approaching San Juan Hills, we heard the colored troops coming up on our right flank and a few of them mixed in with us.

When the Rough Riders "Woods Weary Walkers" (as we came to call ourselves when we found ourselves without horses) at last found ourselves in the jungle at the base of Kettle Hill we formed for the charge to the summit of San Juan Hill proper. There were perhaps twenty-five or thirty colored troopers mixed

up with us and who made the charge shoulder to shoulder with us up to the crest of that famous hill.

The bulk of the colored troops were on our right flank and joined with the white regular cavalry in routing the Spanish from El Caney, from whence all of the U.S. troops approached and entered Santiago after the siege.

—Jesse D. Langdon, "The last Man" of K Troop, 1st U.S. Vol. Cavalry: Roosevelt's Rough Riders.

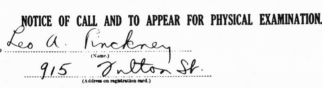

FORM NO. 103, PREPARED BY THE PROVOST MARSHAL GENERAL.

NOTICE OF CALL AND TO APPEAR FOR PHYSICAL EXAMINATION.

To _Leo A. Pinckney_
(Name.)

915 Fulton St.
(Address on registration card.)

You are hereby notified that pursuant to the act of Congress approved May 18, 1917, you are called for military service of the United States by this Local Board from among those persons whose registration cards are within the jurisdiction of this Local Board.

Your Serial Number is __258__, and your Order Number is __1__

You will report at the office of this Local Board for physical examination on the __2nd__ (Day.) day of __August__, 191_7_, at _8_ o'clock A. M. (Month.) (Year.)

Any claim for exemption or discharge must be made n forms which may be procured at the office of this Local Board, and must be filed at the office of this Local Board on or before the SEVENTH day after the date of mailing this notice.*

Your attention is called to the penalties for violation or evasion of the Selective Service law, approved May 18, 1917, and of the Rules and Regulations made pursuant thereto, which penalties are printed on the back hereof.

LOCAL BOARD __44__

By _____ Chairman.

_____ Clerk.

* Date of mailing notice, __28th__ of __July__, 191_7_ (Day.) (Month.) (Year.)

Leo Pinckney, first draftee of World War I

The hero of Pearl Harbor was a black mess attendant, Dorie Miller, who brought down several Japanese airplanes though he had never been trained to fire a machine gun. At that time (1941) blacks were confined in the Navy to menial duties. Today Afro-American youths can aspire to every position in any branch of service.

In July 1972 the Navy launched a U.S. warship named *Dorie Miller* in honor of the hero who lost his life in 1943 when enemy fire sank the *Liscombe Bay* in the Pacific. Two other ships were previously named

for black World War II heroes, the USS *Leonard Harmon* and the USS *Jesse L. Brown*. The latter was named for the first Afro-American naval aviator.

The American custom of separating members of the armed forces according to color resulted in ludicrous situations right up to World War II. In one instance two light-skinned brothers enlisted. The swarthy one was sent to a black unit; his blond brother was given his choice and

elected the Air Force, which then had no known blacks. The "colored" man became an officer in a labor battalion and served throughout the war without the frills provided for members of the Air Force, which always was an elite branch of the armed forces. While keeping the secret, draft-eligible friends of the brothers became much embittered by the government's prejudicial policies, which persisted until civil rights organizations waged a battle that caused the armed forces to relax the rigid discriminatory practices.

Going to take my breast-plate, sword, and shield.... And march out boldly in the field.

TOP: First American privates to receive Croix de Guerre. RIGHT: Black Machine Gunners actually firing on Germans across No Man's Land in France during World War I

TOP: Training Camp, World War I. BOTTOM: Quartette of the 301st Stevedore Regiment attached to the 23rd Engineers, France

Lillian Roth sings "Sing, You Sinners" in Paramount's Honey *(1930).*

One of the greatest roles ever created by Western man has been the role of "Negro." One of the greatest actors to play the role has been the "Nigger."

—Henry Dumas

In MGM's musical comedy A Day at the Races *(1937) starring the Marx Brothers, Duke Ellington's vocalist, Ivy Anderson sings "All God's Chillun Got Rhythm."*

In Old Kentucky, *20th Century Fox (1935), Bill Robinson shows Will Rogers some steps.*

Humphrey Bogart, Dooley Wilson and Sidney Greenstreet in Warner's Casablanca *(1943) Dooley Wilson sang "As Time Goes By."*

like black pearls
trapped
in the white cerebellum
we glisten out of reach
of drum-gun and talking bird

—Henry Dumas

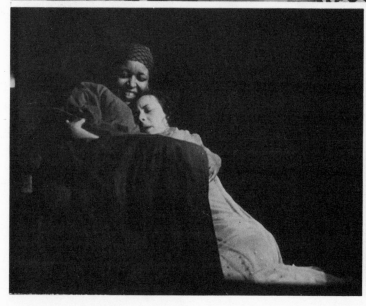

Top row:
The Emperor Jones (1933), starring Paul Robeson with a screenplay by DuBose Heyward based on a play by Eugene O'Neill.
Dancing Feet, Republic Pictures (1936); unidentified dancers.
Cleo Desmond, Edna Mae Harris and Joe Louis in Lying Lips.
Stormy Weather (1943) 20th Century Fox's all-black musical starred Lena Horne, Eddie "Rochester" Anderson, Dooley Wilson and Bill Robinson.

Center row:
An early Paramount comedy, Gasoline Gus (1921), with Fatty Arbuckle also featured a group of unknown vocalists.
20th Century Fox's Sun Valley Serenade (1941) featured the Nicholas Brothers dancing in the "Chattanooga Choo Choo" production number.
Cabin in the Sky, MGM (1943), an all-black musical starring Ethel Waters, Eddie "Rochester" Anderson, Lena Horne and Rex Ingram.

Bottom row:
Ethel Waters and Fredi Washington in Mamba's Daughter.
Katherine Dunham and her dancers in the "Stormy Weather" production number from the film of the same name.
Mantan Moreland, Bud Scott (guitar); Red Callender (bass) and Cee Pee Johnson (drums); from Paramount's Birth of the Blues (1941).

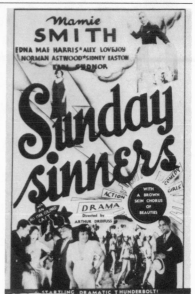

Bottom: The Bennie Moten Orchestra at the Fairyland Park Ballroom in Kansas City around 1930. William "Count" Basie, bottom row, 2nd from left; vocalist Jimmy Rushing, standing to the right of leader Bennie Moten.

I want you to leap high in the sky
with me until we see
yellow trees and the blue gulf.

—Henry Dumas

Top row:
A dance scene in the "Harlem Madness" number from MGM's They
Learned About Women *(1930).*
The Hot Chocolates performing at The Cotton Club, 1936.
*The Brown Buddies, a 1930 revue with a cast headed by Bill Robinson
and Adelaide Hall.*

Bottom:
Female chorus of an unidentified musical, around 1930.
Greenlee and Rogers, a vaudeville act of the 1930's.

...where from bar to bar
where from glass to glass
I drowned my pain
right to the dancefloor
trodden and worn with steps

And there was this adult pain
Down deep in the soul
Because of which was laughter

Lois Gardella, the original Aunt Jemima, 1933

—Ifeanyi Menkiti

THE DOZENS

When slave auctioneers had exceptional merchandise, they sold it separately. When they felt the "items" were flawed in some way—age, illnesses, deformities, etc.—they sold them in lots, frequently of a dozen. Every slave knew that he was included among a *dozen* only if something was physically wrong with him. Thus, to be a part of a dozen was humiliating.

Eventually, the term was applied to a ritualized verbal battle that black people developed to insult and humiliate each other. The focus was on genealogy and the point was total humiliation. Yet the loser was the one who, because his emotions took control or because his insults were too weak, took refuge in physical abuse. The winner was the one with the cruelest wit who managed to keep cool.

A child calls to its mother "O mamma look dat da fulafafa!" The mother, with a superior air says: "Gal, you bin in dis buckle country [buckra is white man] so long, an' can't say wulisapapa." The joke lies in the fact that "fulafafa" and "wulisapapa" both mean woodpecker in an African language.

Went to the river to be baptized
Stepped on a root and got capsized
The river was deep and the preacher
    was weak
So the nigger went to Heaven from
    the bottom of the creek

Joyce Kilmer's Trees

I think that I shall never dig
A spiel as righteous as a twig.
A twig whose scoffish chops are stashed
Right on the apple's pile of trash.
A twig that digs the knock each bright
And spreads its hooks so fine and right.
A twig, Jack, that may in heat time drape
A crib of feathers in its cape.
Upon whose barrel Hawk has squat
Who is so mellow on each spot.
Spiels are laid by lanes like me
But just the Knock can make a tree.

I was standing on the corner when I heard my bulldog bark
He was barking at two men who was gambling in the dark
Stag O. Lee, threw seven and Billy swore that he threw eight
Stag O. Lee told Billy, 'I can't let you go with that
You done won all my money and my brand new Stetson hat.'

Stag O. Lee went home to get his long "forty-four"
'I'm gone kill that nigger,' was the words that he swore.
Stag O. Lee met Billy in that favorite drinking place
He had the look of the Devil in his long skinny face.
Billy started beggin and pleadin for his life
'Stag O. Lee, don't kill me. Oh! Please don't take my life
I got three little children and a very sickly wife.'

Stag O. Lee shot Billy, with slugs from that long forty-four
Billy fell over two tables and like a rag doll he hit the floor.
The bullits went through Billy and into the mirror behind the bar
Stag O. Lee caught a freight and headed where safer places are.
And the police came in and asked did Billy lay bleedin in his own sin
And all the folks asked, 'how many Stag O. Lees since then?'

SHINE AND THE TITANIC

The eighth of May was a hell of a day
When the *Titanic* was sinking away.
Yeah, what a hell of a day, when the news reached the seaport
    town
The *Titanic* was sinking down.
Shine went below deck, eating his peas
Till the water come up to his knees.
Shine went up on deck, said, "Captain, I was downstairs eating
    my peas
Till the water come up to my knees."
Captain said, "Shine, Shine, sit your black ass down.
I got ninety-nine pumps to pump the water down."
Shine went back down below deck, looking through space
Till the water came up to his waist.
Shine went up on deck, said, "Captain, I was downstairs looking
    through space
Till the water came up to my waist."
Captain said, "Shine, Shine, sit your ass down.
Got ninety-nine pumps to pump the water down."
Shine went down below deck eating his bread
Till the water came up to his head.
Shine went up on deck, said, "Captain, I was downstairs eating
    my bread
Till the water came up to my head."
He said, "Shine, Shine, sit your ass down.
Got ninety-nine pumps to pump the water down."
Shine took off his shirt and started to take a dive.
Captain's daughter came over to Shine.
Shine jumped in the water and met up with a shark.
Shine said, "You may be king of the ocean, king of the sea,
You got to be a swimming motherfucker to outswim me."
And Shine swim on.

Ham bone ham bone where you been?
Around the world and back again.

Ham bone ham bone what'd you do?
I got a chance and I fairly flew.

Ham bone ham bone where you stay?
I met a pretty girl and I couldn't get away.

SONGS OF THE HUCKSTERS

Charleston, S.C., had its Catfish Row and the musical songs of the hucksters who sold fruits, vegetables and food both cooked and raw but every urban center came to life when its enterprising black men and women took to the streets with their edibles. Especially inventive was an old Philadelphia woman who sold hot soup. She sang:

"Peppry pot, all hot, all hot!
Makee back strong, makee live long,
Buy my peppry pot."

Nearby a crab man sang his song:

"Crabs, fresh crabs
Fresh Baltimore crabs
Put'em in the pot
With the lid on top
Here, buy my Baltimore crabs."

BILE DEM CABBAGE DOWN

Bile dem cabbage down
Bile dem cabbage down
Look here gal—don' wan' no foolin'
Bile dem cabbage down.

Went to Susy's house
Susy wasn't home
Look here gal—don' wan' no foolin'
Bile dem cabbage down.

My old Missus promis' me
Bile dem cabbage down
When she die she goin' to set me free
Bile dem cabbage down.

She live so long till her he'd got bal'
Bile dem cabbage down
She gib up de idea o' dyin' at all
Bile dem cabbage down.

GO ROUN' THE BORDER SUSIE

The action in this ring-play is directed by the verses. While the first verse is sung, the players join hands in a circle and swing to its rhythm. In the next verse "That turtle dove started," indicates that a girl has begun to move within the ring. "Out goes the hornet," is the signal for a boy to follow her. With "Hist the windah," the players lift their clasped hands. First the girl weaves in and out of the circle, between the uplifted arms. The boy follows suit. "Don't miss no windah," explains itself, and the last verse, "Close in d' 'semble," means to close the window when the boy and girl are both on the outside. The fun then begins, and the chorus may need to be sung several times while the hornet attempts to catch the turtle dove, who turns in one direction, and then in another, to avoid capture:

Chorus: Go roun' the border Susie
Go roun' the border Susie
Go roun' the border Susie
That long summer day.

Out goes the hornet, shoo down my little one
Shoo down my little one, shoo that day
Out goes the hornet, shoo down my little one
Shoo down my little one, long summer day.

That turtle dove started, shoo down my little one
Shoo down my little one, shoo that day
That turtle dove started, shoo down my little one
Shoo down my little one, that long summer day.

Hist the windah, shoo down my little one
Shoo down my little one, shoo that day
Hist the windah, shoo down my little one
Shoo down my little one, that long summer day.

Don't miss no windah, shoo down my little one
Shoo down my little one, shoo that day
Don't miss no windah, shoo down my little one
Shoo down my little one, that long summer day.

Close in d' 'semble, shoo down my little one
Shoo down my little one, shoo that day
Close in d' 'semble, shoo down my little one
Shoo down my little one, that long summer day.

LITTLE SALLY WALKER

Little Sally Walker
Sitting in her saucer
Weeping and crying for some one to love her.

Rise, Sally, rise!
Wipe ya weepin eyes
Put ya hands on ya hips
Let ya back bone slip
Aww shake it to the east
Aww shake it to the west
Aww shake it to the one you love the best.

OLE AUNT DINAH

Ole Aunt Dinah
Sick in bed
Send for the doctor
The doctor said
Get up Dinah
You ain' sick
All you need
Is a hickory stick
An' I ball the jack on the railroad track.

JUBA DIS AN' JUBA DAT

Juba dis an' Juba dat
An' Juba kill d' yalla cat
An' get over double-trouble
Juba!
She served d' meal
She gimme d' husk
Cooked d' bread
She gimme d' crus'
She fried d' meat
Gimme d' skin
That's 'e way momma
Took me in
Now Juba!

SHOUT JOSEPHINE SHOUT

"Josephine! Ma'am?" is sung first as is usual; the leader then tells where the pain (or ornament) is located and the participants instantly try to place their hands on the spot named:

Josephine! Ma'am?
Don't you hear y'o' mammy call you
Why don't you go an' see what she want?
Josephine! Ma'am?
Want to shout? Yes, ma'am.
Shout Josephine—Shout—Shout!
Shout Josephine—Shout!
Get a hump on y'o'self you red-eye' devil
Get a hump on y'o'self you big-eye' coon!
Pain in the head—Shout—Shout!
Shout Josephine—Shout!
Pain in the back—Shout—Shout!
Shout Josephine—Shout!
Pain in the neck—Shout—Shout!
Shout Josephine—Shout!
Pain in the hip—Shout—Shout!
Shout Josephine—Shout!

---

*An old-time hair-do.   **Earring.

Josephine
Ma'am?
Want t' shout?
Yes ma'am
What time?
Right now.
Shout Josephine
Shout!
Pain in the toe
Shout! Shout!
Pain in m' leg
Shout! Shout!
Pain in the heel
Shout! Shout!
Shout Josephine
Shout!
That sore toe
Shout! Shout!
That finger ring
Shout! Shout!
That water fall*
Shout! Shout!

Shout Josephine
Shout!
That ribbon bow
Shout! Shout!
That air ring**
Shout! Shout!
That slipper shoe
Shout! Shout!
That shiny eye
Shout Josephine
Shout!
Now shake the baby
Shake! Shake!
Now shake the baby
Shake! Shake!
Shake the baby—Shake!
The song is closed off with:
A'n' Jinny hoecake
Sweet! Sweet!
Take some an' lef' some
Sweet! Sweet!
A'n' Jinny hoecake
Sweet! Sweet!
Take some an' lef' some
Sweet! Sweet! Sweet!

KNEE-BONE

Knee-bone when I call you
H-a-nnn knee-bone
Knee-bone when I call you
H-a-nnn Lord knee-bone bend.
Bend my knee-bone to the ground
H-a-nnn knee-bone
Bend my knee-bone to the ground
H-a-nnn Lord knee-bone bend.
Knee-bone Zachaniah
H-a-nnn knee-bone
Knee-bone Zachaniah
H-a-nnn Lord knee-bone bend.
Knee-bone when I call you
H-a-nnn knee-bone
Knee-bone when I call you
H-a-nnn Lord knee-bone bend.

Knee-bone didn't I call you
H-a-nnn knee-bone
Knee-bone didn't I call you
Ha-ah Lord knee-bone bend.
Knee-bone in the mornin'
H-a-nnn knee-bone
Knee-bone in the mornin'
Ha-ah Lord knee-bone bend.
Knee-bone in the evenin'
H-a-nnn knee-bone
Knee-bone in the evenin'
Ha-ah Lord knee-bone bend.

"Knee-Bone" is both a shout song and a rythmic work song for oarsmen.

WHEN THE COLLARD GREENS TALKED

... T'other day ... our new minister preached a sermon for us, and you know it's the custom for any man who thinks anything of himself to go up to the preacher and express his opinion of the sermon. I went up to him, and the first thing I knew I didn't know what I was talking about, and very slyly he stole the opportunity to say, "I'll catch you out some day, and I'll measure you on the ground for what you said to me." I tried to say something, but no word would come. I went out wondering at myself. Then I realized that it was a too-much dinner of collards and so and so that had talked to the preacher. My mind kept me awake that night, and the dawn of day found me cussing myself. I got up with the determination to go to the preacher and have it out with him. He had threatened to whip me and I wanted him to keep his word. He lived in a grove not far away, and as soon as I snatched a quick breakfast I started out to look for him.

On the way, I stopped at a creek to wash my hands, for the Lord won't like it if a man hits a preacher when his fits is dirty. I was walking along and somebody yelled out, "Hold on!" I stopped, looked up, and here come the preacher. I had tightened my fist, when he said "I want to beg your pardon for what I said the other day about stretching you on the ground. In fact, it wasn't my mind that was talking to you when I said that I would stretch you on the ground. It was an overindulgence in collard greens." I grabbed him by the arm, and said: "Thank God, brother. That was the matter with me. It was collard greens talking."

RACIAL ETIQUETTE

... He and his pardner were working on top of a high, tall building when he got too close to the edge and he fell off. His pardner called out to him, "Stop, Jim you'se falling." But he sang out "I can't stop I'se done fell."

His pardner leaned over the edge an' call to him an' say "You Jim! You'se gwine to fall on a white lady!" An' Jim stopped and come right on back up. . . .

GETTING INTO HEAVEN

Negro went to heaven by land. Went there an' knocked on the door. St. Peter come to the do' say "Who is that?" Nigger say "This is me." St. Peter say, "You ridin' or walkin'?" Nigger says "I'm walkin." St. Peter says "Well you can't get in here les'n you're ridin'." Nigger left; come on back down the road about five miles meets up wid a white man. Say, "Mr. White Man where you goin'?" White Man say, "I'm goin' to heaven." Nigger say "You can't git in dere walkin'. I just left dere." Nigger say "I'll tell you a way we'll get in dere." Nigger say "Let me be your horse an' you get straddle me an' I'll go ridin' an' carry you up to heaven; an' you knock on de gate an' Salt Peter ask you who you is an' you tell him it's you an' he gonna say 'Bof you all come on in!" White Man says "All right get down." White Man straddles the nigger; nigger goes runnin' back up to heaven wid him. Rode him right up to de door. White Man knocks on de do!. St. Peter say "Who is dere?" White Man say, "Dis is me." St. Peter say, "You ridin' or walkin'?" White Man says "Yes." St. Peter says "Hitch your damn horse outside an' come on in."

THE HOUNDS AND THE LAW

... The fox ... had his eye on a turkey perched in a tree-top. "Hey Brer Turkey" called Brer Fox "is you heard about the new law?—Foxes can't eat no more turkeys and hounds can't chase foxes. Come on down and we'll talk about it." "Nothin doin'," said Brer Turkey "we can talk about it right where we is." Just then some hounds were heard coming over the hill. "Guess I'll be runnin' along" said Brer Fox. Brer Turkey said "I thought you said the new law says no more fox hunts." And Brer Fox said "Thas right—but them dogs will run right over that law."

SANGAREE

If I live
    Sangaree.
Don' get kill'
    Sangaree.
I'm goin' back
    Sangaree.
Jacksonville
    Sangaree.
Chorus: Oh Babe
    Sangaree.
Oh Babe
    Sangaree.
Oh Babe
    Sangaree.
Oh Babe
    Sangaree.
If I live
    Sangaree.
See nex' fall
    Sangaree.
Ain' goin' t' plant
    Sangaree.
No cotton at all
    Sangaree.
Repeat Chorus:
Chicken in the fiel'
    Sangaree.
Scratchin' up peas
    Sangaree.
Dog on the outside
    Sangaree.
Scratchin' off fleas
    Sangaree.
Repeat Chorus:
My husban's got the shovel
    Sangaree.
An' I got the hoe
    Sangaree.
If that ain't farmin'
    Sangaree.
I don't know
    Sangaree.
Repeat Chorus:
If you want t' see a nigger
    Sangaree.
Cut the fool
    Sangaree.
Let him ride
    Sangaree.
A white man's mule
    Sangaree.

We were born on my father's farm near a little town in Alabama. It was a good farm. The soil was good and my father loved growing things. He must have been a better farmer than a business man though, because there came a day when we heard the terrible words "foreclosure" and "mortgage." In what seemed no time at all, we lost the farm and had to move to the city. We, who had always been so free and independent, found ourselves working as hired hands for other people.

Ours was a large family. My oldest sister—a half sister by my father's first wife—cooked in the "big" house. My mother and the two sisters a little older than I worked in the fields. I had to stay home and watch the three younger children. I was eight. The sister who cooked received four dollars a week, and if her "boss" didn't want to pay cash he sometimes paid her with syrup. My other two sisters tied radishes for a penny a bunch. And then, at the end of the week, when we were to be paid, there was always some deduction for rent or some damage we had caused, real or imagined.

My father could never get used to being ordered around, so, one day he told my mother he was going to Pensacola, Florida, to try his luck. He had heard that things were much better there. If he were successful in finding a good job, he was to send for us; if not, he would return. Mr. V— was very angry when my father didn't come to work. He threatened to put us out of the house, and I use the word "house" loosely. My mother pleaded with him and he finally agreed to let us stay. But he was twice as mean. There was hardly any money now. Whatever Mr. V— had too much of, that is what he paid us for our wages.

But no matter what happened, when the school doors opened, those of us of school age were sent off to school. We had to walk miles to the nearest one, but we went.

The school in Alabama was very crowded and all of the grades were jumbled together. The teachers were untrained.

However, with our reduced earning power, my mother's life was made miserable by Mr. V—. He kept insisting that we children be taken out of school to help work out the rent bill. And my father had been gone weeks!

Finally, one day, there was a letter with twenty dollars in it! We were jubilant but we were cautioned not to talk about it because, even then, a plan was beginning to take shape in my mother's mind. She wrote my father that she did not want to go to Florida. She asked him to save carefully what he earned because she had decided to go North where her children could be educated. She wanted something better for us than working in the fields as she was doing.

There were long weeks when she heard nothing from my father. Mr. V— was growing more insistent about taking her children out of school. She finally had to agree to take the older ones out. We had brought a few pieces of furniture with us from the farm. We had my dad's books, I remember. Gradually, these things were disappearing. Somehow my mother found ways of selling them, but she could do this only on a small scale so Mr. V— would not get suspicious. We children did not know exactly what was happening, but we knew something momentous was about to happen.

Then, one day, she told us that soon we were all going on a trip—on a train! We were going North!! But still, there was no word from my father. Then she told us that she had written him that if he ever wanted to see any of us again, he had better be on number 4 when it came through G— on a certain morning in November!

Early that November morning we were bundled up, six of us (my oldest sister was to stay until we sent for her)! Not one of us was over fourteen. My mother had gotten someone with a wagon to come for us and our belongings. And with the greatest excitement I had ever known we were on our way to the station! My father had not answered her letter, so, with sinking hearts, we were afraid we would

never see him again.

We were finally all settled down in our seats. My nose tingled with that odor than only a train coach can give. And then, we were moving! There were tears in my mother's eyes. She had made a big step. We know now that she hadn't even enough money to get out of Alabama. But she was going north of where we were. When her money ran out, she would work until she got enough to go a little farther, but always north. Vague but determined, those were her plans. Courage was needed for that.

The train conductor came through the car and called out the name of the next stop. At last we could stop looking over our shoulders. Until then we felt that any minute Mr. V— would find out about us and we would have to get off the train.

My seat was turned so that I faced the rear of the coach. The train rocked along. I was so excited I couldn't relax. And then the door of the coach opened and there, coming up the aisle, swaying as trains make you do, was Papa! He had been on the train all the time but waited until it was safe to look for us. Such crying and laughing and hugging and kissing! Later he told us how ke knew Mom meant what she said. So he had gotten busy. He had found out about large companies who would transport whole families to different sections of the country and the wage earner could pay the company back for the transportation out of his wages, a little at a time. He had signed up with a coal mining company in Kentucky, but we had to lay over in Birmingham to complete the deal.

While in Birmingham, we had one large hotel room. Our lunch was gone and money almost. There were a couple of anxious days of waiting. Trying to keep six, active, half hungry kids quiet in one hotel room certainly must have been a job.

Then we were in the train station all huddled in the Negro section. There were other families like ours all waiting, not knowing what was in store for us, but it couldn't be any worse than what we had left. We were all hungry. After an eternity, several men came around with the largest baskets I have ever seen. They were full of the most glorious sandwiches! There was milk and coffee! And then on the train again. The farther we went the colder it got. By the time we came to Kentucky it was frigid. We who had never seen snow and had no adequate clothes suffered. The Company furnished our meals all the way.

Finally, we arrived at one of the dirtiest little towns I have ever seen. Coal dust covered the snow. We were assigned to one house in a row of identically ugly houses. One big potbellied stove "heated" the house. We were given commissary books for groceries.

The main thing that I remember about this little town is how cold we were, how dirty my Dad was when he came home, the smell of the carbide head lamps, and that I had a birthday on Christmas. A com-

pany man came by and placed a large box of chocolates on the porch of each family. My first taste of chocolate.

For some reason, we didn't stay there very long. We moved to another town in Kentucky which was much nicer. The men worked hard and, compared with what he had earned before, Papa made good money. It did not take too long to pay the Company back.

The Cumberland Mountains were all around us, but we were warm in the valley. I suppose it was a typical mining town. The people worked hard and played hard. They were friendly and took us right in.

There was a school. It was much closer than the one in Alabama had been, but the standards were worse. We had one teacher for all classes. When she reached the section of the arithmetic that called for long division, she could go no further. My sisters had learned long division, so

she confided that she had never learned it and could they teach her how?

When my mother inquired where she could send the children to get a better education, she was told that they would have to go over the mountain to Lexington. Of course, there were better white schools closer, but that was out of the question. Sending us over the mountain was also out of the question. My mother began planning again.

She added to Papa's income by washing and ironing for single men, selling them lunches and so forth. She was able to save money as never before, but she didn't like the cough my father was developing and the way his shoulders were beginning to look stooped all the time. But most of all she saw no future for her children.

She had a brother in Ohio. In his letters he begged her to come to Ohio; "it was God's country." Work

was plentiful, schools were good and not segregated. But since Papa was working regularly and supporting his family for the first time since he lost his farm, he was not too anxious to go to something he wasn't sure about. But Mom persisted. She saved everything above basic necessities. She kept in close contact with her brother.

He wrote, finally, that there was a new house next door to his and he had a job waiting for my father, so all of Papa's arguments crumbled and once again we were on a train and this time we were really going North.

The day we arrived, our signals had gotten crossed and there was no one to meet us. We knew nothing about the town, or cabs or street-cars. So we walked; Mom, Papa, six children and our luggage.

My youngest brother had on some shoes that were too small and he cried every step of the way.

After literally hours of being lost, we did at last reach our destination. When we got over our weariness we looked around us. So this was God's country! My Uncle's and ours were the only two houses on the street. Ours was new. It was pretty nice except the plumbing was outside.

The job for Papa was watchman in a sewage disposal plant which was not far enough away from our house. However, the wages weren't bad and the work was easy.

But the exciting thing was the school. All those rooms and teachers! The books! We were so excited. So excited that it took us awhile to realize that all was not sweetness and light. Being the second Negro family in this section of the city

there were many children there who had never seen any other Negroes. We created quite a diversion for them. They stared, giggled and made us very self-conscious. That was in school. Outside, we were targets for all kinds of practical jokes. We were called all kinds of names. Of course we were afraid; we were greatly outnumbered and coming directly from the South we didn't know how much fighting back we could do.

Our cousins quickly briefed us. "You are in the North now. You have to let them know you aren't afraid of them. If they call you names, call them names." We were told what names would make what group the angriest. There were many foreigners there who were just as new as we were. Many of them were much older than the American kids because of the language barrier which had kept them behind in school. We had never heard a foreigner talk and they had seen few Negroes. And, of course, the "Americans" were superior to all of us.

There were fights everyday. We were waylaid on the way home. Most of the teachers were wonderful, though. There were times when we were sent out of the room and when we returned we would feel a difference in the pupils, a kindness. We were asked to participate in their games and so forth. Some of the teachers, however, were as prejudiced as their students were. Sometimes, they would actually call *us* names if we got into trouble. They didn't last long though.

How we learned anything, I don't know. But we did. We learned that you gained a certain amount of re-

spect when you would fight back. We learned that all white people were not enemies. We learned that the best teachers may not always have the highest degree. I will never forget some of those teachers in that little Ohio town.

Finally, though, we had to move on. Friction developed between our two families and although we licked the racial differences in our school, we could not overcome the differences between the two families.

We went from bad to worse. It was impossible to find decent housing for seven children (my mother had a new baby and influenza simultaneously and never really got her strength back). Such managing would be quite a chore for anyone, but it would be even more so for a Negro. Some of the places where we had to live are a story all by themselves. I never want to think of them again.

When we had reached a new low, someone told my Dad about the Company here that was transporting families and furnishing housing in a manner similar to the situation in Kentucky, except that it was in a steel town. Arrangements were made. We were given four rooms and an option on another four in the same building. It seemed like heaven compared to some of the holes in which we had lived. And the school? Excellent! There were enough Negroes here so that, although there were some unpleasantnesses, we were not pioneers.

My mother and father lived to see six of their seven children graduate from high school.

—Donnie Woods

SCUPPERNONG WINE

"Now don't look to this not to fail you if you don't do like I tell you. And when I've done told you all I know, then you still got to have a sort o' feelin' about it, and if you ain't got that feelin', you just as good go buy your wine some'eres for you cain't make it.

"Now you mash your Scuppernongs the very same day you pick 'em. Don't you go pickin' 'em of an

evenin' when the sun's low and the day's coolin', and then you go traipsin' off some'eres, sayin', 'I'll start my wine come mornin'.' You pick 'em fust off in the mornin', with the dew on 'em, and you mash 'em with a bread roller. Put 'em in a deep crock. A keg? Well, yes, I've used a keg, but a crock's better. Now you sprinkle sugar or honey over 'em. How much? Now I cain't no more tell you that than why a bird sings.

Just sort of kiver 'em light-like, and honey's the best. I'd say flat-woods honey. Palmeeter honey is a mite too dark. Now you let 'em stand three to seven days. I cain't tell you which, nor what day in betweenst. They git a certain look.

"Now some folks, when that time comes, skim off the pummies. That ain't my way, and you kin do as you please. When that time comes, I put 'em in a flour sack and I squeezes

hell outen 'em. Then I puts the juice back in the crock and I adds sugar slow, powerful slow, stirrin' all the time. How much sugar? Now if you like your wine sweet, you put the sugar to the juice until a egg'll float. I don't fancy it that sweet. I like wine to lay cool and not sickly on my tongue. I put in sugar to where a egg don't quite float, to where it sort o' bubbles around, and mebbe just raises itself oncet almost to the top.

"Now some folks leaves it lay in the crock. I don't. I put it right now in the bottles, without no tops on. I keep some back in the crock. I kivver the bottles with a cloth. The wine'll work and it'll shrink down, and ever' mornin' come sun-up I'll add some from what I've helt back in the crock. I do this until it quits workin'. Then I cork it tight and lay it down on its side in a dark place. Now that ain't the way of a heap o'folks, but it's my way."

BOILED OKRA
1 pound fresh small okra pods
Salt and pepper
¼ cup melted butter
Vinegar (optional)

Wash the okra. Cut off the tops of the stems, being careful not to cut into the pods. Leaving some of the stem keeps the okra in shape, and prevents it from becoming gummy.

Barely cover the okra with boiling salted water, and simmer, covered, until tender (about 8 minutes). Drain. Season with salt and pepper to taste. Pour the melted butter over the okra, and sprinkle it with a little vinegar, if desired.

HOE CAKE—ON A HOE
Stand in the shade near the edge of the field. Light a fire from whatever brush and twigs there may be. On the greased blade of your hoe, mix meal and water until it is thick enough to fry. Add salt if you remembered to bring any. Lean the hoe into the fire until the top side of the bread bubbles. Flip it and brown the other side. If you do it without a hoe, you have to make suitable changes in the kitchen.

Almond Soap—fifty lbs. fine white tallow soap; 20 ounces bitter almonds (essence): Process: melt by steam and combine.

Axle Grease—one pound finely ground black lead; 4 lbs. lard; small amount gum camphor, powdered: Process: combine and mix thoroughly until smooth.

Perfection Hair Oil—one gal. of 90% proof essence Cologne spirits; one spoon each oil of lemon, orange and bergamot; 40 drops extract vanilla: Process: shake well until perfectly blended, then add 1½ pts. soft water.

Florida Water—½ pt. 90% proof spirits; 2 drachms oil of lemon; ½ drachm oil of rosemary: Process: combine.

Royal Washing Powder—Combine any amount soda ash with equal amount carbonate soda. Prepare then decoction linseed oil and add to soda until thick. Spread out on a board in a warm place to dry. When dry shake well so it will pack nicely.

White Tooth Powder—one ounce cloride of lime; 15 ounces prepared chalk; ½ ounce powdered Peruvian bark; five drops attar of roses.

Tun Mush: Pour cornmeal into boiling water and salt. Cook for about 10 or 15 minutes. It comes out like hominy, but stiff. Pour milk over it—eat with a spoon. (Asked if it was good, Mary Singleton said it used to be good—a long time ago—if you were hungry.)

Maumee: When you plant a crop of sweet potato and one comes up about the size of a human head—they don't come up smooth, but cracked or crinkly—it's called a maumee.

Incidentally, to store sweet potatoes for the winter—or rutabagas or turnips—when you harvest them bank them in a circle as big as a room. Bank them with pine needles, cover with dirt, and they're put up for the winter.

Come to a party: When waves of black immigrants moved from the rural South to the urban North and especially during the great Depression years, some tenants raised money to pay the inflated rents by giving "parlor socials." These were also aptly called "house rent parties." The party-givers would get cards printed for distribution among friends, acquaintances and strangers, then lay in a store of "soul food," ice and bootleg liquor which would be sold to guests. The printed cards bore amusing lines such as:

———

Get your kicks where it is groovy
Finer than a 10¢ movie.

———

This Sat. Nite at Mabel's
16 A W. 133 St., 2nd fl. rear on
 right. 9 p.m.

———

Party all night after the setting sun
Where there won't be no cuttin done
At Bubba's place Sat. May 10th
10 Governor Pl. rear—Come on
 down

———

Pig feet, corn bread, rice and gravy,
Country girls—boys from the navy,
Music, soft lights, whiskey, gin
Bring yourself, bring friends and fall
 on in
At 1313 First St. top floor front—
 9 p.m.—until?   The Social Five

The goose hangs high and so am I
And you will too, this Sat. nite at
Ceremony Sam's Jumpin Jack Pad
Special guest—Hospitality Hazel
452 Bradhurst Av. basement—Oct.
 14—9 p.m.

———

Colonel McKee was a Negro millionaire who left in his will certain stipulations as to the distribution of his wealth; $800,000 was to be used to found a military school for white and black orphans. The provision was that if the school no longer operated the money was to be returned to his estate and collected by his heirs and descendants.

His grandson, T. John McKee, had gone to Yale, become a lawyer and was passing for white. When he read in the newspaper that the McKee estate was searching for the heirs to return the money to them, he promptly changed back to his race and put in a claim for the money.

see the <u>New York Daily News</u>, February 20, 1948.

FANCY HAIR-DRESSERS

The *creme de le creme* of sable artists in wool are the Misses Mahans, at their residence Thompson street, near Spring. Pompadours, waterfalls, cascades, a la contraband, rats, mice, etc., are the principal fashions.

—The New York Citizen, August 5, 1865.

Hodgson, the Great African Hair Unkinker, invented a process to straighten hair and expected great financial rewards. He hired a hall on Spring Street in New York City and labored hard to distribute circulars inviting all sons and daughters of Ham to a live demonstration. The program got off to a late start as only a handful of skeptical blacks showed up and it was a difficult task to get one to come forward and serve as a guinea pig for the demonstration.

A dishpan with a mysterious concoction was put over a gas burner, and when the potion got warm it was applied to one side of a woolly head. What had been tight curls was suddenly "straight as a coon's leg; as glossy as a wet beaver's back; and several inches in length." Then began the fireworks.

One woman announced she wouldn't desert her race to get straight hair even though she had "Indian features." Others insisted on knowing what was in the concoction. What broke it up and caused Hodgson to flee was a man with a head almost as bare as a billiard ball who demanded that Hodgson prove the efficiency of the "unkinker" by straightening the remaining few hairs on his head.

———

From <u>The New York Times</u>, February 9, 1859.

Dreams, dreams, play my dreams.

All numbers dreamed of should be played for three days.

Ability—To dream of possessing this characteristic is a very good sign to all except prisoners. It promises riches and prosperity, and also that you will be called upon to perform a highly esteemed task which will not only bring you wealth, but also fame. **012**

Accumulate—To dream that you accumulate wealth denotes heavy losses by fire. **315**

Accurate—To dream that you count very accurately is a sure sign that your friends are unfaithful and that they are trying their utmost to ruin your reputation. This can only be avoided by keen judgment on the part of the dreamer. **375**

Acid—To dream of acid is a sure sign of drunkenness. It also indicates lawsuit in which you will have a very poor chance to win. To throw acid on anyone denotes envy. **215**

Adrift—This is a very good dream. To a young girl it indicates that she is admired by many prominent young men who mean to marry her. To a man it indicates that he will marry a pretty girl of fortune and high standing. **520**

Afraid—To dream that you are afraid to walk denotes courage and elevation in society; you will become prominent and very active in social circles. **678**

Ague—Denotes that your friends are unfaithful. It also denotes danger from an unexpected source. **605**

Alligator—To dream of this harmful creature denotes that you will be engaged in a terrible fight in which you will be the winner. **181**

Almonds—To dream of ripe almonds signifies happiness; young almonds denotes the reverse in business. **167**

Alum—To dream of using alum denotes false love, followed by worries and unpleasant visits from friends and relatives who despise you greatly for your ambition. **748**

Ammonia—To dream of ammonia denotes that you will receive a declaration of love from your sweetheart. This is a very good dream from lovers as it indicates true love followed by the union of great happiness which no man can change. **120**

Ankle—To dream that you have a swollen ankle denotes grief. To dream that your ankle has grown smaller denotes bad luck on the following day and that you should not conduct any business for at least three days. To see others with swollen ankles is a sign of riches. **923**

Ants—To dream of ants denotes money in abundance. To dream that they bite you denotes good business relationship on the following day. **230**

Ape—To see one in your sleep denotes that you are being robbed out of your labor. **500**

Apple—To see an apple in your sleep denotes joy and happiness. To see ripe apples denotes health and wealth. **940**

Armed Men—To dream that you see armed men indicates that you are strong and powerful and that you are not afraid to fight for your rights. **385**

Arms—To dream of hairy arms are signs of riches in proportion to the amount of hair on the arms. **563**

To see skinny hairy arms denotes trouble from a friend or relative. This is a dream of watchfulness. **367**

Withered or broken arms signify quarrels and probably separation. **569**

Ass—To see one denotes hard work but good pay. To hear one bray denotes sad news. To ride one, profit. **811**

Awl—To dream of an awl denotes wasted time, which can be made use of in some other way. **825**

Baby—To dream you see a baby denotes joy and much happiness accompanied by health and wealth in abundance. To hear one cry denotes that you will have a baby boy shortly. **112**

Bacon—To dream of seeing a large amount of bacon denotes that you will have many beautiful and loving children; three boys and two beautiful girls. These children will be the pride of your old age and will be the source of your support throughout the remaining years of your life. **320**

Balsam—To dream of seeing this plant grow denotes that you will suffer loss by rain. **639**

Banana—To dream that you see a bunch of yellow bananas is a sure sign that you are going to be very successful in games of chance. If the bananas are green, it indicates losses. **017**

Bandy—To dream you see a bandy person denotes that someone is trying to take away your husband. To a man it indicates someone is trying to make love to his wife. **100**

Basin—To dream of seeing one denotes the death of a friend. To give one away denotes losses by theft. **823**

Bath—To bathe your skin signifies that you are deeply in love. **618**

Beans—To dream of beans denotes lawsuits in which you will lose. To eat them signifies deceit and slander. To buy them is a sign of courage and determination of your plans. **781**

Bear—To dream of a bear is a very pleasant dream to farmers, it denotes a good crop. To others it denotes hardships. **890**

Bed Bugs—To see them denotes that your friends are unfaithful. To kill them denotes grief. **501**

Beef—To dream that you see plenty of beef denotes death, generally a friend or relative. **522**

Bicycles—To dream of a bicycle denotes that you will not recover your losses, despite the fact that you may know the one who robbed you. **644**

Biscuits—To dream of brown biscuits denotes gain. White ones, losses, generally loss of position. **852**

Boar—To see a wild boar denotes unpleasant weather, generally snow storms and earthquakes. **693**

Boots—To dream of new boots signifies a declaration of love. **918**

Bow-Legged—To dream that you are bow-legged, denotes a surprise. **551**

Bread—To dream of wheat bread denotes riches and excellent health. White bread denotes that you will be very unfortunate. **081**

Bride—Signifies an unpleasant affair. **507**

Buffalo—It is a sign of approaching marriage. **863**

Butter—Signifies riches by dishonest means. To eat it on bread or any food denotes that you will be heavily insured in the near future. **178**

To give butter away, denotes long life and much prosperity. **544**

Buying—To dream that you are out shopping denotes that you are being deceived by your sweetheart. **210**

Cabbage—To dream of eating cabbage denotes that you will grow very rich. To see it, and not eat it denotes a troubled mind. **453**

Candy—Denotes a false sweetheart. To eat it denotes shame. To give it away, happiness. **683**

Carrots—To dream of carrots denotes a change of employment for the better. **961**

Castor Oil—To dream of castor oil denotes your lover is unfaithful. To drink it denotes that you will be cheated out of your savings in some way. To see others drink it denotes sudden wealth. **108**

Cat—To dream of a black cat is extremely hard luck. A white one signifies that you will persuade a friend to commit an act of injustice. To kill one is a warning of reform. **422**

Chair—To dream of a chair indicates that you will form the acquaintance of an infamous person. **976**

Chow Chow—To dream of chow chow is a sign of approaching danger from an unexpected source. **238**

Christmas—Signifies that you will have a beautiful son and two darling girls who will be very religious. They will be the joy of your old age. **285**

Cockroach—Denotes gain in all kinds of games and chances. **393**

Colored People—This is an excellent dream for all. It promises riches and extraordinary good health. To those in business, great success. To prisoners, a speedy release; to farmers, good crops; to the broken-hearted, courage. **725**

Commode—Denotes unrequited love. **303**

Crabs—Signify sly friends, who will betray you for the sake of a dollar. **100**

Dragon Fly—To dream of one denotes that you will be attacked with a filthy disease. **841**

Drum—To hear one denotes a funeral. To play one yourself is a sign of happiness. **107**

Never step over a baby less than a year old; it will stunt his growth.

If the child's fingernails are cut before he is a year old he will be a thief.

A piece of money tied around the ankle will insure the wearer against poverty.

From *American Negro Folklore,* J. Mason Brewer; Quadrangle Books, 1968.

Numbers to play

If You:
foot itches	422
hand itches	333
beat case	754
burn self	618
buy dress	402
pay insurance	346
pay bills	685
cut foot	318
fall down	697
escape death	318
find money	498
have fight	324
leave wife	160
see ghost	632
sign papers	209
visit sick	427

If You Get:
moved	419
new lover	386
parcel	432
pregnant	617
lost	214
telegram	724
the blues	195
belly ache	479
ear ache	900
eye ache	921
rheumatism	676
sick	377
accused	723
arrested	417
bonds	101
days	700
divorce	957
drunk	971
engaged	003
fired	114
gun	040
hit	680
job	198
letter	437
lousy	803

Automobiles:
Auburn	671
Buick	353
Cadillac	245
Checker Cab	971
Graham Paige	121
Hudson	672
Hupmobile	617
Lasalle	604
Pierce Arrow	685
Studebaker	551
Lincoln Zephyr	387

Believe me, I loved you all
Believe me, I knew you, though faintly,
And I loved, I loved you all

—Gwendolyn Brooks

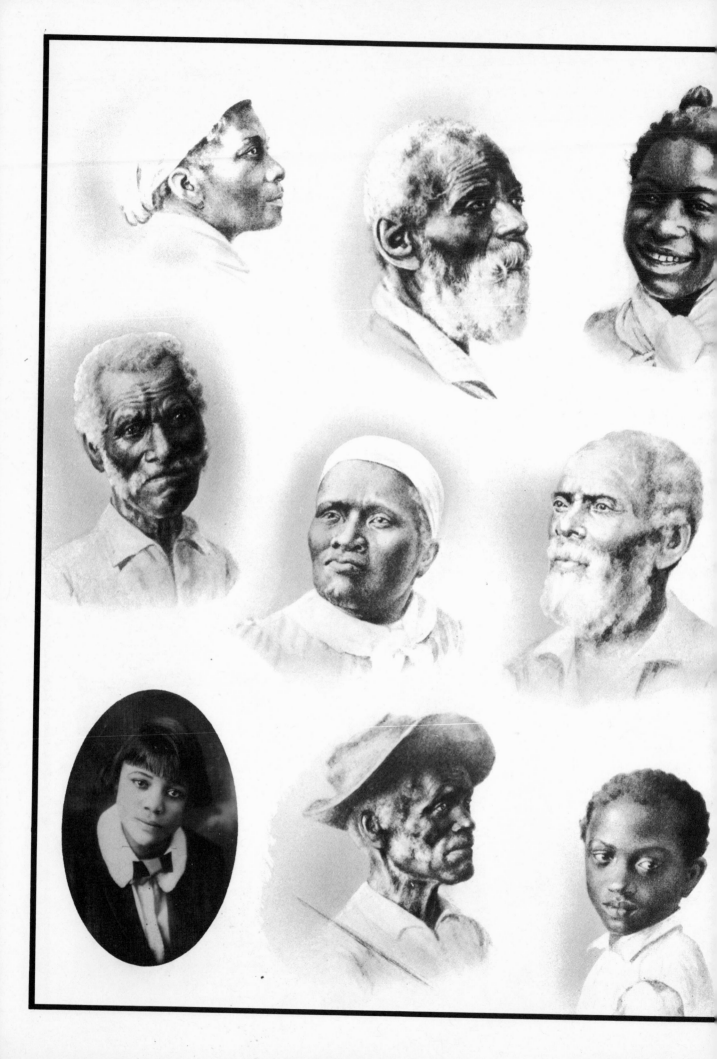

We have a journey
to take and little time;
we have ships to name
and crews.

—Henry Dumas